THE CIVILIZATION OF EXPERIENCE

The Orestes Brownson Series
on Contemporary Thought and Affairs

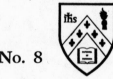

No. 8   1973

THE CIVILIZATION
OF EXPERIENCE:

A WHITEHEADIAN THEORY
OF CULTURE

David L. Hall

FORDHAM UNIVERSITY PRESS
NEW YORK

To
LEMUEL, DAVID,
and CHRISTOPHER

ACKNOWLEDGMENTS

I am pleased to acknowledge here the assistance of those who have aided me most in my investigation of Whitehead's philosophy: first, Widick Schroeder of Chicago Theological Seminary, who introduced me to the intricacies of Whiteheadian studies; and secondly, William Christian of Yale University, who, with awful patience and rigor, criticized the manuscript which formed the principal ancestor of this work. In addition, George Allan of Dickinson College and Delwin Brown of Anderson College provided imaginative and pertinent criticisms of my penultimate draft. These criticisms I have gratefully, though sometimes painfully, accepted, if not always successfully met. To each of these men I offer thanks and the hope that they will not have occasion to feel compromised by having their names associated, in however indirect a fashion, with my work.

I gratefully acknowledge the permission of the respective publishers for the use of quoted material from the works of Alfred North Whitehead listed on the next page. I also wish to thank the University Research Institute of the Graduate School of the University of Texas at El Paso for assistance in the completion of this project.

DAVID L. HALL

The University of Texas
at El Paso

ABBREVIATIONS

The following abbreviations are employed in the notes. They are also given parenthetically, with page references, in the body of the text. In all other cases, regular footnote procedures are employed. The notes will be found at the end of their respective chapters.

AE   *The Aims of Education*. New York: The Free Press, 1967.
AI   *Adventures of Ideas*. New York: Macmillan, 1933.
CN   *The Concept of Nature*. Cambridge: Cambridge University Press, 1920.
ESP   *Essays in Science and Philosophy*. New York: Philosophical Library, 1948.
FR   *The Function of Reason*. Boston: Beacon, 1958.
MT   *Modes of Thought*. New York: Free Press, 1968.
PNK   *An Enquiry Concerning the Principles of Natural Knowledge*. Cambridge: Cambridge University Press, 1925.
Prin. Rel.   *The Principle of Relativity*. Cambridge: Cambridge University Press, 1922.
PR   *Process and Reality*. New York: Macmillan, 1929.
RM   *Religion in the Making*. Cleveland: World, 1960.
SMW   *Science and the Modern World*. New York: Macmillan, 1925.
S   *Symbolism: Its Meaning and Effect*. New York: Macmillan, 1927.

CONTENTS

INTRODUCTION

I

THE IRONY OF WHITEHEADIAN SCHOLARSHIP is its tendency to degenerate into an eager scholasticism. The complexity of Whitehead's thought, couched as it is in an extremely technical language, militates against the speculative employment of his metaphysical categories. So much effort must be expended merely in understanding Whitehead's fundamental concepts that little time or strength remains to experiment with, or to develop extended applications of, the metaphysical categories.

In this work I have sought, on the one hand, to provide an exposition of basic philosophic concepts of Alfred North Whitehead which would serve to introduce the breadth and profundity of his philosophic endeavors, and, on the other, to develop the outlines of a Whiteheadian theory of culture. Most of the published works on Whitehead concentrate upon the nature and implications of his mature metaphysical system to the exclusion of his somewhat less formal social and cultural philosophy. The developed theory of culture presented in this volume is meant to provide the proper context for the presentation of the broad range of Whiteheadian concepts. The analysis of the relationship of experience and culture; the meaning of cultural agents, objects, and aims; the development of a theory of the cultural interests of art, morality, religion, science, and philosophy; a consideration of the meaning of civilization, and a discussion of those factors in experience (individual, social, and cultural) which enhance or frustrate the realization of civilized societies—these topics constitute the primary subject matters of this work.

I have utilized a constructive and synthetic, rather than a dialectical or analytic, approach to Whitehead's philosophy. That is, I have subordinated the goals of the clarification of concepts via analysis, and the criticism of his theories through dialectical arguments, to the aim of the construction of a theory of culture through the analogical extension of certain of Whitehead's concepts and theories. In so doing, I do not mean to imply that

Whiteheadian philosophy could not be subjected profitably to analytical or dialectical modes of exposition. But the inclusion of critical excursions at all the relevant points in the following discussions would have compromised a sharply focused consideration of Whitehead's thinking on the topics of culture and civilization.

Because of my expository method, almost every chapter abounds in interpretations with which some Whiteheadian scholars might wish to argue. And though I should be more than willing to defend my interpretations of Whitehead in another context, the purpose of this volume is not polemical. I have sought, on the contrary, to direct Whiteheadian thought outside the sphere of conflicting scholastic interpretations and closer to the mainstream of intellectual culture where the philosopher may be read, understood, and found relevant to the understanding of critical issues of life, society, and history.

By considering Whitehead from the perspective of a theory of culture, I believe I have uncovered an extremely accessible path into the complexities of Whitehead's thought. For Whitehead, as we shall have occasion to note in Chapter I, is primarily a philosopher of culture. To ask after his views on the theory of culture is, I believe, to ask the single most important question concerning his philosophy.

There is no simple route into the heart of Whitehead's philosophy. All roads lead through complex metaphysical concepts. Since the ultimate actualities for Whitehead are submicroscopic, issues germane to cultural experience and expression obviously cannot proceed unless we indicate first the relationship between the microcosm and the macrocosm of the Whiteheadian universe. This we shall do. We shall find in Chapter II that an analysis of the theory of "concrescence," the growth of experience, will provide an understanding of the primary analogate from which experience in its cultural modes may be understood. The cultural aims—"Art," "Adventure," "Truth," "Beauty," "Peace"—which define a civilized society will be shown to be paradigmatically present in each microcosmic occasion of experience. "Cultural Interests"—the human interests of art, morality, science, religion, philosophy—which organize and focus the cultural energies of individuals will likewise be shown to be grounded in distinct abstractive emphases of individual experience.

Mere repetition of certain Whiteheadian insights is hardly sufficient for providing an understanding of Whitehead's contribution to a theory of culture. If one concentrates upon the less speculative portions of Whitehead's writings and gives merely an orderly restatement of his views on any given topic, it is possible to provide specificity and concreteness in the characterization of the subject matter, but one is unable to consider adequately the far-reaching consequences of Whitehead's metaphysical scheme. Thus A. H. Johnson's discussion of Whitehead's theory of civilization[1] considers Whitehead's explicit statements on issues involved in his theory of civilization, but provides only minimal reference to the metaphysical underpinnings of these issues. The approach here taken, on the other hand, omits detailed consideration of Whitehead's specific statements on cultural experience and expression, and concentrates instead on the way in which the meanings of such terms as "culture," "civilization," "art," "morality," "science," "religion," "philosophy," etc., may be characterized in terms of speculative concepts essential to Whitehead's metaphysical scheme. The advantage of this approach is its conceptual generality and its concern for the subtleties of Whitehead's metaphysical theories.

It is important to recognize that the expository approach which I have employed depends upon the assumption of a continuity in Whitehead's thought. Such an assumption may seem of rather doubtful validity when we realize that Whitehead's professional concerns ranged over the subjects of mathematics, logic, philosophy of science, metaphysics, and theory of civilization. It is necessary, therefore, to provide some support for my assumption that such a continuity does, in fact, exist.

If we approach Whiteheadian thought historically, we may speak of the development of Whitehead's philosophy by attending to the chronological sequence of his writings. Such an approach usually divides his work into three periods: (1) 1891–1913, the mathematical period, dominated by the appearance of *Principia Mathematica*; (2) 1914–1923, the period of philosophy of science, which produced *The Principles of Natural Knowledge*, *The Concept of Nature*, and *The Principle of Relativity*; (3) 1924–1944, the speculative period, to which belong *Science and the Modern World*, *Religion in the Making*, *The Function of Reason*, *Process and Reality*, *Symbolism: Its Meaning and Effect*, *Adventures of Ideas*, and *Modes of Thought*.

It is quite possible to see a continuous development of Whiteheadian thought from his early mathematical and logical constructions through the systematization of a natural philosophy in his middle period and finally to a metaphysical synthesis incorporating the results of the former periods. Indeed it is clear that while writing in the philosophy of science Whitehead was already planning to incorporate the results of his natural philosophy into a broader metaphysical scheme.[2] Such a reading of Whitehead finds little by way of repetition in his writings from one period to another. Likewise, rarely is a primary scientific or metaphysical concept reinterpreted in anything like a radical manner.

It is because of this basic understanding of his philosophic development that I am disposed to find concepts and theories in Whitehead's earlier writings which adumbrate propositions in the speculative period, and to employ his mature speculative concepts to interpret aspects of his earlier philosophy. Such an employment of Whiteheadian literature conflicts with a widespread methodological device, introduced by William Christian in his work *An Interpretation of Whitehead's Metaphysics*,[3] which requires at least a provisional separation of pre-systematic, systematic, and post-systematic statements. This approach to the study of Whiteheadian texts is based upon the famous "airplane" metaphor used by Whitehead in explanation of his speculative enterprise. "The true method of discovery is like the flight of an aeroplane. It starts from the ground of particular observation; it makes a flight in the thin air of imaginative generalization; and it again lands for renewed observation rendered acute by rational interpretation" (PR 7). The airplane takes off from pre-systematic experience, flies into the air of systematic generalization, and comes to rest again on some post-systematic runway. The three areas remain reasonably distinct; the vocabularies in use in each differ significantly. On this view it is important not to ground any interpretation of Whitehead's writings on a confusion of these forms of statements.

The principal advantages of this method are its clarity and the fact that it maintains Whitehead's metaphysical scheme intact by calling constant attention to the categoreal scheme as the systematic focus from which all serious expository attempts are to begin. This method assumes a theory of types in which one set of propositions (systematic, for example) can refer to another set (post-systematic), but not to themselves. But metaphysical concepts are propositions. A metaphysical system is a complex proposition or set of propositions. "Propositions" are contained, formally defined, among the categories of existence in Whitehead's categoreal scheme. The interpretative power of Whitehead's theory insofar as it explains the meaning of propositional states of affairs must explain itself as well. Whitehead's metaphysical system has the ontological status of a "proposition" as defined by that system, and aims, therefore, at self-referential consistency. This fact renders the distinction between pre- and post-systematic propositions (based as it is upon a theory of types) inappropriate for the interpretation of Whitehead's philosophy as a whole. It seems to me, moreover, that such a procedure, though it may be reasonably sound as a method for interpreting *Process and Reality*, fails as an approach to the broad scope of Whitehead's philosophy. Whitehead's philosophic method, as I shall demonstrate, is much more complex than one would suppose from a consideration of the methodological statements contained in *Process and Reality*. My use of Whitehead's concepts and theories to develop a theory of culture will be based upon the presumption of an internal coherence of his published writings throughout his long career. And though I have given some philosophic support for this assumption, its validation must, in the last analysis, be pragmatic. If a coherent theory of culture can be constructed employing such an approach, the procedure will have been justified.

If I am at all successful in this work, I should establish several intrinsically related conclusions concerning the adequacy of Whiteheadian philosophy for the construction of a theory of culture and civilization. First, Whitehead's metaphysics provides a balance between realist and idealist philosophic tendencies and thereby avoids any form of radical metaphysical dualism. Thus, his theory of experience grounds a naturalistic philosophy in which the characterization of all types of experience is derived from the fundamental concept of the "actual entity." Whitehead's theory of the types of order is able, therefore, to allow definitions of human persons, societies, and cultures which are continuous with, but distinct from (according to certain specific teleological characteristics), all forms of natural occurrences.

Also, Whitehead's form of naturalism, supported by the complex metaphysical categories in terms of which his philosophy is expressed, allows for the characterization of highly general aims definitive of civilized experience and expression. These abstract value-concepts are categoreally based notions which serve as the criteria in terms of which one may judge the relative success or failure of human societies in achieving a balanced complexity of experience.

Thirdly, Whitehead's concept of the unitary character of experience, coupled with his theory of abstraction, permits the construction of a theory of cultural interests which supports the autonomy and interdependence of cultural enterprises, while at the same time affirming their metaphysical unity as perspective abstractions from experience. Such a theory steers a middle course between the reductionistic tendencies of the positivists and idealists, and the non-systematic approaches of contemporary analytic philosophies.

Finally, rational religion, which has suffered in this century from the attacks of neo-orthodox theologians, the reductionist onslaught of the positivists, the anti-rationalism of the existentialist movement, and, latterly, the modesty and triviality of many of the claims and accomplishments of analytic philosophers, is given powerful support by Whitehead's metaphysically elaborated theory of religion. In both his diagnosis of the cultural problem and his characterization of the religious insight which is meant to aid in its solution, Whitehead has developed a theory of culture and religion which succeeds in promoting the qualities of a civilized society and in overcoming the effects of finitude and uprootedness which threaten the cultural milieu.

II

The tone and character of the following work is, in large part, a function of certain specific circumstances qualifying the nature and role of philosophy in contemporary culture. In our present period, most professional philosophers remain content with the examination of issues which are relevant only to the profession itself. Few are concerned, as philosophers, with concrete issues outside the realm of pure philosophic speculation or analysis. Their refusal to address themselves directly to contemporary social problems has led to a dearth of significant interpretations of culture and, largely because sound philosophies of culture are lacking, contemporary thought has been inundated by amateur philosophers armed with easy, off-hand solutions to our cultural dilemmas. This "book-of-the-month" approach to philosophy of culture simply must give way to a more patient and restrained examination of the problems of contemporary culture. I hope this presentation of a Whiteheadian theory of culture will be a move in that direction.

I have written this work with a specific apologetic task in mind: to help bridge the gap between scholastic understandings of Whiteheadian philosophy and "non-philosophical" reductionistic approaches to cultural problems. Thus I have attempted to divert the attention of professional philosophers toward a confrontation of theory with concrete cultural phenomena and to illustrate to those in non-philosophical disciplines the adequacy of a philosophic theory for interpreting cultural phenomena. Professional philosophers, particularly Whiteheadian scholars, may find the book frustrating because I omit detailed analysis and a defense of my many extensions of Whitehead's philosophy. Others, interested more in the very real issues involved in the meaning of human culture and civilization, may find the work tedious at times because of the apparently unnecessary excursions into complex metaphysical issues. Of the former group I beg indulgence. I have offered here *a* Whiteheadian theory of culture and do not claim, therefore, to have established the orthodox interpretation of Whitehead's philosophy of civilization. "Wide is Madrid"; surely a philosopher of Whitehead's type is open to a number of consistent and important interpretations. Of the latter group I ask patience. Though the arguments of Parts I and II are sometimes difficult to grasp because of the unfamiliar Whiteheadian language, the chapters of Part III are meant to apply the Whiteheadian concepts in such a way as to illumine not only the significant problems of human culture, but the meaning of the metaphysical concepts themselves. That is to say, the entire work should become clear when the theory of culture constructed from Whiteheadian categories is given application in the final chapters.

Both groups of potential critics, I hope, will gain a sense of the interpretative power of Whiteheadian categories when they are applied to cultural situations. I hope this will stimulate some Whiteheadian scholars to leave their cloisters and to move into the world of concrete experience where they may relate to the significant problems confronting contemporary man. And those already confronting these issues I hope will take time out for a "retreat" into Whiteheadian thought to gain some new tools for dealing with our contemporary cultural situation. If either or both of these results is in some measure occasioned by this book, my apologetic effort will have been successful.

NOTES

1. Johnson, *Whitehead's Philosophy of Civilization* (Boston: Beacon, 1958).

2. In the preface to the second edition of PNK (1925), Whitehead indicates his plan to produce a "more complete metaphysical study" which would embody the various topics of speculative physics considered in PNK, CN, and *Prin. Rel.*

3. Christian, *An Interpretation of Whitehead's Metaphysics* (New Haven: Yale University Press, 1959).

PART ONE

METHODOLOGY

Chapter I

SPECULATIVE METHOD

WRITING IN *The Philosophy of Alfred North Whitehead* of his inability to reply in detail to the various critiques of his philosophy which form the substance of that work, Whitehead said:

> The absence of any direct expression of my reaction to these chapters is but a slight loss. The progress of philosophy does not primarily involve reactions of agreement or dissent. It essentially consists in the enlargement of thought, whereby contradictions and agreements are transformed into partial aspects of wider points of view.[1]

In this characteristic statement Whitehead reveals his basic methodological stance to be that of a benign rationalist who expects to find fundamental agreement between himself and the dominant philosophic traditions, and who sees philosophic progress as a function of the enlargement of thought rather than as dialectical refutations based upon presumed irreconcilable differences. Anyone even cursorily familiar with Whitehead's thinking will acknowledge the essentially non-dialectical character of his argumentation, a fundamental aspect of Whitehead's methodology which makes the study of his philosophy such an extremely worthwhile venture. For essential to any philosophy of culture is the constructive endeavor to make sense of the varied and often conflicting aspects of one's intellectual environment.

The irenic nature of Whitehead's speculative method does not mean that he tries to be all things to all men, but it does mean that in Whiteheadian thought we have one of the few serious attempts on the part of a contemporary philosopher to treat the data of intellectual culture in an undogmatic and non-reductive fashion. I shall have occasion in this chapter to provide some support for the view that such a benign rationalism as Whitehead's

4

provides an important approach to the problems of developing a theory of culture.

1. *Scientia Universalis* AND *Ontologia Generalis*

In the twentieth century, speculative philosophy has divided its attention between questions of the nature of being and of the organization of the principles of thought and action; or, as Gottfried Martin has termed it, between *ontologia generalis* and *scientia universalis*—general ontology and universal science.[2] Most speculative philosophers have attempted to combine both concerns, with the unhappy result that one of the two usually dominated. The most ambitious twentieth-century speculative endeavors—those of Martin Heidegger and of Alfred North Whitehead—are remarkable examples of these two complementary philosophic approaches.

For Heidegger, philosophy is the endeavor to frame a general ontology which aptly characterizes the importance of Being. To this task Heidegger has brought an acute appreciation of the history of philosophy and of the relation of philosophy to the language of a given culture. Heidegger's thought, judged by the criteria of originality, profundity, and breadth of purpose, would seem to offer a valuable approach to the problems of culture. But examining his philosophy on that score leads to grave disappointment. As exciting as the adventure of reading Heidegger may be, one is soon overcome by the feeling that Heidegger has failed utterly because of a tragic flaw contained within his fundamental approach to thinking. For Heidegger's "destruction of ontology" is, at base, merely one more attempt to make philosophy speak German.

Heidegger has diagnosed the problem of Western culture with greater insight, perhaps, than has any other twentieth-century thinker. The phenomenological analyses of *Dasein* and its world have provided us with concepts with which to understand the transforming effect of the technological state of mind upon our cultural heritage. His essay entitled "The Question of Being," written in response to Ernst Jünger's analysis of the philosophic nihilism which has been the characteristic European response to advanced technology and its encroachments upon the life of man, is surely one of the most significant contributions to the existential revolt against the technological demon. The tragic element of Heidegger's thought becomes all too clear, however, when we search for prescriptive judgments and programs to lead us out of the well-defined cultural dilemma. In this regard Heidegger's *An Introduction to Metaphysics*[3] is perhaps most significant. Originally prepared in 1935 as a lecture, and revised for publication in 1953, the work dramatically illustrates the fact that Heidegger's theory of culture is tied all too closely to German language and culture. After acknowledging "the spiritual decline of the earth" and claiming that only Europe can save the world from collapse, Heidegger identifies Germany as the "center" of Europe, the "most metaphysical of nations" possessed of a language which, along with Greek, "is (in regard to its possibilities for thought) at once the most powerful and most spiritual of all languages." [4] The historic being-there of Germany, asserted to be the center for Europe itself, is the context within which the asking and answering of the question of Being must take place. The cultures of America and Russia are rejected, seen as "the same dreary technological frenzy, the same unrestricted organization of the average man." [5]

Quite clearly, Heidegger has expressed a kind of inadmissible provinciality in his approach to culture philosophy. Even if one might, at one time, have been willing to accept salvation from the technological demon at the hands of the Germanic messiahs, it is clearly no longer possible. For what has been so aptly termed Heidegger's "demonic honeymoon with the Nazis," was nothing more, read philosophically, than an investment of his energies on the side of the drive for German cultural hegemony. The attempt to expand Germany's political and geographical influence in accordance with her presumed cultural influence did not succeed. It is no accident that since that failure Heidegger's thinking has increasingly moved toward a quietistic, poetic mysticism and away from the systematic concerns of his *Dasein-analysis*. "The destiny of a language," says Heidegger, "is grounded in a nation's *relation* to *being*." [6] Failing in its historical task of establishing cultural hegemony over Europe, Heideggerian thought accepts the passive role history has determined for it. No more sublime failure has been seen, perhaps, in all our philosophic tradition.

Heidegger's philosophic program, in spite of this failure, has made quite clear the limitations of Western philosophy as *ontologia generalis*: the explication of Being must occur within a specific semantic context in which the concreteness of man's existence is fully expressed. We have lived for two millennia by the concept of Being derived from the Greek linguistic context. The kind of ontological revision sought by Heidegger is possible only within a new semantic context. But the cultural disunity of the West renders impossible the employment of any one language as an adequate substitute for the Greek. The kind of radical program outlined by Heidegger was, of necessity, a failure. For the ontological revision he sought must await the development of a unified cultural milieu in which a single language of Being may be spoken. We must turn to the philosophy of Whitehead to find a more viable, and ultimately more fruitful, philosophy of culture.

The basic difference between Heidegger and Whitehead as philosophers of culture may be noted in terms of the fundamental issue from which each philosophy begins. For Heidegger, the primary question is: "Why is there something rather than nothing at all?" In place of this *ontological* question, Whitehead asks a *cosmological* question: "What kinds of things are there?" Heidegger's approach is certainly the more radical, but it is grounded in a necessary revision of ontological categories in terms of a semantic structure (the German language) which is not general enough in scope to be applicable to diverse cultural contexts. Whitehead's method, ideally, avoids this cultural relativity in two ways: first, by accepting a less radical program—that of a delineation of cosmological principles, rather than of ontological structures; and, secondly, by basing his descriptive generalizations in large measure directly upon scientific concepts which, because of their broad acceptance throughout Western culture, have the advantage of transcending any particular linguistic structures.

Whitehead characterizes experience by appeal to an interpretive scheme which symbolizes and organizes experiences, individual and cultural. A beginning point of philosophy is immediate experience in all its vagueness and complexity. "The elucidation of immediate experience is the sole justification for any thought; and the starting point for thought is the analytic observation of components of this experience" (PR 6). Thus, immediate experiences are the fundament out of which systematic philosophy originates. But the purpose of philosophy is not to celebrate the vagueness of experience, but to focus upon the clarification of experience which leads to understanding.

> We must start with some insights. Rationalism then "cuts their hair; washes their faces and fixes them up" so as to be presentable in the available universe of discourses. In particular, mystic insights are not "damned nonsense." The nonsense comes in when mystics claim no rational explication is possible.[7]

The rationalism of the speculative philosopher, according to Whitehead, does not allow contentment with vague mystical intuitions. Whitehead holds that in principle no important notion is closed to discovery and rational explication. Having said this, however, the philosopher should remain humble in the face of the obvious weakness of insight and the deficiencies of language which lend to every philosophic proposition its character of metaphor "mutely appealing for an imaginative leap" (PR 6). That is, in spite of Whitehead's heuristic rationalism, the end result of the speculative attempt is always to be judged as inadequate. Whitehead cites as the primary error in philosophy, that of "overstatement" (PR 11). Alternately, he claims the chief danger to philosophy to be "narrowness in the selection of evidence" (PR 512). Examining both sides of this coin will lead us more deeply into an understanding of Whitehead's philosophic method.

A narrow selection of philosophical evidence is almost impossible to avoid. Individual temperament and the limitations of social groups and schemes of thought providing the context of individual thinking lead to biases in the selection of evidence. One way Whitehead attempts to avoid such narrowness is through application of what he terms "the metaphysical rule of evidence: . . . we must bow to those presumptions, which, in despite of criticism, we still employ for the regulation of our lives. Such presumptions are imperative in experience. Rationalism is the search for the coherence of such presumptions" (PR 229).

The criteria for the selection of evidence must be pragmatic. For instance, the selection of the ultimate ideals defining actuality leads to the acceptance of a range of evidence which is characterized by more than mere truth-value. The least biased selection of evidence is one in which "the chosen stage of exemplification [is] such as to compel attention, by its own intrinsic interest, or by the intrinsic interest of the results which flow from it" (PR 512). That which is interesting in itself or by virtue of its *import* in producing interesting things stands out as evidence for philosophic speculation.

If Whitehead's primary concern were with truth, he would have to admit defeat from the very beginning. For, as he stated, "If we consider any scheme of philosophic categories as one complex assertion, and apply to it the logician's alternative, true or false, the answer must be that the scheme is false" (PR 12). The function of a speculative system of philosophy is not the establishment of truth, but the provision of a system from which true propositions applicable to particular circumstances can be derived. But even false propositions serve important philosophic functions. For those propositions which are non-conformal to the actual world "pave the way along which the world advances into novelty" (PR 284). The primary function of philosophy in its propositional form is the evocation of novelty by serving as a "lure for feeling." To avoid reading Whitehead's philosophy of culture altogether too narrowly, one should keep in mind that the four primary qualities of propositions—*validity, truth, interest,* and *importance* —illustrate the four basic modalities in which philosophic evidence is expressed.

"Validity," or correct logical form, is, of course, desirable. One reason Whitehead constructs a philosophic *system* is that the logical form itself allows for rigorous inferential moves to be made. Whitehead's respect for logic in philosophic argument is illustrated by the fact that he explicitly constructed his *Process and Reality*, at least in part, in critical response to the failure of philosophers to avoid arbitrary deductions in *ex absurdo* arguments and to reject the belief that logical inconsistency can result from anything but antecedent errors. This logical failure, evidenced in nineteenth-century Idealism and repeated with a slightly different tone in this century's existentialist philosophy, signals nothing for Whitehead but bad philosophy. Thus propositions which form a philosophic system are to be placed in logical form. The system is then employed as a matrix of propositions from which inferences can be drawn which may then be applied to circumstance for interpretative purposes. "The use of such a matrix is to argue from it boldly and with rigid logic" (PR 13). But validity in and of itself is worthless in philosophy; unless propositions have, in addition to validity, some truth, interest-value, or importance, they are sterile and impotent.

After the logical form of a proposition has been protected and the validity of propositional arguments assured, it is important to ask whether or not the propositions are true or false. The truth or falsity of a proposition is first suggested by its relevance to the field of experience from which the proposition derives. Though relevance to some experience in no way insures relevance to additional kinds of experience, some relevance does provide the basis for truth-relationships. But a true, or conformal, proposition which, in addition, is expressed in correct logical form is a candidate for yet further philosophic scrutiny. Philosophy has little use for bare, formal truths. For, in addition to being true and valid, propositions may be interesting and important.

The interest-value of a proposition is measured by the subjective attachment felt for the proposition. "The primary mode of realization of a proposition . . . is not by judgment, but by entertainment" (PR 287). Propositions may be entertained with joy, horror, sadness, relief, boredom, etc. Propositions are interesting if the mode of entertainment of an individual holding the proposition is one of intense, or focused, emotion. If a proposition evokes boredom, it can have little effect upon the entertaining subject. Without interest there is no efficacious entertainment of the proposition. Truths packaged in dull propositions are much less useful than interesting falsehoods which can at least stimulate reflection leading to broader speculations.

The fourth significant quality of propositions is *importance*. Granted it is more important that a proposition be interesting than that it be true: it is at least as important that a proposition be *important* as that it be interesting. "Interest" is a quality relating to the form of subjective commitment with which a proposition is entertained; "importance," however, is an objective quality of propositions concerned with their import in the actual world. Importance is "interest, involving that intensity of individual feeling which leads to publicity of expression" (MT 8). A proposition is important if it is the public expression of a perspective upon the totality of experience. Our culture has grown in accordance with certain public expressions of perspective. "Morality," "art," "religion," etc., are the names of species of importance. But "no one of these specializations exhausts the final unity of purpose in the world" (MT 12). That is, no single perspective can be taken as *the* perspective from which importance is obtained.

Whenever interest leads to public expression, importance exists to some extent. Philosophy of culture asks the question: "What have been the significant human interests which have consistently led to public expression?" The answer which will be given to this question in this work will be in terms of the dominant species of importance which are the result of "cultural interests." The philosophy of culture, from a Whiteheadian perspective, is the philosophy of "importance"—that is, it is the consideration of the principal species of importance and their emergence as public expressions of perspectives placed upon the universe of things in accordance with the quality of "interest." Over-concern with truth, characteristic of the systematic philosophies of the nineteenth century, has led to a situation in contemporary philosophy in which, by way of reaction, objective truth is considered of little concern to the philosopher. This fact has led philosophers to turn away from the search for truth toward the goals of clarity and consistency (validity) or to the ego-celebration of personal immediacy (subjective interest). But Whitehead's philosophy of culture is not undermined by the hiddenness of truth. Philosophy of culture, as the philosophy of *importance,* begins with the consideration of those species of importance which dominate human cultural expression, recognizing that beneath the importance of a proposition is the interest which gave rise to it, and realizing, as well, that one quality which evokes interest is the quality of "truth." Cultural experience and expression, the result of the qualities of interest and importance, contain propositions which are to be analyzed in terms of their conformity to the actual world—i.e., their truth. Placing the quality of truth in proper perspective allows Whitehead to construct a philosophy which has as one of its systematic criteria that of valid logical form, while allowing him to be free of the false conclusion: "clarity is enough," or even "truthfulness is enough." For in addition to validity and truth there are propositions, cultural expressions, which are important by virtue of some quality other than truthfulness. When we approach the question of what constitutes philosophic evidence for the construction of a theory of culture, we find that such evidence is comprised of all the species of importance currently extant in the cultural milieu.

Consequent upon the failure to select broadly enough in gathering philosophic evidence is the philosophic failure of *overstatement.* A philosopher overstates his case in two significant ways. One way restricts thought to only a selection of the categories descriptive of actuality without recognizing the resultant abstractness of thought. And since a specialized science "is confined to one genus of facts, in the sense that no statements are made respecting facts which lie outside that genus" (PR 14), speculative philosophy functions by making the sciences aware of the degree of abstraction at which they operate, as well as by systematizing the various ways of knowing through the use of yet more general principles.

The second form of overstatement results from the "false estimate of logical procedure in respect to certainty, and in respect to premises" (PR 11). Whitehead states explicitly that deductive procedures are secondary to philosophy used primarily to test the scope of general principles. Philosophy is primarily descriptive, not deductive. This important point, which Whitehead made repeatedly, deserves stress since the hypothetical-deductive scheme which introduces the systematic portions of *Process and Reality* seems to align Whitehead closely with the tradition of seventeenth-century rationalism which accepted the mathematical method of deduction as basic for philosophy. The rationalism of Whiteheadian philosophy is balanced by a humility regarding the actual success of philosophic endeavors. This type of rationalism expressed by Whitehead's philosophy has strong pragmatic overtones. "The verification of a rationalistic scheme is to be sought in its general success, and not in the peculiar certainty, or initial clarity, of its first principles" (PR 12).

Whiteheadian method is an attempt to avoid overstatement by avoiding narrowness in the selection of evidence. For if one selects as broadly as possible from all the viable sources of philosophic evidence, the danger of overstating the importance of any given type of evidence is thereby reduced. If one sees the speculative endeavor primarily as *scientia universalis,* then the sources of philosophic evidence will be found by a survey of the entire *speculum mentis,* private, historical, and cultural.

2. ANALOGICAL GENERALIZATION

The primary tools of philosophic method are three: analysis, dialectic, and analogy. The method of analysis discriminates the elements of a complex in order to demonstrate the character and role of each part, thereby uncovering the principles which found inferences from cause to consequence. Dialectical method contrasts elements with their alternatives which have been discovered in analysis or conceptual hypostatization in order to clarify X and or its alternative, $\bar{X}$; to establish the validity of X by the rejection of its alternative; or to synthesize X and $\bar{X}$ by some more inclusive concept. In the first and second instance a synthetic move is required. The progression from part to whole within a complex is achieved either by recourse to universals or by analogy. The former is a dialectical procedure; the latter is based upon a special kind of generalizing procedure—descriptive, or *analogical,* generalization. Analogical generalization operates by the selection of a primary analogate, a root-metaphor concept, which serves as the fundamental reality governing the movement from part to whole, or whole to part. Whitehead's primary philosophic method is that of analogical generalization. Analytic and dialectical procedures are subordinated to the use of analogy.

In the following examination of Whitehead's method of analogical generalization, I shall be depending for my extended applications of the concept of analogy upon the discussion of Dorothy Emmet in *The Nature of Metaphysical Thinking.*[8] The thesis of that work is that all metaphysical thinking is in some sense analogical. In the defense of this thesis Professor Emmet articulates five kinds of metaphysical analogies: deductive, projective, hypothetical, coordinating, and existential. Whiteheadian method draws heavily upon each of these types of analogy, with the exception of the projective.[9] In what follows we shall discover that the fundamental sources of philosophic evidence from which Whitehead begins his philosophizing require the assumption of analogical relationships existing among all elements of reality.

There are two primary sources of philosophic evidence for Whiteheadian philosophy which seem, prima facie, quite divergent. The first is implied in Whitehead's formal definition of speculative philosophy as "the endeavour to frame a coherent, logical, necessary system of general ideas in terms of which every element of our experience can be interpreted" (PR 4). Philosophy, so considered, begins with "general ideas." The principal sources of such ideas are the various interests characterizing intellectual culture, such as art, science, or religion.

Cultural interests serve as the repository of general ideas from which the systematic procedures of the speculative philosopher begin. Such a philosophic endeavor should produce "the genus, for which the special schemes of the sciences [i.e., ways of knowing] are the species" (FR 76). This procedure refers to " 'the utilization of specific notions, applying to a restricted group of facts, for the divination of the generic notions which apply to all facts' " (PR 8). This procedure involves the use of analogy as a means of coordinating various elements of experience in terms of the extension of a key notion derived from a single element of experience.[10] This, as we shall see, is Whitehead's primary analogical ploy.

Such a method presupposes that relations exist among the various interests of intellectual culture such that, regardless of the discipline selected as the source of general ideas, these ideas will have relevance to each of the other disciplines. This assumption is the bedrock of the dominant traditions of Western philosophy stemming from both Plato and Aristotle. For Plato the abstract generality of mathematical forms was the basis of all intellectual culture. "The Good" was that formal principle which united all knowledge and practice. Insight into the important formal principles undergirding human knowledge provided an understanding of the relationships of the various interests of intellectual culture. Aristotle, whose organization of the sciences stressed the autonomy of theoretical, practical, and productive enterprises, nonetheless found in logic, *The Organon*, a tool of analysis and inquiry relevant to each of the disciplines. The logical principles employed in each of the cultural interests were fundamentally the same. For Aristotle, intellectual culture illustrated a basic logical patterning.

Whitehead's acceptance of a fundamental structure discoverable in any topic of human interest places him squarely within the classical rationalist tradition. The novelty of Whitehead's philosophy consists in his detailed examination of the grounds for presupposing such a common structure. One dominant theme of Whiteheadian thought from *Principia Mathematica* to *Modes of Thought* is the examination of reasons for assuming a fundamental set of analogical relationships existing among the data of experience.

Whitehead's attempt in *Principia Mathematica* to ground mathematics in a tautological base would have provided, quite apart from its contribution to the fields of logic and mathematics, an enormous boost to the rationalistic method. And the fact that Whitehead conceived this attempt to have been a failure[11] is significant precisely because it sets limits to the formal, mathematical rationalism of his method. The partial success of this attempt, however, is sufficient to provide Whitehead with the belief that logic and mathematics express general truths about the world which are reflected in every topic of intellectual culture. "The generality of mathematics is the most complete [abstract] generality consistent with the community of occasions which constitutes our metaphysical situation" (SMW 38). The examination of the general ideas discoverable in any topic of human interest—from physics to philosophy—should disclose a basic mathematical or formal set of relationships. Whitehead's own philosophic investigations, considered both systematically and biographically, are extensions of his mathematical and scientific researches and speculations. The need for specialized grounding as the basis of descriptive generalization is often emphasized by Whitehead. Grounded in the classical traditions of logic, mathematics, and physics, and acutely aware of, as well as partly responsible for, the revolutionary changes in these disciplines in the early twentieth century, Whitehead employs the conceptualizations of physics and mathematics as a basic source of evidence from which to construct his cosmological system.

The deductive and analytic function of Whiteheadian method is discerned in the hypothetical-deductive nature of his categoreal scheme in *Process and Reality*. The categoreal notions are axiomatically organized, allowing for relevant deductive procedures which define the limits of applicability and the mutual coherence of the various notions within the scheme itself. The explication of the categoreal notions in the text of *Process and Reality* and, within limits, in some of Whitehead's other writings, may be reintroduced into the categoreal scheme and deductively manipulated, exposing new relationships and possible discrepancies. Deductions employing the categoreal scheme are in fact analogical procedures in which empirical phenomena are interpreted in terms of the morphological scheme of *Process and Reality* based upon the presumption of analogies between certain factors in experience and formal aspects of the categoreal scheme. The type of procedure involved, therefore, presupposes that analogical relations exist between the nature of the cosmos as a whole and some specific class of phenomena within it. And since the entire cosmos can never be the object of experience, the analogies can be no more than hypothetical.[12]

Whitehead's second source of philosophic evidence is the private psychological field. This matrix of private experience, accessible via immediate apperceptive intuition, serves Whitehead at crucial points to test the reasonableness and existential import of concepts or intuitions and provides a wealth of subjective data for philosophic construction. This second source of philosophic evidence is not nearly so far removed from the first as might appear to be the case. For the mathematical relationships presupposed in intellectual culture are expressed in immediate experience as well. The "full universe, disclosed for every variety of experience, is a universe in which every detail enters into its proper relationship with the immediate occasion" (SMW 38). The relationships within and among the various fields of specialized interest are found to exist at the most primitive experiential level. The "reasonable harmony of being, which is required for the unity of a complex occasion, together with the completeness of the realisation (in that occasion) of all that is involved in its logical harmony, is the primary article of metaphysical doctrine" (SMW 40). The relationship of one occasion to another is determined by the fact that the general conditions discoverable in one occasion are necessary for the ingression or passage into other occasions. "Either we know something of [another] occasion by the cognition which is itself an element in the immediate occasion, or we know nothing" (SMW 38).

The generality of mathematical and logical forms discoverable within an experience "is imposed alike on external reality, and on our abstract representations of it" (SMW 39). Thus employing the private psychological field as a source of philosophic speculations is merely the other side of the coin from beginning with some generalized topic of human interest. "The world within experience is identical with the world beyond experience . . ." (AI 293).

The private psychological field provides the primary grasp of reality; the specialized fields of human interest represent abstract representations of reality. Whitehead constructs his philosophy, via coordinating analogies, drawn from reality both as immediately experienced and as abstractly represented in mathematical physics. The analogies between private experience and our abstract representations of nature provide the grounds for this twofold procedure. The "direct evidence as to the connectedness of one's immediate present occasion of experience with one's immediately past occasions can be validly used to suggest categories applying to the connectedness of all occasions in nature" (AI 284). There is a necessarily direct analogical relationship between the formal relations within and among specialized topics of intellectual culture and those relations discoverable within the private psychological field. "An occasion of experience which includes a human mentality is an extreme instance . . . of those happenings which constitute nature" (AI 237). From the analysis of physical science Whitehead derives the basic structure of the hypothetical-deductive scheme of *Process and Reality*. In the introspective analysis of the private psychological field he discovers the basis for the concept of the aesthetic events which are the fundamental entities forming nature in its widest sense.

In addition to introspective analysis and the conceptual constructions of mathematical physics, Whitehead employs three other sources of philosophic evidence. But whereas the first two sources are employed constructively—i.e., as means of constructing basic philosophical categories and organizing them in a hypothetical-deductive scheme—the remaining sources of evidence are used in a "limiting" fashion as means of validating the fundamental notions derived from introspection and from natural science. These three sources of "limiting" evidence are: alternate philosophical schemes, the language of metaphor and imagery, and what Whitehead terms "the width of civilized experience."

One basic way in which Whitehead seeks to validate his fundamental philosophic insights is through a comparison of his own ideas with alternative understandings. Such a confrontation indicates the need for a partial revision of certain classical philosophical categories and vocabulary. Throughout the second part of *Process and Reality* Whitehead introduces new terms and expressions into philosophic vocabulary and in so doing revises some of the more sophisticated notions of classical philosophy. For instance, the introduction of terms such as "prehension," "actual occasion," "eternal objects" is meant to facilitate a reformulation of the categories of causality, particulars and universals, subject and predicate, etc., as these categories arise in the philosophic programs of such philosophers as Plato, Descartes, Locke, and Hume.

The discussion of alternate scientific and philosophic theories in the development of his system provides Whitehead with a partial check of the rationality of some of his insights. Dialectical comparison of his thought with that of other constructive theorists provides him with some sense of the analogies existing between his and other serious thinking. That some such analogies should exist is important to Whitehead because of his principle of rationality. For if reason is in principle capable of penetrating to the nature of things, 2400 years of philosophic activity in the West should have produced thinkers who have found some significant truths. A philosopher who claims to be a rationalist and claims, as well, to have radical novelty of insight, yet sees his fellow philosophers as "wrong-headed," must face the uncomfortable question: "If reason is such a good instrument, why has it achieved worthwhile results only in *my* philosophy?" Some agreement from the truly great philosophers is essential in order to sustain one's rationalism and one's sense of making a significant contribution to philosophy. Thus what John Dewey has called Whitehead's "excessive piety toward those historic philosophers from whom he has derived valuable suggestions" [13] is nothing more than an expression of this basic rationalistic impulse.

Though a rationalist in principle, Whitehead is convinced of the limits of rationality. In philosophic understanding a "givenness" is always presupposed beyond which no rational inquiry can be made. For Whitehead, apart from such givenness there is no basis for reasoning, and the fact of givenness implies the necessity of deciding on a starting point for philosophy. That is, givenness leads to "decision," and decision implies exclusiveness and selectivity. While it is the case that we must have a world, the reason *why* we have a world is ultimately undeterminable through philo-

sophic analysis. Here we have the fundamental reason why Whitehead refuses to make a full-scale attempt to answer the ontological question, and
remains satisfied with the cosmological question. Nonetheless, philosophy
as Whitehead sees it leads to the very edge of understanding. For this reason
Whitehead often resorts to poetic and metaphorical language.

Another source of limiting evidence is illustrated by the use of metaphor
and imagery. Whitehead is convinced that concerning that which cannot be
said one must in no wise remain silent, but that one must attempt to employ forms of linguistic expression which point beyond literal significances
and evoke experiences which can only be intuited. Because of his conviction
that these intuitions are shared by members of our cultural tradition and
expressed in the poetic visions of civilized literature, Whitehead sometimes
employs language in an evocative manner. His prose style is often a mixture
of original aphorisms and poetic metaphor borrowed from aesthetic expressions common to Western man.

The employment of metaphorical or imagistic language serves two
philosophic purposes. Whitehead wishes to evoke some sense of that which
is literally inexpressible. Resort to poetic metaphor provides some tools
whereby such evocation is possible. But Whitehead wishes at the same time
to demonstrate that certain insights are at present incapable of finding literal
expression. In other words, he uses non-literal language in order to gain
partial access to insights not completely accessible to his reason. Such language serves both as a signpost pointing beyond and a boundary preventing
further penetration. Analogies which characterize experiences capable of
only partial rationalization express the penumbral limit of Whitehead's
philosophical thought.[14]

Literal language is altogether too abstract to deal with all the aspects of
experience. As we shall see in dealing with Whitehead's theory of experience, the greater part of our experience is primitive, emotional, and, ultimately, non-verbalizable. "For this reason, philosophy is analogous to imaginative art. It suggests meanings beyond its mere statements" (MT 117).
There is reason, therefore, to term philosophy mystical since philosophy
shares with mysticism direct insight into unspoken depths. But philosophy
is mystical in a distinctly different way from religion or poetry. The religious mystic enjoys and attempts to evoke the experience of individuality
sub specie aeternitatis through the use of imagery which relates to a system
of belief. The poet seeks through meter to penetrate to the depths of experience indifferent to any systems of belief. Philosophy employs not meter
but mathematical pattern to plumb experience in order to construct a rationally coordinated mysticism. Religion, art, philosophy—each in its own
way seeks to deal with the unspeakable.

Whitehead's use of metaphor and imagery in order to penetrate beyond
the limits of explicit language may be illustrated by recourse to his characterization of philosophic evidence in *Process and Reality*. Whitehead is

discussing the proposition which begins Chapter I of Part V, entitled "The Ideal Opposites": "Philosophy may not neglect the multifariousness of the world—the fairies dance, and Christ is nailed to the cross" (PR 513). The multifariousness of the world which may not be named or characterized may nonetheless be sensed through such imagery. Between the boundaries of the noble and the tragic, the historical greatness of events and the trivial fantasies of immediate joy, lie the subject matters of philosophy. Here philosophy allies itself with poetic imagery to evoke the sense of the inconceivable multifariousness of things. What is claimed is that the contrast between the extremes of experience metaphorically expressed is analogous to the contrasts between extremes within the context of the totality of experience which forms the source of philosophic evidence.

The most significant use of limiting evidence by Whitehead is to be found in his appeal to "the width of civilized experience." We shall consider the use of this evidential source in some detail since it is so closely related to Whitehead's development of a theory of culture. A developed philosophic system finds its context not only among other cosmological systems. More importantly a philosophy has the broad cultural context as its fundamental locus. In the appeal to "civilized experience," we have one of the major sources of philosophic evidence concerned with theory of culture. For Whitehead continually philosophizes against the background of a positive affirmation of the Western cultural tradition.

> Philosophy is the search for premises. . . . When applied to concrete instances, it is a tentative procedure, finally to be judged by the self-evidence of its issues. This doctrine places philosophy on a pragmatic basis. . . . Pragmatism is simply an appeal to that self-evidence which sustains itself in civilized experience. Thus pragmatism ultimately appeals to the wide self-evidence . . . of what we mean by "civilization" [MT 105–106].

The appeal to "civilized experience" is one reason for Whitehead's claim that philosophy is based in pragmatism. One of Whitehead's concerns in his criticism of modern philosophy has been to indicate the way in which philosophies—particularly those of the classical British empiricist branch and their issue—have arbitrarily suppressed, or failed to note, ranges of human experience. Whitehead claims, as we have noted, that the besetting sin of philosophy is narrowness in the selection of evidence. Philosophers have tended to find in "clear and distinct" reflections, or in the "primary deliverances of the senses," or in "ordinary language," the sole repository of philosophic evidence. Such approaches to philosophy are reductionist in nature. Granted that *all* philosophy is reductionist since philosophers are finite beings with interests, perspectives, and abilities which entail a limited capacity for encompassing the real in philosophic reflection: the aim of the philosopher, nonetheless, must be to select as broadly as possible in seeking the evidence upon which to found a speculative system.

The appeal to the practices of mankind is a strong affirmation of the pragmatic character of philosophy. It is an explicit denial of the orthodox meaning of rationalism illustrated by the great speculative philosophers of the seventeenth century as well as a rejection of the narrow introspective biases of the sense-data philosophers. Philosophy must appeal to "widespread, recurrent experience" (PR 25). The function of philosophy is "to promote the most general systematization of civilized thought" (PR 25–26). The importance of human beliefs is not questioned by Whitehead, for beliefs constitute one source of evidence about the human experience of the nature of things. The philosopher then must consider the width of human experience, and the validity of any scheme developed must depend ultimately on the adequacy of that scheme to interpret human experience and expression in all its forms. The width of experience is comprised of "language, social institutions, and action, including thereby the fusion of the three which is language interpreting action and social institutions" (AI 291).

The appeal to experience in Whitehead is, thus, an appeal to experience in all its modes. The speculative reason of the philosopher "seeks to build a cosmology expressing the general nature of the world as disclosed in human interests" (FR 85). The close contact required between a speculative system and the concrete reality it seeks to describe requires that account be taken of the institutions which constitute, and have constituted, the structures of human society. "It is only in this way that we can appeal to the widespread effective elements in the experience of mankind. What those institutions stood for in the experience of their contemporaries, represents the massive facts of ultimate authority" (FR 85).

Whitehead considers his philosophic method to be that of the working hypothesis in which the pragmatic appeal to the self-evidence of civilized experience serves as one basis for the validation of philosophic premises. Just how seriously we are to take his claim to a pragmatic method may be suggested by showing the similarities between Whitehead and John Dewey on the issue of philosophic method.

In his *Quest for Certainty*,[15] Dewey traces the conflict between theoretical and practical conceptions of reason back to its origins in Greek culture. The bifurcation in the social and political realm of the intellectual leisure class and the laboring masses provides the *fundamentum in re* for the philosophical distinction between theory and practice. This is a good illustration of Dewey's genetic-functional interpretation of the origin of philosophical concepts and their dependence upon cultural states of affairs. The role of philosophy is not to provide a fixed and stable conceptual framework from which to argue; rather philosophy facilitates the practice of that form of inquiry which uncovers "leading principles." Dewey's revolution in philosophy had concerned itself precisely with this subject of method. And the pragmatic turn he helped to give to philosophy led to the union of the theoretical and practical forms of reason by recourse to a revised concept of "practice."

Like Existentialism and linguistic analysis, Dewey's form of pragmatism owed its development largely to reaction against Idealism. Dewey's earliest works, especially his *Outline of a Critical Theory of Ethics*,[16] reflected a type of idealism which was in large part rejected by the time, twelve years later, he published his *Studies in Logical Theory*.[17] Dewey's genetic-functional approach was a product of the impact of Darwinian theory upon philosophic thought. The functional, operational approach to biology was extended to all topics of philosophy, even logic. Thus philosophic concepts and theories possessed the same mutability attributed by Darwin to all biological species. The theory of cultural interests which derives from such a philosophic method is one in which the separation between the so-called theoretical and practical disciplines is overcome and dominance is given to the practical, functional activities as the origin of all speculative interests. Dewey's *Quest for Certainty* is a brilliant attempt to provide a genetic account of the origins of the bifurcation of theoretical and practical forms of reason (and of the origin, therefore, of the cultural divisions between knowledge and action). In this work he sought to provide, as well, the foundations of a method for the ultimate union of knowledge and action through the practice of philosophic inquiry which demonstrates knowledge to be only one among many modes of action.

This theory has been criticized as incapable of bringing into proper balance the elements of "status" and "function" in a culture. The emphasis upon "change" over "permanence" means that cultural interests and activities are seen largely as methods of progressive realization of types of experiences each within the bounds of its own particular issues and problems. Such an operationalist approach to culture emphasizes function over status, an emphasis which has been vigorously criticized by many theorists of culture because of its failure to allow to philosophy, or to any other cultural enterprise, a normative function.[18] Dewey's form of pragmatism shares with linguistic analysis and logical positivism a certain immanental bias which refuses to recognize a need for corrective norms transcendent of any actual state of affairs.

These philosophies are, in fact, types of positivism in which a cultural given is posited and never critically evaluated. Logical positivism posits the scientific world-view of physics and its epistemological foundations. Linguistic analysts posit ordinary language which is to be accepted as normative of philosophic analysis. ("Philosophy may in no way interfere with the actual use of language; it can in the end only describe it. . . . *It leaves everything as it is*." [19]) The pragmatism of Dewey posits a pluralistic society which allows freedom of inquiry and is open to change. Philosophy then concentrates upon "meaning" and "significance" rather than upon truth since the work of philosophy is the progressive adjustment of traditions constituting the funded experience of man to novel scientific and political tendencies incompatible with received authority. That the actual mind of man is composed of a body of traditions means that transitions which occur in human beings occur only within a given society. Disagreements among philosophers are not a sign of the difficulty of any search for truth, but a manifestation that truth itself is not the proper goal of philosophy. Variations in philosophies signal variations of role in the social complex. The plurality of philosophical systems arises from the inherent plurality within society. According to Dewey, if the ruling and the oppressed elements in a society were to have the same philosophy, one would be skeptical of its intellectual integrity.

Dewey's stress upon the genetic and functional approach as the only proper philosophical method carries the implication of a type of operationalism which denies to reason the ability to discover formal definitions and postulates which have relevance to the passing flux of actuality. Thus Dewey appreciated that part of Whitehead's philosophy which was based upon empirical methods—i.e., descriptive generalization—but criticized Whitehead whenever he supplemented descriptive generalizations by abstract schemes of morphology. Dewey's instrumentalism stems from the emphasis upon the empirical operations of actuality and de-emphasis upon all abstract theoretical schemas not immediately pertinent to such operations. In a critique of Whitehead's philosophic method, Dewey claims that "there must be something homologous in the material of physical science and that of feeling, ideas, emotion and enjoyment as they occur in human experience. But . . . all that is needed in the way of homology is correspondence of *functions*." [20]

Whitehead, like Dewey, looks to civilized societies as givens from which the philosopher draws his descriptive generalizations and to which he makes appeal for the validity of his philosophy. The difference, however, between Whiteheadian philosophy and Dewey's form of pragmatism is that, for Whitehead, there is a transcendent appeal possible beyond the experiences, aims, and goals of any finite group of societies, since, for the philosopher, "the final court of appeal is intrinsic reasonableness" (PR 63).

Dewey looks upon the plurality of philosophic positions as a function of the varying interests and roles of men in societies. The attainment of significance rather than truth is the criterion by which such philosophies are to be judged. The fundamental unity of cultural interests is a unity of the method of inquiry. For Whitehead, on the other hand, the existence of a plurality of conflicting beliefs and aims is an indication, not of essential conflict, but rather of *identity*.

> The discordance at once disclosed among the beliefs and purposes of men is commonplace. . . . The superficial details at once disclose themselves by the discordance which they disclose. The concordance in general notions stands out. The very fact of institutions to effect purposes witnesses to [the] unquestioned belief that foresight and purpose can shape the attainment of ends. The discordance over moral codes witnesses to the fact of moral

experience. . . . The basis of every discord is some common experience, discordantly realized [FR 85–86].

Whereas Dewey's social philosophy is a generalization of societal operations and functions without any explicitly normative motivation, Whitehead's generalizations involve an explicitly formulated theory which presupposes a common structure of experiencing underlying all separate modes of experience.

The distinction between Whitehead and Dewey's operationalism is drawn even more sharply in their views on the significance of "conventionalism" in regard to the subject of the laws of nature. Dewey conceives a law of nature to be a "formula of description and calculation of interdependent changes" [21] for *"the prediction of the probability of an observable occurrence."* [22] Laws are descriptions of functional relationships between observed phenomena. Again in his concern for the constitutive nature of law, Dewey's theory of the immanence of law becomes indistinguishable from the positivist concept of law as pure description. Such a conception of law eschews all metaphysical or ontological considerations in favor of as simple and direct a statement of observed regularities as possible. Whitehead's doctrine of the immanence of law manifests a tendency of a different sort. Whitehead makes a concession to the concept of conventionalism in the interpretation of natural law. The concession is grounded in the notion of the finitude of the human intellect and the relatively small number of actual sciences which have been developed in the history of civilized man. Accordingly, Whitehead makes the declaration that "there are an indefinite number of purely abstract sciences, with their laws, their regularities, and their complexities of theorems—all as yet undeveloped" (AI 177). Until we need or desire to develop the sensitivities to the type of regularities to look for in nature, these sciences will remain undeveloped. The emergence of science depends in part upon convention. "The order of emergence depends upon the abstract sciences which civilized mankind have in fact chosen to develop" (AI 177).

One significant contribution of Whitehead's methodology is found in his attempt to combine the broad-based empiricism implied in his notion of analogical generalization with the speculative and rationalistic concern for the discovery of generic permanences within the flux of experience. Whitehead combines the genetic-functional method praised by Dewey with the mathematical-formal method which seeks to discover an abstract scheme of morphology normatively relevant to experienced process.

The historic process of the world, which requires the genetic-functional interpretation, also requires for its understanding some insight into those ultimate principles of existence which express the necessary connections within the flux. . . . To hold necessity apart from accident, and to hold form apart from process, is an ideal of the understanding. The approxi-

mation to this ideal is the romantic history of the development of human
intelligence [ESP 94, 99].

Here is a classic Whiteheadian statement of method. The dichotomy of
rationalism and empiricism is a false dichotomy. There is no necessity to
choose one form of thinking over the other. To hold rational necessity apart
from empirical contingencies is not a task performed in order to save
ideals from the taint of empirical circumstances. On the contrary, the two
elements of experience are mutually interrelated in that the ideas or forms
of process interpret those concrete experiences which constitute the only
reason for the development of a speculative scheme. Whitehead is not prepared to accept as final either the seventeenth-century mathematical-formal,
or the twentieth-century genetic-functional, method.

Such are the outlines of Whitehead's complex method of analogical generalization. I have noted that at least five separate sources of philosophic
evidence are employed and that Whitehead exploits the peculiar analogical
relations existing within and among these separate evidences. The analogical relations presupposed between the data of immediate experience and the
general character of nature allow Whitehead to extend generalizations concerning data discoverable in experience in order to construct coordinating
concepts of general philosophic import. Similarly, coordinating analogies
suggest relations between the specialized field of mathematical physics and
the basic concepts involved in other cultural interests. Whitehead's developed system then can be exploited through the application of its general
hypothetical interpretation and the explicit deductive employment of the
categoreal scheme. The "existential" analogies existing between metaphorical language and experiences transcending literal description provide another basis for philosophic explanation. Finally the presumed relations between Whitehead's views and the broad presuppositions of civilized experience, as well as the more specific relations existing between Whitehead's
philosophy of creativity and other philosophical views, confirm the adequacy
of a speculative philosophy which illustrates profound relevance for the interpretation of Western cultural experience.

NOTES

1. *The Philosophy of Alfred North Whitehead,* ed. Paul Schilpp (New York: Tudor,
1941) [664].
2. "Metaphysics as *Scientia Universalis* and as *Ontologia Generalis,*" in *The Relevance
of Whitehead,* ed. Ivor Leclerc (New York: Macmillan, 1961), pp. 219–231.
3. I have used the edition published by Doubleday in 1961.
4. *Ibid.,* p. 47.
5. *Ibid.,* p. 31.
6. *Ibid.,* p. 42.
7. Quoted in A. H. Johnson, "Whitehead as Teacher and Philosopher," *Philosophy
and Phenomenological Research,* 29, No. 4 (1968–1969), 353.

8. Emmet, *The Nature of Metaphysical Thinking* (London: Macmillan, 1944), pp. 8–17.

9. "Projective" analogies are grounded in the presumed relations existing between elements discoverable within experience and "transcendent"—i.e., non-experienceable—objects. For example, when Kant, characterizing the noumenal realm, speaks of "things-in-themselves," he is applying, perhaps inadvertently, a concept ("plurality") derived from the world of phenomena to a transcendent realm. Whitehead does not employ such analogies for the simple reason that he does not presume the existence of non-experienceable entities.

10. See Emmet, *Metaphysical Thinking*, pp. 12–13 for the discussion of "coordinating" analogies.

11. See "Indications, Classes, Numbers, Validation," in ESP 239–240.

12. See Emmet, *Metaphysical Thinking*, pp. 8–12, for the discussion of "hypothetical" and "deductive" analogies.

13. In *Philosophy of . . . Whitehead,* ed. Schilpp, pp. 659–660.

14. Emmet terms such analogies "existential." See *Metaphysical Thinking,* pp. 13–15.

15. Dewey, *Quest for Certainty* (New York: Capricorn, 1960), Chapters I and IV.

16. Dewey, *Outline of a Critical Theory of Ethics* (Ann Arbor: Register, 1891).

17. Dewey, *Studies in Logical Theory* (Chicago: University of Chicago Dicennial Publications, 1903).

18. See Robert Weaver, *Ideas Have Consequences* (Chicago: University of Chicago Press, 1948), especially Chapter II, for this type of criticism; as well as Herbert Marcuse, *One-Dimensional Man* (Boston: Beacon, 1964), pp. 1–18, 85–120; and Paul Tillich, *Systematic Theology* (Chicago: University of Chicago Press, 1963) III 28–29.

19. Ludwig Wittgenstein, *Philosophical Investigations* (New York: Macmillan, 1953), p. 49 (italics mine).

20. In *Philosophy of . . . Whitehead,* ed. Schilpp, p. 660.

21. Dewey, *Reconstruction in Philosophy* (Boston: Beacon, 1957), p. 61.

22. *Quest,* p. 206.

Chapter II

THE PRIMARY ANALOGATE

"IN ALL PHILOSOPHIC THEORY there is an ultimate which is actual in virtue of its accidents" (PR 10). The ultimate to which Whitehead refers is the principle or intuition which grounds philosophic theories. Examples of such ultimates in philosophic theory are Plato's "Form of the Good," Aristotle's "Prime Matter," and Spinoza's "God." The ultimate notion serves as the fundamental metaphysical or epistemological principle. It is the alpha and omega of philosophic theory in the sense that argument presupposes the notion, elaborates upon it through analytic, dialectical, or analogical means, and employs the notion as the principle which justifies the primary philosophic arguments. Philosophers who employ the method of analogical generalization, as Whitehead does, utilize this ultimate as the basis for the construction of a "primary analogate"—i.e., a conceptual construct from which are made the principal analogical moves leading to the construction of a systematic philosophical interpretation of experience.

1. THE AESTHETIC EVENT

The philosophic ultimate from which Whitehead's primary analogate is constructed is the notion of "creativity." The analogate is that of "aesthetic event," possessing the qualities of *freedom, transience,* and *novel purpose.* In discussing Whitehead's method of analogical generalization, I have already adumbrated the concept of aesthetic events which, under the name "actual entities" or "actual occasions," constitute the primary subject matter of Whitehead's philosophy. We shall begin with a brief characterization of that concept in a relatively informal manner; then we shall discuss the concept in some detail employing Whitehead's technical language. But before we consider Whitehead's primary analogate, it will be well to note some of the alternatives to the Whiteheadian philosophy which have established themselves in the Western philosophic tradition. For besides philosophies which draw upon the concept of creativity, as Whitehead's does, there are such alternative visions as those of the materialist, naturalist, idealist or volitional philosophies which employ quite different primary analogates or "root metaphors." [1]

The materialist vision is grounded in a concept of material or conceptual simples, basic building bricks, comprising the nature of things. Classical atomism with its assumption of least material units from which derived the basic world-view of seventeenth- and eighteenth-century science, has given way to slightly more subtle forms of psychological or linguistic atoms as fundamental realities. The Freudian vision of man and culture couched in terms of primal instincts or drives, themselves fundamental and unanalyzable, is a perfect example of the materialist paradigm. Logical atomism, similarly, is a materialist vision grounded on the supposition that atomic facts, answering to Humean simples, form the basis of our understanding of the nature of things.

The materialist vision with its mechanical world-view involves an affirmation of determinism. "Nature," conceived as atoms and empty space, or physiological drives, or linguistic units, is reductively explained. All relations are extrinsic, no room is provided for human freedom in the ordinary sense of the word. Freedom is best understood in its psychotherapeutic sense —i.e., as the freedom from responsibility for that which one has become. Materialism is backward-looking in the sense that to understand the past is to account for the present. Causal analysis is the primary philosophic method. The philosophy of culture which is grounded by such a philosophy is best exemplified by Freud's *Civilization and its Discontents*, a reductive explanation of human culture as the sublimated products of repressed libidinal impulses. On such a view, cultural objects such as poetry, mathematical schemas, etc., are the result of isolatable impulses within the physiological make-up of the cultural agent.

The formalist vision, paradigmatically expressed by Plato, characterizes reality in terms of an unchanging set of forms, ideas, or essences, the intrinsic interrelations of which constitute the essential structure of things. The understanding of things is obtained by dialectical thought which moves from particularity to universality in search of the primary principle, a principle of relatedness. Human agency is seen in terms of knowledge, its pursuit, and obedience to its dictates. Social and cultural experience are understood in terms of the fundamental ideas which guide the thought and action of individuals and epochs. For such a vision, the primary analogate is the principle, or principles, which informs thought at its highest level —for Plato, the principle of the Good.

Another paradigm with which Whitehead's thought has some similarities is that of the naturalist viewpoint. "Naturalist," as I am using the term, has reference to the philosophic vision grounded in the concept of biological organism. It is the biological world-view which received its most significant modern expression by those nineteenth- and twentieth-century philosophers who rationalized the Darwinian evolutionary theory.

According to this view, an organism is a whole whose parts functionally interrelate to achieve some purpose. The purpose defines the manner in which the various parts function. This biological metaphor, which is employed to understand not only living things, but social and political institutions as well, approximates the Whiteheadian paradigm, since to understand the nature of all things by recourse to the concept of a growing thing is similar to understanding it in terms of aesthetic events.

Volitional philosophy customarily affirms the arbitrary power of human decision and action as the fundamental reality. Man is the measure of all things. "Reality" is that which "great men" decide. Great men are those capable of persuading others of the validity of their convictions. In our century it is Existentialism which best exemplifies this perspective. All relations are power-relations. The paradigm for understanding social and political issues in the ruler–ruled relationship. On this view the primary analogate is *expression*—as *atoms* were for the materialist, *ideas* for the formalist, and *organisms* for the naturalist. Man's being is self-made via expression. Language is the matrix through which the power-relations of men are established. The importance of language and the necessity of rhetorical persuasion are illustrated in existential philosophers such as Sartre, Camus, Heidegger, who draw heavily upon the use of plays, novels, poetry, etc., to make many of their most significant and subtle philosophic points.

In contradistinction to the materialist, naturalist, formalist, and volitionalist paradigms, Whiteheadian philosophy begins with the notion of "creativity," "the pure notion of the activity conditioned by the objective immortality of the actual world" (PR 46–47). Whitehead claims that this concept of creativity functions *systematically* much as does Aristotle's concept of "prime matter" in that each is without a character of its own. He explicitly contrasts his concept with Aristotle's since creativity, unlike prime matter, is "divested of the notion of passive receptivity" (PR 46). Thus creativity is without character, but it is not *passively* so. That is to say, creativity in itself is uncharacterized; nonetheless, it *characterizes*! " 'Creativity' is the universal of universals characterizing ultimate matter of fact" (PR 31). A number of different issues must be sorted out before we can decipher these rather confusing statements. First, it is necessary to distinguish between "creativity" as a *concept* and as the source of a fundamental intuition. Then we must determine the way in which creativity functions in each of these roles.

When Whitehead characterizes creativity as the "universal of universals" or identifies it as an "ultimate notion" (PR 31), he is speaking of it as a concept whose role is as "The Category of the Ultimate" in his metaphysical system. As such, it is comparable to Aristotle's "matter" or Plato's "Form of the Good" as that principle which explains the ontological situation characterized by a philosophical system. Plato's fundamental principle explains existence as a rational totality of a permanent world of forms. Aristotle's principle explains a changing world of forms with a *substantial* permanence. Whitehead's principle explains a world of change in which process has taken priority over substance as the fundamental ontological given. As an explanatory principle, Whitehead's concept of creativity is directly analogous to Plato's "Form of the Good," Aristotle's "matter," Spinoza's "God," etc. Part of the difficulty in understanding Whitehead's principle in this manner is that classical first principles have tended to be concepts of substances rather than processes. Our philosophic dispositions lead us to think that a concept of a process is a contradiction in terms. A concept of a process is, after all, not just an abstraction but a falsification as well. This leads to difficulties in understanding which are not encountered in substance philosophies.

John Cobb, an otherwise competent expositor of Whitehead, falls victim to this substantialist bias in a comparison of "creativity" and "prime matter." [2] Making the distinction between *what* things are and *that* things are, Cobb states that Aristotle's prime matter, since it is subject to any form whatsoever, cannot explain the *what* of things. The question asking why there is anything at all is in some sense answered, however, by the reply that prime matter is eternal and demands some form. Cobb concludes that prime matter functions as an explanatory principle, since "once we have intuited the idea of prime matter we see that from the Aristotelian perspective there must be something eternally unchanging at the base of the flux of the things." [3] But Cobb claims that Whitehead's denial of any underlying substance which is the substrate of change means that creativity cannot function as an explanatory principle analogous to prime matter. Since the Aristotelian prime matter seems to provide a ground beneath the flux of phenomena, Cobb questions the significance of any analogous notion in Whitehead when the ontological situation itself is in flux. Cobb claims that "there is a radical and evident contingency about the existence of new units of creativity (actual entities) that is not characteristic of new forms of prime matter." [4]

Cobb concludes, therefore, that creativity explains neither what things are nor that things are, and that to seek an explanation on Whitehead's terms one must look elsewhere. Such a conclusion does real injustice to Whitehead's philosophy. To say, as Cobb does, that there is a radical contingency about the existence of new actual entities which is not characteristic of new forms of prime matter and that creativity, therefore, does not *explain* in a fashion analogous to prime matter is to miss the point of

Whitehead's analogy. There is no more reason to assume that becoming will cease than to think that being will suddenly lapse into non-being, *unless* one insists upon thinking in terms of a substance ontology. But this is precisely what is at issue. Cobb has manifested a clear substantialist bias in his interpretation of Whitehead's notion of creativity. Creativity functions to express why things *become* in the same manner in which prime matter functions as an explanation of why things *are*. There is a contingency about both ontological substances and processes. The notions of both Aristotle and Whitehead are meant to meet these contingencies. Clearly, creativity explains *that* things are for Whitehead in a sense analogous to Aristotelian prime matter.

The explanatory power of an ultimate principle is always limited. The ultimate principle is precisely a limiting concept. It cannot be explained, because it is the limit of explanation. All explanations are more specialized than itself (v. PR 47). Thus Plato's form of the Good is sometimes spoken of as "beyond Being" and as the object of something like a mystical intuition.[5] The principle of the Good as an explanatory principle points in two directions—toward the world of forms, the objects of its explanatory power, and toward an extra-ontological datum grasped only by intuition. Whitehead's concept of creativity functions in like manner. Besides its character as a concept,[6] creativity is the source of a concrete intuition. As such it is described as the "creativity whereby the actual world has its character of temporal passage to novelty" (RM 88). As an intuition, creativity expresses the ongoingness of things as a passage into novelty. For Whitehead, "the universe is . . . a creative advance into novelty" (PR 339–340). As an intuition, creativity is a sense of radical contingency which derives from a basic incompleteness. "Nature is never complete. It is always passing beyond itself" (PR 442). Also, creativity requires novelty. Creationist philosophy is grounded in the metaphysical assumption that self-creative aesthetic events are the primary realities of which the world is made.

The fundamental characterizations of aesthetic events are freedom, transience, and novelty. These qualities are essential to any creationist philosophy since creativity, as the intentional production of novelty, depends upon a radical indeterminism. As a thing loses its uniqueness once it has come fully into being, reality is *process*. The beings of which the world is made, therefore, must be free centers of aesthetic growth whose *becoming* is their final reality. The primary analogate for Whitehead's philosophy, therefore, is the concept of aesthetic events, *free, novel* and in *process*. We may clarify this concept of "aesthetic event" by comparison to the alternative philosophic visions, introduced earlier, to which Whiteheadian philosophy bears some resemblance.

Though certainly not materialist in the classical sense, Whiteheadian philosophy shares certain basic insights of that tradition. "Actuality is incurably atomic" (PR 95). "The ultimate metaphysical truth is atomism"

(PR 53). Whiteheadian philosophy is a philosophy of *process,* but this process involves the coming into being and passing away of discrete particles. " 'All things flow' . . . [but] all flow of energy obeys 'quantum' conditions" (PR 471). The aesthetic events of which all things are comprised are analogous to the basic building blocks of materialism not only because of their discreteness, but because they are in one aspect externally related. "In so far as concerns their disclosure by presentational immediacy [i.e., ordinary conscious perception], actual entities in the contemporary universe are causally independent of each other" (PR 188).

Regarding his relations with the formalist tradition, Whitehead affirms that his philosophy is an attempt to "render Plato's general point of view with the least changes made necessary by the intervening two thousand years of human experience" (PR 63). The philosophy of organism characterizes a world in which the "things which are temporal arise by their participation in the things which are eternal" (PR 63). Though temporal things participate in eternal forms, these forms are not the sole reason for the existence of temporal entities. The "reasons" for the existence of actuality, on the contrary, are the actualities themselves. "Thus the search for a reason is always the search for an actual fact which is the vehicle of the reason" (PR 64–65). These actual facts, as we shall see, are self-creative, aesthetic events not completely rationalizable by recourse to formal analysis.

The formalist vision is close to Whiteheadian philosophy. But for Whitehead it is precisely the radical understanding of creativity which limits his allegiance to Platonic philosophy. The forms, which for Plato are the final realities, are for Whitehead the structural components of what is in fact even more real: changing, becoming, aesthetic events. The radical freedom of these fundamental actualities sets limits to the rationalizability of things.

The difference between naturalism and creationism is to be found in the distinctions which may be drawn between biological and aesthetic events. The "organic unity of experience" spoken of by both Dewey and Whitehead has significantly different meanings. Both for Whitehead and for Dewey the unity is that of *purpose.* For Dewey, experience is the result of an interaction between organism and environment which signals a satisfactory adjustment to environmental circumstances. The basic understanding of all things is grounded in biological metaphor. For Whitehead, however, the fundamental unity of experience is aesthetic. The categoreal structure of occasions of experience is understood in terms of aesthetic and logical, rather than biological, concepts. The concept of a living organism, in the biological sense, is derivative from the more basic categories of intensity, novelty, and aesthetic contrast.

"Creativity," from the volitional perspective, is the unique contribution of a man to history. Creativity is a making. It is quite close to the Whiteheadian concept of creativity except that the volitionalist vision does not accept the underlying ontological commitments to the categoreal structure of experience accepted by Whitehead. The concept of expression is fundamental to Whitehead's philosophy. "Expression is the diffusion, in the environment, of something initially entertained in the experience of the expressor" (MT 21). Such expression is basic to the continuity of experience. "The creative advance of the world is the becoming, the perishing and the objective immortalities of those things which jointly constitute *stubborn fact*" (PR ix). Expression, as "the activity of finitude impressing itself on its environment" (MT 20), is the way in which the objective immortality of the primary actualities is achieved. The continuity of becoming is a function of the diffusion of actualities via expression. "History is the record of the expressions of feelings peculiar to humanity" (MT 27).

We must not overrate the importance of Whitehead's proximity to the volitionalist viewpoint. Volitional philosophy is philosophic anthropology. It is a doctrine of *man*. But for Whitehead actual occasions are the measure of all things. The radical freedom of actualities is not just a characteristic of human beings. Even in recognizing that fact, however, we must acknowledge that there is a strong volitional element in Whiteheadian philosophy. The distinction to be drawn between the volitional and creationist philosophies might well be made in terms of the concept of freedom. For the volitionalist, freedom is the exercise of power over others in order to establish one's own reality as *the* reality. For the philosophy of creativity, freedom is the freedom of self-creativity. The first type of freedom is the freedom of the political figure or the man of action; the second, the freedom of the artist.

Whitehead's concept of aesthetic events shares significant relations with the atomist, naturalist, formalist, and volitional viewpoints, but it is significantly different from the fundamental vision of each. Nor is it merely a combination of these viewpoints. The concept of "creativity" is distinctly different from the primary visions of nature, knowledge, law, and power expressed by the alternate philosophic viewpoints. We shall soon have opportunity to see in some detail the unique contribution a philosophy grounded in the concept of aesthetic event provides by way of constructing an adequate understanding of human culture.

2. THE STRUCTURE OF EXPERIENCING

The first step in understanding Whitehead's theory of culture is to analyze in some detail the primary analogate from which his analogical generalizations derive. This leads us to the concept of "concrescence"—the growth of experiencing occasions.

Much of the difficulty in understanding Whitehead's philosophy results from his complex and detailed analysis of the process of concrescence. It is tempting to gloss over his involved and sometimes involuted discussions of the growth of experience, if for no other reason than that such a discussion is sure to strain the attention of even the most dedicated reader. But it is essential that we avoid this temptation since so much of our discussion of problems relating to culture and civilization will depend upon the fundamental metaphysical categories to be uncovered through a discussion of Whitehead's concept of the actual occasion. Because of the analogical method employed, Whiteheadian philosophy cannot well be discussed segmentally. An understanding of any specific aspect presupposes an understanding of all other principal components. Unlike the philosophy of Kant, for example, in which the critiques of science, morality, art, and religion can be reasonably well understood in isolation one from the other, Whitehead's philosophy of culture must be approached as a whole. We must therefore begin the rather tedious project of tracing the various threads which run through the analysis of the aesthetic events which comprise experience and reality itself. The rewards of such a procedure should become evident as we proceed to construct a theory of culture in the following chapters.

In our consideration of the Whiteheadian conception of experiencing as aesthetic event we shall be concerned both to set the stage for a natural progression from the concept of "experience" to the subjects of "culture" and "civilization" (considered in later chapters) and to illustrate the crucial terms and concepts which are necessary for any fundamental understanding of Whiteheadian philosophy.

In the following consideration of the structure and aim of experience, both the complexity and the richness of Whitehead's thinking will be evident. The relevance of many of the concepts discussed in this chapter to the development of a theory of culture may not be clear until applications of these concepts are made in later chapters. Suffice it for the present to state that just as the concept of aesthetic event is the concept from which Whitehead, by analogical generalization, constructs his novel metaphysical theories, so the detailed analysis of experiencing as self-creative process provides the analogical foundation for the construction of a Whiteheadian theory of culture.

John Dewey, in a classic article entitled "An Empirical Survey of Empiricisms," [7] sought to reconstruct the concept of experience through a critical appraisal of two dominant tendencies in the history of philosophy, the first stemming from the Greeks, the second from the British empiricist tradition beginning with Locke. According to Dewey, Greek philosophy—and here he is thinking particularly of Aristotle—tended to identify experience with a storehouse of information, skills, and techniques deriving ultimately from memories of sense-impressions and proximately from acquired habits and customs. In such a view, experience, derived from sense perception, is contrasted with reason, which is grounded ontologically upon an intellectual intuition into the nature of reality. Such a concept of experience dominated philosophy, according to Dewey, until the seventeenth century.

British empiricism, said Dewey, reverses the roles of reason and experience. Reasoning is derivative from experience, which gives one direct contact with external reality through sensations. From Locke to Hume a progressively smaller role was given to reason. Hume's skepticism left reason only the power to reflect upon analytic, tautological truths or upon the bare deliverances of the senses. Such an empiricism transposed the Greek conceptions of the relations of reason and experience without bringing them into integral relationship.

Whitehead would accept Dewey's characterization of these two tendencies in philosophic tradition toward the separation of reason and experience and would, with Dewey, seek a concept of experience which would overcome the limitations involved in such a separation. For Whitehead well saw that philosophic idealisms had often succeeded (in the works of Hegel and Bradley, for example) in uniting reason and experience, but only by emphasizing the ability of the mind functioning at its highest reflective level to overcome all conflicts and distinctions apparent at the level of phenomenal existence. On the other hand, realisms, accepting the coercive power of objective existents, had tended to overestimate the passivity of the mind to experience and, in so doing, had lost any concept of the rational activity involved in the acquisition of knowledge. Whitehead's theory of experience is an attempt to find a way of uniting reason and experience without resorting either to the idealist or to the realist type of philosophic reduction. For this reason Whitehead claims that his philosophy attempts to present "a transformation of some main doctrines of Absolute Idealism onto a realistic basis" (PR viii).

For Whitehead the world is in a continuous state of flux. The basic building blocks out of which the universe is made are constantly in process of coming into being and of passing away. The experienced permanence, or relative permanence, of objects of ordinary human experience belies the transience of things as viewed from the perspective of the fundamental entities of which they are composed. If, therefore, we seek the most basic understanding of the constitution of things, it is necessary for us to leave the world of ordinary human experience and to follow Whitehead into the world of the "actual entity."

The universe, according to Whitehead, is composed of "actual entities"— microcosmic centers of energy, non-permanent as individuals, whose life span is the process whereby they come to be. The life of an actual entity consists in its attempt to achieve a certain aim or goal. This goal is termed the "subjective aim" of the actual occasion. It is provided the occasion by virtue of its entertainment of certain ideals or patterns of action. These ideals are termed "eternal objects." This process of entertainment Whitehead

terms "prehension." Prehensions are of two main types, relating to two of
the structural components of each actual occasion, the physical and the conceptual poles.

Prehension is the manner in which an actual occasion grasps the data
which supply it with its subjective aim and with the means of achieving
that aim. Prehensions of concrete data, other actual entities of the past,
constitute the physical pole of the occasion. The prehensions of abstract
data, or eternal objects, are conceptual prehensions and constitute the conceptual pole. There is a third main type of prehension, a hybrid physical
prehension, which occurs whenever an actual occasion prehends conceptual
data, yet receives them into physical feeling.

The actual occasions of the world range hierarchically from those in
which the physical pole is dominant and the mental pole is almost non-
existent, to those in which the mental pole dominates. The dominance of
the mental pole in an actual occasion implies that it is free to introduce
novelty into its received data, and that it is able, with the proper environment, to entertain abstract possibilities and decide relevantly among them.
Physically dominant occasions are those forming so-called empty space and
the lower "inorganic" forms. Societies of these occasions are characterized
by undifferentiated endurance. Occasions of conceptual dominance are
those which play a part in the higher organisms and are responsible for
the emergence of the human conscious self.

Thus the universe is comprised by societies of actual occasions and societies of such societies. An atom is a society of occasions. A molecule is
a "structured" society of occasions. The human body is a group of societies
with differing defining characteristics. And the human self is a "personal
order" of occasions serially strung out through time.

The general concept of an actual entity refers to both temporal and non-
temporal entities. The former are termed actual *occasions*. Thus, for Whitehead, "God" is an actual entity, but a non-temporal one. When we think
of God we must do so with His two natures in mind. God's primordial
nature, His conceptual pole, consists of the organized and patterned structures of pure possibilities. This is the "realm" of eternal objects. God's
primordial nature, thus organized, constitutes the lure which draws the
actual occasions of the world toward transcendent goals. Each occasion ac-
quires from God the aim or goal which is most suitable to it, given its particular circumstances.

The physical pole of God, termed His consequent nature, is that aspect
of God concerned with the prehension and harmonization of the data from
the actual occasions of the world. God's subjective aim is derived from a
complete envisagement of the eternal objects. Thus He knows what harmonies are possible, and His satisfaction is obtained by harmonizing the
data received into His consequent nature. Unlike other actual entities, which
have only a brief span of existence, God is everlasting. It is the concept of

"God" whose primordial nature is comprised by ordered possibility and whose consequent nature is composed of harmonious actuality, which is the foundation of the coherence of Whitehead's metaphysics.[8]

The actual entity is, in a very real sense, *causa sui*. It selects from among available data that which conforms to the more or less definite subjective aim which it derives from God. In achieving its aim, it reaches satisfaction and passes away, becoming objectified as a novel datum for other actual occasions. Thus is Whitehead's universe a world in process, patterned by freedom and novel purpose.

According to Whitehead, an occasion of experience may be analyzed into two primary pairs of contrasting characters: "There are the physical and the mental poles, and there are the objects prehended and the subjective forms of the prehensions" (AI 268). In addition to these, there is a third contrast, which, though important, as we shall see, is not as fundamental as the first two. This is the contrast between Appearance and Reality. In this section I shall consider the two primary contrasts; in section three I shall discuss Appearance and Reality.

An occasion of experience is a process of becoming. This process is constituted by "the reception of entities, whose being is antecedent to that process, into the complex fact which is that process itself" (AI 229). There are three principal stages in the growth of an occasion of experience, internally considered: datum, process, and satisfaction. The objective content of an experience is its datum. This datum as received into experience is indeterminate as regards that particular occasion of experience. The process of becoming moves toward an increased definition or determination of the indeterminate content. The final determinate unity achieved by an actual occasion is its satisfaction.

Whitehead's characterization of the datum of experience is crucial to his entire philosophical program. "[The whole philosophical system depends on] the character to be assigned to the datum in the act of experience" (PR 238). According to Whitehead, it is precisely in the characterization of the datum of experience that modern philosophy has failed most disastrously.

Two epistemological assumptions account for many of the defects which Whitehead finds in modern philosophies. The subjectivist principle entails the belief that the datum in an act of experience can be adequately analyzed purely in terms of universals, while the sensationalist principle holds that "the primary activity in the act of experience is the bare subjective entertainment of the datum, devoid of any subjective form of reception" (PR 239).

Whitehead cites three premises which underlie the sensationalist principle, each of which he denies: first, that the substance-quality concept expresses the ultimate ontological principle; second, that Aristotle's definition of primary substance must be accepted always as a subject and never as a predicate; and third, that the experient subject is a primary substance. Thus, traditional philosophy included the element of extreme objectivism which implied that the subject–predicate form of a proposition expresses a fundamental metaphysical truth.

Whitehead thinks that, beginning with Descartes, this traditional view was altered in at least one respect. For although Descartes maintained an emphasis upon the substance-quality modes of thought, he introduced a subjectivist bias which qualified the premises of sensationalist epistemologies. Descartes held that the subjective states of the philosopher are the primary data of philosophy. According to Whitehead, had this discovery been fully elaborated, the history of modern philosophy would have been significantly different. As it was, Descartes, Locke, and Hume continued to analyze subjective functionings in terms of the substance-quality forms of thought. Whitehead wishes to rectify this fault by formulating an "objectivist" principle for the datum of experience in order to balance Descartes' subjectivist bias. This will provide a reformed subjectivist principle. Whitehead's "objectivist" principle entails the denial that the datum of experience can be adequately analyzed in terms of universals. An analysis of experience reveals actual entities as well.

The datum of an act of experience is whatever is given for feeling. The process of experiencing consists in the reception of such data into subjective feeling. Such reception of a datum on the part of an occasion of experience is termed "prehension." There are three factors comprising each prehension. There is the subject which prehends, the datum which is prehended, and the "subjective form" of the prehension. The subjective form is simply the manner in which a subject prehends a datum. Thus the growth of an occasion of experience is the becoming of a subject. That growth is due to the reception, via a specific subjective form of feeling, of a datum which is antecedent to it. Experience then may be said to be a becoming of subjectivity which is derived from an objective, antecedent world.

The contrast between objective content and subjective form in experience is here revealed. The objective content of experience is the datum of a prehension. The subjective form is "the affective tone determining the effectiveness of that prehension in that occasion of experience" (AI 227). In human experience we are made aware of this contrast whenever we realize that our emotional reaction to a given event has been markedly different from that of another observer or participant in that event.

The basic fact of experience "is the rise of an affective tone originating from things whose relevance is given" (AI 226). That is, the affective tone which determines the effectiveness of a prehension in an occasion of experience is derived, initially, from the datum of that prehension and not from the experiencing occasion itself. There is continuity, therefore, between the subjective form of the past occasion and that of the prehending subject. This broad-based continuity of the form of feeling between past and present experience establishes one basis for expecting the continuance of the past. This doctrine, as well, explicitly rejects the sensationalist principle cited above. The sensationalist principle, and the sensationalist theory of perception in general, requires the view that emotional experience is a subjectively determined response to the datum of experience. Whitehead holds that the affective response of a subject to its data derives, originally, from the data themselves.

The stress upon the objectivity of the datum of experience indicates not only that experience is fundamentally physical in origin, but that primitive experience is emotional. Though in human experience emotion is often overlaid with the selective and interpretative character of consciousness, it is the emotional elements in conscious experience which most closely resemble the basic elements of all physical experience.

Most philosophers have not seen this aspect of experience as the most fundamental. Rather, conscious perceptions and judgments have been emphasized in classical and modern philosophical treatises. Because of the de-emphasis of the primitive casual feelings, experience has been misread. Emotional and purposeful experiences have often been thought consequent to bare sense-data. The errors involved in such an approach to the analysis of experience have been discussed by Whitehead in terms of the *Fallacy of Misplaced Concreteness*.

Unless one accepts the view that "the order of dawning, clearly and distinctly, in consciousness is not the order of metaphysical priority" (PR 246), then the traditional philosophic theory of "vacuous actuality" (i.e., that some actualities are devoid of subjectivity) and substance-quality doctrines are bound to emerge. By accepting these as metaphysical principles, one has taken as fundamental the results of a high degree of abstraction and has committed the Fallacy of Misplaced Concreteness. For the data of clear, conscious experience are not primary; they are, rather, derivative modifications of the initial data felt in the primitive phases of experience.

In this section we are attempting to understand something of Whitehead's theory of the structure of experience. Two sets of contrasts within experience are being considered. Thus far we have dealt with the contrast between objective content and subjective form. This has led us to consider Whitehead's reformed subjectivist principle. There are three related implications of this principle which are germane to our later discussions of culture. First, one aspect of Whitehead's reformed subjectivist principle is its reconciliation of important elements of classical and modern philosophies. Considered in terms of broad tendencies, the classical tradition was realistic, while in modern philosophy, beginning with Descartes, the idealist tendencies have been strongly affirmed. Whitehead's version of the subjectivist principle attempts to emphasize both idealist and realist elements in experience. The primary datum for philosophy is oneself experiencing.

This expresses Whitehead's agreement with the idealist tendency of Descartes. But this is not the whole story. The primary datum of philosophy is oneself experiencing *objects*. The realistic tendency is here equally affirmed. The idealist tendency expressed in the concept of subjective form and the realist tendency expressed in the concept of objective datum are combined in the subject–object contrast within experience.

A second relevant point is that this balance of idealist and realist elements is grounded upon Whitehead's denial of metaphysical dualism implicit in his treatment of the relation of subject and object. The subject–object relation has been placed by Whitehead within the context of an occasion of experience. Any dualism such as that of the thinking and extended substances of Descartes, for example, is rejected. The notion of the dualism of subjects and objects is a derivative abstraction from the unity of experiencing occasions. Since experience is constituted by the union of subjective form and objective datum, subjects or objects considered by themselves are abstractions from that unity.[9]

A third important implication of Whitehead's subjectivist principle is that it provides the key to understanding the relation between the concept of the actual occasions of experience and specifically human experience. Modern philosophers, such as Descartes for example, hold a theory of experience which applies, for all practical purposes, only to *human* experience. But Whitehead refuses to accept the metaphysical dualism implied by such a view. As we have seen, he holds human experience to be a specialized form of primitive emotional experience. Thus he is faced with the problem of explaining the relation of human experience to experience per se.

Just as Descartes' *cogito* entails the view that the primary data of philosophy are the subjective states of the philosopher, so Whitehead's reformed subjectivist principle suggests that human experience is the basis for the construction of the philosophic concept of the actual entity. Whitehead holds that any metaphysical theory which stresses the continuity of human and natural experience is forced to find in the analysis of human experience at least some elements which are found in the less specialized types of experience in nature. At least some of the features held in common between general and specialized occurrences must be generic. Therefore, we may conclude as Ivor Leclerc has done in his discussion of Whitehead's theory of experience, that "the generic features of all actuality are to be found exhibited in human experience."[10]

Besides the contrast between objective content and subjective form, experience manifests a second important contrast: the physical and the mental. We noted above that the three principal stages in the growth of an occasion of experience are datum, process, and satisfaction. In our discussion of the contrast of objective content and subjective form, we were concerned mainly with the datum. In order to examine the physical-conceptual contrast, we must consider the stage of process. For it is in the process of growth from the initial datum of a concrescing occasion to its final satisfaction that the dynamic functioning of an actual occasion is manifest. The process of concrescence contains three successive prehensive phases. These are termed the "conformal," the "conceptual," and the "comparative" phases. The division of the growth of experience into phases is meant mainly as a heuristic device to aid in the explanation of the complex types of feelings which comprise a concrescing subject. These phases do not have any ontological status; they are simply ways of organizing the three principal types of feelings—the physical, the conceptual, and the comparison of the physical and the conceptual. The analysis of these types of feelings will provide the basis for understanding the second of the two primary contrasts illustrated in experience, the contrast between the mental and the physical poles.

The initial phase of concrescence is the phase of physical feeling, also termed the "conformal" phase. In this first phase, the actual world is received as objective datum for synthesis. According to Whitehead's principle of relativity (v. PR 33), every being serves as a potential for each becoming; the entire past actual world is felt by each concrescence. If A is an actual entity in the past actual world of B, it is felt *conformally*. That is, B, in process of concrescence, feels, in its first phase, a prehension x which conforms to A's prior feeling of x. This is the basis for the translation of cause into effect. The past lives in each present. This is Whitehead's doctrine of objective immortality.

The distinction between initial datum and objective datum should be noted. The initial datum of a physical feeling is the entire actual entity felt by the subject; the objective datum is the prehension of the actual entity as objectified by one of its component feelings. The initial datum consists of an as yet unintegrated set of actual entities. The task of the phase of physical feelings is to integrate that initial datum into a felt unity.

There are two principal types of physical feelings: simple and transmuted. Transmuted feelings will be considered in section three of this chapter in connection with the discussion of the Appearance–Reality contrast. At present, therefore, we are concerned only with simple physical feelings. Simple physical feelings are of two types: pure and hybrid. We have provided an outline view of the pure physical feeling in our discussion of the initial datum above. The data of simple physical feelings are actual entities in the past of the prehending subject. The hybrid physical prehension is somewhat more complex and therefore must be considered in some detail.

There can be no process of concrescence unless there is an "aim" in terms of which concrescence proceeds. An actual occasion may be said to aim at "intensity of experience," a phrase to be explained gradually in the following pages. The real possibility of the attainment of such an aim is determined by the state of the past actual world of a given concrescence

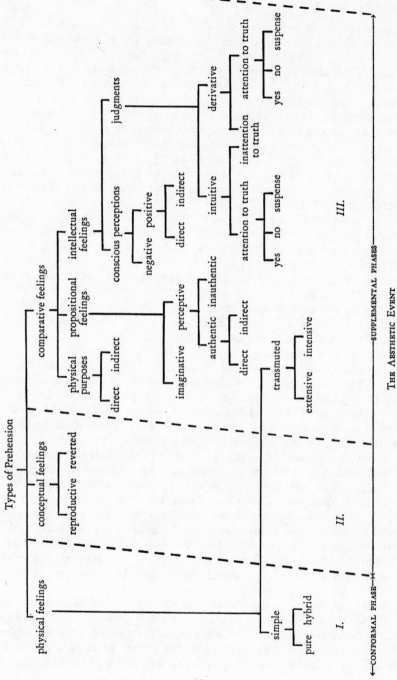

The Aesthetic Event

38

at the moment of its initiation and by the freedom of the concrescing subject. The initial aim of an occasion of experience will provide the relevant possibilities which act as potentialities for its realization.

It is a fundamental principle of Whitehead's philosophy

> that every condition to which the process of becoming conforms in any particular instance, has its reason *either* in the character of some actual entity in the actual world of that concrescence, *or* in the character of the subject which is in process of concrescence [PR 36].

This "ontological principle" means that all possibilities, both "real" and "abstract," must be *somewhere*. The possibles contained in the initial aim of a concrescence cannot be in that concrescence since the aim initiates the concrescent process. And they cannot be in the past actual world of objectified temporal entities, for if the objectively immortal past actual world constituted the sole source of possibilities there could be no explanation of real novelty in the world. The locus of eternal objects functioning as possibilities for the concrescence of temporal actual occasions must be a nontemporal actual entity which is never fully determinant. This actual entity possessed of the full range of possibilities and capable of selecting the relevant possibilities for each concrescent occasion is termed "God." The primordial nature of God is the locus of abstract possibility from which are derived the initial aims provided for the temporal creatures.

The initial aim of an actual occasion is obtained through a hybrid physical prehension of God. Through such a prehension the actual occasion in its first phase objectifies God in terms of the eternal objects which have graded relevance for its concrescence. The initial aim determines the kind of experiencing which the concrescence will realize, but only within certain limits. The occasion is able to modify its initial aim to a greater or lesser degree depending upon its intrinsic capacity for introducing novelty.

The hybrid physical prehension of God is the physical feeling of an eternal object or eternal objects derived from God's "primordial" nature. As "primordial," God houses the realm of abstract possibilities; as "consequent," He has physical prehensions of the actual occasions of the temporal world. In His "superjective" function, God orders the realm of eternal objects according to the possibilities of order determined by His physical prehensions of the temporal entities. God, as do all actual entities, aims at intensity of experience. His graded envisagement of the realm of eternal objects is determined by this aim at intensity of experience in accordance with the conditions of the temporal world. The initial aim derived via a hybrid physical prehension by each concrescing subject provides a vision of the viable potentialities for its achievement of the greatest intensity of experience commensurate with the state of its past actual world. This hybrid prehension of the initial aim provides an intuition of the order of things which serves as the basis for the hypothesis of a primordial non-temporal actual entity as the source of that order.

Thus far, we have been concerned with the physical side of the actual occasion. But each occasion is dipolar—having a conceptual as well as a physical pole. The second phase of concrescence introduces the conceptual pole. The two types of conceptual feelings of the second phase are functionings expressive of two distinct categoreal conditions of Whitehead's metaphysics. These functionings are termed conceptual valuation and conceptual reversion.

In conceptual valuation there is the reintegration of a conceptual feeling for each of the physical feelings in the initial datum. A reverted conceptual feeling is a feeling of proximately novel eternal objects partially identical with and partially diverse from the eternal object forming the data in the conceptual valuation. The relevance of these novel eternal objects is determined by the initial aim which is given via a hybrid physical prehension of God. The ideal according to which the actual occasion shapes its growth consists of the provision of ordered possibilities relevant to the achievement of maximal intensity of feeling on the part of a concrescence. The initial aim of an occasion may be altered by the occasion to introduce novel conceptual feelings—i.e., those feelings not immediately obtainable by conceptual reproduction of physical feelings in the initial datum.

A valuation is the subjective form of a conceptual feeling, either reproductive or reverted. A valuation may be such as to intensify or to attenuate the given conceptual feeling as regards its role in the final satisfaction. Whether or not the datum of a conceptual feeling is adverted (valued up) or averted (valued down) is a function of the subjective aim of the occasion in accord with the aim at intensity of experience.

The comparative feelings characteristic of the third phase of a concrescent process provide the final selection and intensification which issue in the satisfaction. Since this phase of concrescence involves a comparison of the two fundamental types of prehensions, it is necessary that we introduce Whitehead's concept of "contrast" to explain the method whereby the physical and conceptual feelings are synthesized in concrescence. A contrast is a mode of synthesis in which there is an entertainment of two or more compatible components in the objective datum, or in which one and the same eternal object is contrasted with itself in two modes of functioning. This latter case is that of "identification" which, in Whitehead's theory, is derivative from the more generic notion of "contrast" (v. PR 145, 251). A contrast is a mode of unification in which diverse elements are held in unity in order to maintain complexity of feeling, which is one prerequisite of intensity. The alternative to the introduction of contrasts is to eliminate via negative prehension one or the other of the diverse data.

"Physical purposes" are the simplest type of comparative feeling. A physical purpose contrasts the initial datum and the conceptual feeling derived either through reproduction, or reversion, from that datum. If the conceptual feeling is a reverted feeling, the physical purpose derived from a contrast utilizing that feeling is termed "indirect"; otherwise it is "direct." Two additional aspects of the conceptual feeling determine the character of physical purposes and their distinction from the more complex comparative feelings. (1) In the comparative phase, the conceptual feeling may be felt either transcendently or immanently—i.e., it may be held apart from the physical feeling, thereby retaining its indeterminate relevance, or it may be allowed to unite itself with the physical feeling. If the former occurs, the feeling will constitute a "propositional" feeling; if the latter, a physical purpose. (2) As a valuation, the subjective form of the conceptual feeling may be *averted* or *adverted*. In a physical purpose, the result of aversion is to attenuate the efficacy of the physical feeling beyond the given concrescence; adversion, however, tends to heighten its efficacy and to promote its inheritance beyond the subject in question.

The most common, and for our purposes the most interesting, type of physical purpose is that which involves a reverted feeling. In such a case the physical purpose involves: (1) a physical feeling, (2) a conceptual feeling derived by reproduction from the physical feeling, (3) a reverted conceptual feeling. If the reverted feeling has experienced a heightened intensity (through adversion), then it becomes the focus of novelty in the occasion, having introduced the contrast between the integration of the physical feeling and its primary conceptual derivative and the integration of the physical feeling with it. The aim of experience, as we shall see, is balanced complexity in the satisfaction, and two factors determine its concrescent harmony: (*a*) its concern for the immediate present, and (*b*) its desire for the maintenance of intensity in the relevant future. The contrast introduced by the heightened relevance of reverted feelings in a concrescence characterized by physical purpose insures that the first aim will be satisfied. If the concrescence is to satisfy its second criterion of intensive satisfaction, however, it must seek to maintain intense experience beyond itself. This may be done in the following way: the novel reverted feeling of occasion A becomes the physical feeling of occasion B in its immediate future. The most relevant reversion possible to B, in attempting to procure immediate intensive enjoyment of contrasts, is that which recapitulates the pattern of physical feeling of the initial datum of A. A successive string of occasions, A, B, C, D, etc., which form an enduring object may, therefore, be characterized by alternation of the roles of original and reverted patterns within the successive occasions. The regularity of alternation insures stability; the alternation itself insures heightened intensive satisfactions.

This type of physical purpose introduces the central aesthetic component of Whitehead's theory of experience. "All aesthetic experience is feeling arising out of the realization of contrast under identity" (PR 427). On this criterion, all experiences are aesthetic insofar as their subjective aims seek to maintain a complex of contrasts within a general pattern. "An actual fact is a fact of aesthetic experience" (PR 427) since the physical purpose, which aims at intensity and stability, realizes contrast within a pattern of identity.

The second principal type of comparative feeling is the propositional feeling. To understand propositional feelings, one may compare them to the simpler type of comparative feeling just discussed. Whereas in a physical purpose, the conceptual feeling is felt immanently in the third phase of the concrescence, in a propositional feeling the conceptual feeling is felt transcendently—i.e., it is held aloof from the physical feeling, thereby maintaining its indeterminateness. The proposition felt in the third phase is an integration of the physical feeling, which now indicates the "logical subjects" of the proposition, and the eternal object which is relevant to the potential determination of these logical subjects, acting as "predicative pattern." In a proposition the actuality of the logical subjects is abstracted from, and the occasions comprising the physical feeling are thus reduced to, a multiplicity, each member of which has some hypothetical relevance to the predicative pattern potentially determinate of these logical subjects. It is clear now that the full indeterminateness of an eternal object acting as predicative pattern is lost; *qua* predicate of a proposition the eternal object has potential relevance only for its logical subjects. The concrescence containing the propositional feeling is a part of the locus of the proposition felt. More generally, all actual occasions whose actual worlds contain the logical subjects of a proposition together constitute the locus of that proposition.

A propositional feeling originates through a rather complicated process occurring in the earlier phases of concrescence. One physical feeling presupposed by a propositional feeling is termed the "indicative feeling," since it includes (therefore "indicates") in its objective datum the logical subjects of the proposition. Another physical feeling must include in its datum a given eternal object to be conceptually reproduced, and *possibly* reverted, in the second phase of concrescence. The second physical feeling is termed the "physical recognition." Either the reproduced, or the reverted, conceptual feeling derived from the physical recognition serves as the predicative pattern of the proposition and is termed the "predicative feeling." The feeling constituted by the integration of the indicative with the predicative feeling is the propositional feeling.

Two types of propositional feelings are important: the "perceptive" and "imaginative" varieties. The distinction between perceptive and imaginative propositional feelings is not drawn sharply. If the physical recognition and the indicative feeling of the propositional feeling are identical, then the propositional feeling is termed perceptive; if they are not identical, then there is an imaginative propositional feeling. But since there are all degrees of difference possible between the two physical feelings, the distinction between the two types of propositional feelings may be vague.

Perceptive feelings are of three species. "Unauthentic" perceptive feelings derive from a predicative feeling which has arisen by reversion in the subject. This introduction of subjectivity causes a distortion in the integration of the predicative and indicative feelings. If there is no reversion in the subject, the feeling is "authentic." But there may yet be complications which introduce error if there is reversion in the datum. A perceptive feeling including reversion in the datum is termed "indirect." Only direct authentic perceptive propositional feelings are certain of being true.

Imaginative feelings require diversity between the physical recognition and indicative feeling so that the predicative pattern will be derived from a nexus which differs from the nexus which is the objective datum of the indicative feeling. Without this diversity no free play of imagination is possible. The unauthentic perceptive feeling is the product of a reversion in the subject which gives rise to the predicative feeling. This reversion brings about a limited diversity between the physical recognition and the indicative feeling, though there is still only one physical feeling serving as basis of the origination of feeling. Thus the unauthentic perceptive feeling is close to the imaginative feeling, and may, in fact, be termed "tied" imagination (v. PR 400–401). Imaginative feelings, though usually serving as lures for feeling in a concrescence, may have as data true propositions. Since truth is not dependent upon the identity of physical recognition and indicative feeling, novelty may occur in an occasion without necessitating a concomitant loss of truth.

A single verbal expression can indicate a number of different propositions. Language functions to evoke propositional feelings, and the principal problem involved in language is that of evoking the proper propositional feeling. The conscious entertainment of a proposition is achieved *via* judgment. The judgment is evoked by the spoken or written expression and by the context or environment within which it is expressed and entertained. This being the case, the type of indicative feeling which is evoked is determined by the subjective functioning of the prehending occasion as well as by the objective character implied in the verbal expression. "Meaning" and "reference" are thus functionally dependent. Still "meaning," in the sense of the propositional value of a verbal expression, is a function both of the objective environment and of subjective functioning.[11]

Propositions *qua* data of propositional feelings may be of two types: conformal or non-conformal, depending upon whether or not the proposition conforms to what is in fact the case. A conformal proposition is true; a non-conformal one is false. Both conformal and non-conformal propositions serve a valuable purpose—the former principally in mathematics and logic; the latter in the arts, in speculative philosophy and religion, and in the imaginative hypotheses of science. The distinction between conformal and non-conformal propositions is straightforward. A conformal proposition is entertained in much the same way as are the initial data in the conformal phase of concrescence. "The reaction to the datum has simply resulted in the conformation of feeling to fact" (PR 284). A non-conformal proposition introduces novelty since an alternative possibility of the complex predicate is entertained and synthesized with the "fact" of the data constituting the logical subjects of the proposition. Both conformal and nonconformal propositions are entertained below the level of consciousness. Thus it is absurd to claim that propositions function mainly as materials for judgment. By introducing novelty into the occasion, non-conformal propositions function in this concrescence phase much as the reverted feeling of the second phase. But in accordance with the increasing complexity of experience of the latter phases, propositional novelty has a broader range of variation than have reverted feelings.

None of the feelings discussed so far need involve conscious attention. Consciousness emerges at the final stage of Whitehead's analysis—the stage of perceptions and judgments. The phase in which consciousness is important is dominated by the third type of comparative feeling, termed by Whitehead "intellectual feeling." The two main types of intellectual feeling are conscious perceptions and judgments. The element of novelty with which we have been concerned in this analysis is most characteristic of this phase of the concrescence. In an intellectual feeling there is a contrast between a propositional feeling of the comparative phase and the physical data of the conformal phase, part, or all, of which form the logical subjects of the proposition. The element of consciousness emerges by virtue of the complex comparison of "fact" (the nexus physically felt) and the "supposition about a fact" (the propositional feeling). This is the affirmation-negation contrast which is the basis of all conscious experience. Conscious perceptions thus may be divided into positive and negative types, the negative being the more fundamental type. For example: "round-red-now" might describe the perception of a red ball in the positive form of conscious perception. But this, in turn, is an instance of a more special case of the negative perception which would take the form "not-red, not-round, now."

The reason for the primacy of negative perceptions and judgments in consciousness is illustrated by the fact that the perception, for example, of a red ball as "red-round" is *conformal*. Conformal feelings presuppose the primacy of primitive receptive experience as illustrated by the conformal phase of concrescence. In the case of a negative perception, "not-red, not-round," "red," and "round" are received as conceptual novelties which constitute alternate possibilities. Thus, for Whitehead, the negative perception or judgment constitutes consciousness. "Consciousness is the feeling of negation" (PR 245). The recognition of Y as $\bar{X}$ where Y, for example, is the color red and X any other color opens up the consideration of a wide range of possibilities, each of which constitutes a potential alternative propositional feeling for the given occasion. Such an introduction of alternate possibilities increases the complexity and contrasts within the given occasion and "finally rises to the peak of free imagination, in which the conceptual novelties search through a universe in which they are not datively exemplified" (PR 245). The most sophisticated employment of the negative perception is in the exercise of dialectical reflection which consciously generates "P" for every "P" perceptively entertained.

With respect to judgments, Whitehead distinguishes between "intuitive" and "inferential," or "derivative," varieties. Judgments per se result from the contrast between an imaginative propositional feeling and the feeling of the physical nexus of the conformal phase. The intuitive judgment occurs when the contrast between the datum and the proposition is such as to allow a feeling of the complexity of the relations of identity or diversity between the datum and the proposition. The subjective form of the feeling of the datum conforms to what is, in fact, there to be felt. Error can arise only if the indicative feeling, one of the factors to be integrated, involves a reverted feeling. In this case the judgment is derivative. Error is common in derivative judgments since in this type the integration of the physical datum with the proposition allows a detailed feeling of the proposition, but not of its comparison in detail with the physical datum.

Judgments per se are made about the judging subjects. As such, a judgment feeling is a feeling in the process of the judging subject itself. But just as, in the intuitive judgment, the full, complex, detailed comparison of the proposition which partially transcends the judging subject with the physical datum is given, so the judging subject is seen to be more intimately implicated in this judgment than is the case in the derivative judgment wherein the comparison with the physical datum is not detailed.[12]

Derivative and intuitive judgments may be made with one of two different purposes in mind. One may either attend or not attend to the question of truth. If attention to truth is absent, or at a minimum, conscious imagination of a free speculative type is achieved. If attention is given to the truth of a proposition, three types of judgments are possible; these types are termed by Whitehead the "Yes," "No," and "Suspense" forms. The negative and suspense forms are, of course, those which introduce novelty and contrast into the occasion. The negative judgment recalls the negative perception; the suspended judgment, however, has a special role to play in the higher phases of experience. It is the hypothetical form which comprises the hypotheses and tentative suppositions of the sciences and of all reflective thought. Metaphysical systems, Whitehead would hold, should be constructed on a foundation of hypothetical, rather than of dogmatic, judgments.

It is possible to approximate Whitehead's distinction between intuitive

and derivative judgments by comparing it with the ordinary distinction
between empirical and logical statements. An empirical judgment in the
strong sense of that term is a judgment which is based upon a direct appeal to experience. A logical judgment, on the other hand, is, on the whole,
"deductive" in character. One facet of the distinction between "empirical"
and "deductive" judgments is that the empirical judgment is concerned
with the immediacy of experienced fact, while the deductive judgment is
a judgment derived from immediate experience by virtue of the introduction
of an assumption about the character of the experienced data. In Whiteheadian language: a judgment feeling is the feeling of a contrast between
the physical feeling transmitted from the first phase of concrescence and a
propositional feeling of the third phase. Among the possible propositions
open to the judging subject is one in which the logical subjects comprise
the full complex physical nexus involved in the physical feeling and in
which the predicative pattern is the eternal objects derived through valuation and reversion from the physical nexus. The awareness of the contrast
between the physical feeling and that propositional feeling so derived is an
intuitive judgment and is "empirical" since it refers to immediate experience. On the other hand, if one compares a proposition and a physical
feeling in such a way as to leave unexperienced the full complex detail of
the physical nexus, then the only way a more than vague judgment can
be made about the contrast between a proposition and the nexus is by assuming something about the physical nexus in relation to the proposition
which was, in fact, not experienced. A deductive process is thus involved
in a derivative judgment. Thus:

> Logic is the analysis of the relationships between propositions in virtue
> of which derivative judgments will not introduce errors, other than those
> already attaching to the judgments on the premises [PR 292].

Consider, for example, the *modus ponens* form:

$$p \supset q$$
$$\frac{p}{q}$$

The logical guidelines provided by the *modus ponens* form seek to pro-
tect the derivative judgment "q" from error providing the judgments
"p⊃q" and "p" are not in error.

Intuitive judgments are, often, "psychological"—i.e., judgments relating
to description of personal subjective states. For this reason, most judgments
in the human social world are derivative in nature. Nevertheless the search
for philosophic certainty has often led to the attempt to found philosophy
upon intuitive certainty, usually with little success. The most famous intuitive judgment in philosophic literature—the *cogito* of Descartes—was
an attempt so to found speculative thinking. Since Descartes, volumes have
been written in the attempt to decide whether the *sum* which followed the

intuitive *cogito* was, in Whitehead's terms, an intuitive or a derivative judgment.

The difficulty of founding philosophy upon the self-evident and certain character of intuition was clearly recognized by Whitehead. It is in relation to this difficulty that the undogmatic character of Whiteheadian philosophy is most clearly and significantly affirmed. The aim of philosophy is to evoke intuitive judgments concerning the nature of things. Inference, or derivative judgments, play a necessary, though secondary, role in philosophy. Whitehead's aim is that of the great rationalists of the seventeenth century, but his philosophy is set apart from that type of speculative endeavor by his realization of the practical futility of the dogmatic belief in any final and complete realization of the goal. "Proofs [i.e., inferential arguments] are the tools for the extension of our imperfect self-evidence" (MT 50).

With the analysis of the types of judgment feelings, Whitehead characterizes the pinnacle of intellectual activity in high-grade actual occasions of the type dominating the thought-processes of human beings. But Whitehead is quick to point out that the purpose of complex intellectual feelings is not at all to provide a set of beliefs or hypotheses for intellectual entertainment. Thought is not an end in itself. "The main function of [intellectual] feelings is to heighten the emotional intensity accompanying the valuations in the conceptual feelings involved, and in the more physical purposes which are more primitive than any intellectual feelings" (PR 416). Not a very ennobling conception of the role of reason and intellect; nonetheless a point of pivotal significance for the understanding of Whitehead's theory of experience. The purpose of aesthetic events is *aesthetic* intensity, not high-grade intellectual activity. Such activity is without significant value unless it has "cash value" in terms of emotional intensities. "Intellectual feelings, in their primary function, are concentration of attention involving increase of importance" (PR 416). Failure to understand this can only lead one to assume that the complex analysis of the growth of experience which we have just rehearsed has as its sole purpose to show the way in which high-level intellect originates in experience. Such is our vested interest as human beings who unavoidably overstress the importance of conscious experience.

Enough has been given of Whitehead's complex analysis of concrescence to provide the outlines of his concept of experience as aesthetic events. I have noted two principal contrasts in experience: the contrast between objective content and subjective form and that between the physical and conceptual poles of concrescence. Examination of a third important contrast will complete my preliminary analysis of Whitehead's primary analogate.

3. APPEARANCE AND REALITY

For Whitehead, the contrast of Appearance and Reality is not fundamental to the characterization of primitive experience. The physical–mental contrast and the contrast of objective content and subjective form are the primary factors defining the structure of experience. It is only *conscious* experience which is dominated by the Appearance–Reality contrast. Whitehead, therefore, emphasizes two issues in his characterization of the relation of Appearance and Reality: first, the centrality of the relation as the basis for understanding conscious experience and, second, the need to provide a discussion of the relation which gives proper emphasis to the other two, metaphysically prior, contrasts in experience.

"Reality" for a given concrescence is the actual world from the standpoint of that concrescence—i.e., the physical data, conformally felt, or excluded, by negative prehensions. Reality is the givenness of the past. Through the supplemental feelings of the initial datum, the initial objective content (reality) is integrated with the novel conceptual data selected in accordance with the subjective aim of the occasion and given its peculiar tonality of qualitative feeling by the subjective form of the concrescing occasion.

The objective content of the later phases of the concrescence is thus transformed by integrations with conceptual valuations. In high-grade actual occasions comparative feelings involve further contrasts which heighten the complexity of the original datum. Increasing the complexity of the datum increases the difference between the initial and the final objective contents. "Appearance" is a function of the difference between the initial datum of the conformal phase and the objective content of the final phase which results from the transformation of the physical world by conceptual activity. It is through Appearance that novelty enters effectively into the world. But the novel rendering of the objective datum functions in two ways: it serves as Appearance for the concrescing subjects; but it is, also, an ingredient in Reality for concrescences subsequent to its own. We shall see when I come to discuss human persons that, in the sequence of occasions constituting a person, past occasions in the sequence are peculiarly relevant to any present occasion. Human experience, therefore, provides an illustration of a complex interweaving of Appearance and Reality throughout the route of occasions constituting the "soul" of a human person.

Two concepts, as yet undiscussed, are relevant to a proper understanding of the Appearance–Reality contrast in conscious human experience. These are the concepts of "transmutation" and of "symbolic reference." The essence of the concept of transmutation is embodied in a "categoreal obligation" of the philosophic system found in *Process and Reality*. Because of the importance of this concept to the discussions of the following chapters, I shall quote this categoreal obligation at length.

> When . . . one and the same conceptual feeling is derived impartially by a prehending subject from its analogous, simple, physical feelings of various actual entities in its actual world, then, in a subsequent phase of integration of these simple physical feelings together with the derivate conceptual feeling, the prehending subject may transmute the *datum* of

this conceptual feeling into a characteristic of some *nexus* containing those prehended actual entities among its members, or of some part of that nexus. In this way the nexus (or its part), thus characterized, is the objective datum of a feeling entertained by this prehending subject [PR 40].

The process of transmutation takes place in the following way: in the second phase of concrescence a single conceptual feeling may be derived from the simple physical feelings of the subject. Then, in the third phase this datum may be transmuted so as to characterize a nexus, or part of a nexus, containing those entities physically felt. In this way there has been a transition from the prehension of many individual entities to a nexus of entities. Thus is the move from the microcosmic to the macrocosmic accomplished. Transmutation supplies the rationale in terms of which Whitehead is able to explain why we perceive the world as continuous rather than in its atomic character. As an instrument of high-grade mentality, transmutation reduces the complexity of our feelings of derivation (physical feelings). Appearance is a simplified version of Reality; transmutation is an instrument of simplification.

Almost every perception involves transmutation. Consider the brown color of a desk top, or the green color of a forest in spring. The colors belong to the desk and the forest respectively, but not necessarily to every actual entity comprising the desk or the forest. A valid transmuted perception depends only on the fact that some, or most, of the entities are qualified by the proper eternal object. Without the possibilities for simplification provided by transmutation, we should be lost amid the unimaginable variety and complexity of the microcosmic world of actual entities.

The importance of transmutation is obvious; without it there could be no perception of the world as a community expressing a given type of order, by virtue of analogies among its actual entities. We come to an understanding of our world only when we realize the possibilities of order inherent within it. The distortive character of transmuted feelings is likewise evident. We understand only by ignoring irrelevant distinctions among actual entities and attending to their analogous elements. But "irrelevance" is a relative concept. In some cases it might be precisely the individual differences which are most important.

To understand Whitehead's theory of transmutation more fully, it is necessary to consider his theory of sense-perception. For it is here that transmutation plays its fundamental role in conscious human experience. Whitehead's theory of sense-perception is given a very sophisticated and detailed exposition in several places in his writings.[13] For the present I shall be concerned only with those aspects of the theory which relate directly to his concept of transmutation.

According to Whitehead there are three modes of perception—two pure and one mixed. The first and most primitive mode is that identified with the perception of the causally efficacious past actual world of a given subject. A second pure mode, termed presentational immediacy, occurs when, in the supplemental phases of the concrescence, a transmuted conceptual feeling is utilized in order to objectify a contemporary nexus. The datum of the conceptual feeling ("the sensum") is derived from feelings in the immediate causal past or from a reverted feeling relevant to those causal feelings, and is projected onto a region in the present of the concrescing subject. This mode of presentational immediacy allows perception of an extensive region qualified by *sensa*.

The mixed mode of symbolic reference occurs when the causally efficacious feelings are united with the presentational perception in order to provide a clear, articulate presentational perception, with vague emotional undertones indicating direct derivation from the past. This is the normal form of perception for human beings. The relation between the two pure modes of perception illustrates the Appearance–Reality contrast quite well. Appearance involves transmuted and elaborated causal perceptions; Reality is these causal perceptions. The failure to maintain the proper attention to the contributions of each of the pure modes of perception can result in significant distortion of the perceptual situation and in a consequent imbalance between Reality and Appearance in experience.

The principal distortion involved in sense-perception derives from an overemphasis upon the clear, distinct data of presentational immediacy. Since contemporary actual occasions are causally independent of one another (causality being defined in terms of the efficacy of the past), the type of information derived from presentational objectification concerns the world as comprised of potentials for concrescence. That is to say, the actual world is atomic and in process; the world of presentational immediacy is continuous and in the state of mere passive potentiality. Concentration upon the data of presentational immediacy will entail a consequent de-emphasis upon the world of active centers of valuation expressing the character of derivation from the past and anticipation of the future. Thus one of the distortions introduced by transmutation concerns the transmuting of a sensum onto a necessarily passive continuous region which belies the true nature of the actual world.

The negative effects of the distortion involved in the transition from Reality to Appearance in an occasion of experience are precluded only if there is a proper appreciation of the contributions of the causal, as well as of the presentational, mode of perception. One of the prerequisites for gaining such an appreciation is to understand the general way in which Appearance and Reality differ in an occasion of experience.

> The divergencies between reality and appearance depend on the type of social order dominating the environment of the occasion in question. All our information on this topic, direct and inferential, concerns this general epoch of the Universe and, more particularly, animal life on the surface of the Earth [AI 270–271].

As we shall see in the following chapter the discussions of human individuals and human social orders will, in fact, provide some understanding of the general relation of Appearance and Reality in a fully human person.

A brief comparison of the Whiteheadian and Kantian approaches to this contrast in experience should help to place Whitehead's theory in some perspective. Kant distinguished two elements in appearance: the pure forms of intuition (space and time), and sensations, the "matter" of intuition. According to Kant, "the former inhere in our sensibility with absolute necessity, no matter what kind our sensations may be; the latter exist in varying modes." [14] Over against these primary modes of appearance Kant placed the doctrine of the *things-in-themselves* which, though unknowable, could nonetheless be thought. He seems to have accepted the existence of things-in-themselves merely on the grounds that there could be no appearances if there were nothing which appeared.[15] Since Kant was concerned, in his first critique, primarily with scientific knowledge—i.e., knowledge of the common, objective world of experience as it is constituted by certain a priori categories—it is appearance, and appearance in this particular mode, which is most emphasized in his epistemology. Thus, though there is a realist element in the Kantian philosophy (the doctrine of the things-in-themselves), it does not enter directly into his discussions of the constitution of experience.

There are significant similarities between Kant and Whitehead concerning the relations of constitution of experience. For Kant, it is not enough to know merely that the phenomenal world is constructed by the experiencing of percipients; one must know *how* such constitution takes place. Similarly, for Whitehead, it is not enough merely to state that the percipient occasion is constituted out of its past actual world; one must know the conditions of that constitution. For Kant, the forms of intuition and the categories of the understanding are the chief elements of the human mind which provide knowledge of the world of appearance. And, for Whitehead, the categoreal obligations, such as the category of conceptual reversion and of transmutation, as well as the particular environment of the given occasion, condition the constitution of appearance from out of reality.

The principal distinctions between Kant and Whitehead on this issue are two. First, for Whitehead, the constitution of an occasion of experience involves the contrast of appearance and reality, whereas for Kant, the constitution of experience is wholly concerned with appearance. Second, whereas both philosophers agree that there is an *objective* world, for Kant, this world is constituted by thought, while Whitehead holds that the objective world is prehended as the primary ingredient in an act of experience. Thus, in Kant's theory, the constitution of experience proceeds from subjectivity to apparent objectivity, while Whitehead's view is that experiencing proceeds from objectivity to subjectivity. The reality of objects is affirmed by Whitehead's objectivist principle. Such reality is denied to the objects of experience on the Kantian view.

There is a third possible contrast between Kant and Whitehead in this connection, though it depends on a questionable point in the interpretation of Kant. If we interpret Kant as holding the view that noumena in some sense condition (not cause!) phenomena, a view he does sometimes seem to imply,[16] then it is relevant here to note that such a conditioning relation is, of necessity, a one-way street. Noumena may condition phenomena, but in no real sense could the reverse be said. According to Whitehead, however, there is a two-way conditioning relation between appearance and reality, since what constitutes appearance for one occasion becomes an ingredient in reality for experience beyond that occasion.

We cannot here pursue the intriguing contrasts between Kant and Whitehead uncovered above. I have contrasted these two figures merely in order to highlight the main points of Whitehead's concepts of Appearance and Reality.[17] And as we shall soon have occasion to see, these concepts are central to much of the discussion which is to follow. For it is the Appearance–Reality contrast which, though of a metaphysically secondary character, is of crucial importance for this essay because of its dominance in conscious human experience.

4. THE AIM OF EXPERIENCE

The actual occasion is an act of self-creativity. As such it is to be understood ultimately from a teleological perspective. The *telos* of the aesthetic events comprising the Whiteheadian universe is expressed in terms of the category of subjective intensity: "The subjective aim, whereby there is origination of conceptual feeling, is at intensity of feeling (α) in the immediate subject, and (β) in the *revelant* future" (PR 41). This category conditions the introduction of novelty into the concrescence. Intensity is a function of both the complexity and the compatibility of contrasts between eternal objects. Thus the subjective aim of a concrescence is at satisfaction characterized by "complexity of contrast" and "by balance," which Whitehead characterizes as "balanced complexity."

> Balanced complexity is the outcome of [the] category of subjective aim. Here "complexity" means the realization of contrasts, of contrasts of contrasts, and so on; and "balance" means the absence of attenuations due to the elimination of contrasts which some elements in the pattern would introduce and other elements inhibit [PR 424].

To achieve complexity, the category of conceptual reversion is utilized in order to introduce as many possibilities for contrast as may be entertained. "Complexity" is necessary if "intensity" is to be achieved. "Balance," on the other hand, requires that no eternal object be entertained by the concrescing subject if by such entertainment potential contrasts between other eternal objects in the datum are thereby eliminated.

The introduction of novelty is somewhat complicated by the fact that the aim of a given occasion partially transcends its individual concrescent process by virtue of the presence in it of a concern for its relevant future. The relevant future of an occasion is simply the "real" potentialities for effectiveness in the anticipated future which the occasion receives through the hybrid physical prehension supplying its initial aim. These feelings of anticipation associated with the relevant future comprise at least part of what Whitehead means by the feeling of "objective immortality." In higher organisms the utilization of conceptual reversion can introduce these futurely relevant possibilities into efficacy in the present concrescence.

There is a "pre-established harmony" in experience categoreally expressed in terms of "subjective unity" and "subjective harmony." This pre-established harmony is the categoreal rationale in terms of which the attainment of balanced complexity may be understood. The Category of Subjective Unity states that the feelings belonging to any incomplete phase of an actual entity in process are compatible for integration by reason of the subjective unity of the concrescing occasion. The Category of Subjective Harmony does for the subjective forms of the conceptual feelings what the Category of Subjective Unity does for the objective data by requiring that these subjective forms be "mutually determined by the adaptation of those feelings to be contrasted elements congruent with the subjective aim" (PR 41). The fundamental way in which balanced complexity is achieved is through the introduction of rhythmic pattern into experience.

Actual occasions arise out of the realization of contrast under identity by recourse to comparative feelings. Physical purposes involving reverted feelings provide the primary method whereby the rhythmic vibratory character of physical nature is achieved. Rhythm in nature is the best illustration of contrast under identity which provides intensity of experience within a patterned context allowing for balance in experience. There is a heavy price paid for balance achieved through physical purposes. Negative prehensions exclude much of the data from the past actual world since an occasion dominated by physical purpose is unable to initiate many of the more complex types of contrast involved in comparative feelings without the loss of the stable, rhythmic pattern. In a later chapter, when I discuss the importance of the quality of "Adventure" to the production and maintenance of civilized societies, I shall have occasion to stress the necessity of the transition from one type of perfection to another. There we shall see that the introduction of rhythmic patterns, variations on a main theme, is not the only way to achieve complex, balanced intensity. Besides the way of rhythm, there is the path of transience from one type of complexity to complexity of a wholly different type. But the analysis

of these ways of attaining the aim of experience must await the discussion
of civilization in Chapter IV.

The relative potentiality of an actual occasion is, in large measure, a
function of the actual world from which it grows. The datum from
which a concrescence proceeds is the actual world from the standpoint
of that concrescing subject. Thus the "environment" of an occasion places
intrinsic limitations upon the type and quality of realization which is possible to an occasion. Even in those occasions of greatest complexity, intensity, and greatest potential for self-determination, there can be no complete
transcendence of the datum. Obviously the type of environment, the actual
world, out of which an occasion grows differs widely from occasion to
occasion. And "the degree of order in the datum is measured by the degree of richness in the objective lure" (PR 136).

Whitehead classifies the satisfactions of occasions by reference to four
aspects: triviality, narrowness, vagueness, width (PR 170). Each of these
aspects is conditioned by qualities inherent in the initial datum. The
actual world of each concrescence, which supplies the occasion its initial
datum, is comprised of a congeries of types of order, some of which are
more relevant to the concrescing subject than others. It is possible to
divide the environment of an actual occasion into three elements: foreground, *relevant* background, and *remote* background.[18] The distinction
between these various elements is a relative matter. Quite obviously the
terms "foreground" and "background" should not be interpreted in any
simple sense as referring to spatial or temporal perspectives. Rather, these
terms are to be taken as providing a description of the context within
which an occasion achieves whatever depth of satisfaction it is able to
realize. The foreground is the datum as discriminated and mutually contrasted and as relieved, *via* negative prehensions, of irrelevant diversities.
The relevant background is characterized by vagueness and massive uni-
formity. Vagueness implies a lack of differentiated contrast. This characteristic is the result of the process of transmutation. The remote background is trivial insofar as it is directly objectified in the actual entity in
question.

Triviality arises because of a lack of coordination in the factors of the
datum. Incompatibility is dominant in a trivial environment. Triviality
implies width (discrimination and contrast) but without narrowness (intensification of the relevance of common characteristics) in the higher
phases of experience. Vagueness and triviality express opposite characteristics of the datum. Whereas vagueness results from transmutation issuing
in an identification of formerly differentiated factors, triviality results
from incompatibility arising from the fact that "no feeling arising from
one factor is reinforced by any feeling arising from another factor" (PR
170). Narrowness presupposes vagueness and builds upon it by intensify-
ing (through aversion) the relevance of common factors in the datum.

Width implies a broadly differentiated initial datum capable of yielding discriminations and contrasts which could supply a versatility in regard to the problem of harmonizing incompatibilities introduced in the initial datum without recourse to negative prehensions.

The principal categoreal conditions relevant to the achievement of those various qualities of a satisfaction are those of conceptual valuation, conceptual reversion, and transmutation. Aversion and adversion stress common characteristics and produce narrowness. Transmutation produces vagueness as a ground for narrowness. Reversions may introduce novelty which can bring variety into the data providing a width of experiencing for integration by the higher phases of experience.

The ideal environment for an experiencing subject is one in which the foreground provides the possibilities for relevant discriminations and contrasts in the initial prehensions, while the relevant background provides a proper balance of vagueness and narrowness. The datum arising from such an environment will provide the most varied possibilities for elaboration and intensification by the concrescing occasion, and will promote the achievement of the aim of experience which is balanced complexity and intensity. As I noted earlier, the character of the relationship between Appearance and Reality in an occasion of experience is a function of the type of social order dominating that occasion's environment. The achievement of the aim of experience likewise depends upon the environment within which a given occasion comes into being. Insofar as we are concerned about the structure and aim of conscious experience, we must learn more about the types of order manifest in the world of human experience.

The search for an environment in which the *telos* of experience is most efficiently achieved leads to a discussion of the types of order dominating this actual world. An examination of these types of order, to be undertaken in the following chapter, will indicate that it is in human persons and societies of persons that the aim of experience is best fulfilled. Thus the attempt to characterize that environment which best contributes to the balanced intensity of experience leads to the consideration of cultural experience and expression which are, of course, grounded in analogical extensions of the concept of aesthetic events into the realm of persons and society.

NOTES

1. Stephen Pepper (*World Hypotheses* [Berkeley: University of California Press, 1966]) and Richard McKeon (*Freedom and History* [New York: Noonday, 1952] and *Thought, Action and Passion* [Chicago: University of Chicago Press, 1954]), among others, have concerned themselves with a characterization of fundamental philosophical visions based upon "root metaphors," or primary analogates, which determine the philosopher's choice of methods, principles, and subject matters. My account of the five variant semantic

contexts is loosely based upon the work of these men, as well as on that of Robert Brumbaugh, a student of McKeon's.

2. Cobb, *A Christian Natural Theology* (Philadelphia: Westminster, 1965), pp. 203–214.

3. *Ibid.,* p. 210.

4. *Ibid.,* p. 211.

5. See Book VI of *The Republic.*

6. A. H. Johnson (*Whitehead's Theory of Reality* [Boston: Beacon, 1952], Appendix B, p. 221) claimed, apparently with Whitehead's approval, that creativity is an eternal object—i.e., a *concept.* This has caused some Whiteheadian interpreters anxiety (see Cobb, *Theology,* p. 209, n. 73). But creativity is "conceptual" in only one of its two primary roles—i.e., insofar as it may be considered something akin to an "explanatory principle."

7. *John Dewey on Experience, Nature and Freedom,* ed. Richard Bernstein (New York: Liberal Arts, 1960).

8. Whitehead's use of the term "God" can be misleading if we understand it solely in a religious sense. For even though the concept "God" does serve to interpret religious experience, "the concept of religious feeling is not an essential element in the concept of God's function in the universe" (PR 315–316).

9. See also Ivor Leclerc, *Whitehead's Metaphysics* (New York: Macmillan, 1958), p. 155.

10. *Ibid.,* p. 131.

11. See the discussion of "meaning" in terms of "intensive transmutation" in Chapter III.

12. W. Mays holds this view in *The Philosophy of Whitehead* (London: Allen and Unwin, 1959), pp. 145, 153–156, 159–160.

13. The most concise and provocative account of this theory is contained in S, Chapters I and II. The best technical discussion is to be found in PR 225–279. In AI 274–282, Whitehead clarifies the relations between the concepts of transmutation, symbolic reference, and the Appearance–Reality contrast in his theory of perception.

14. *Immanuel Kant's Critique of Pure Reason,* trans. N. K. Smith (New York: St. Martin's, 1961), A42–43 (B60–61); A225–226 (B272–273). See also H. J. Paton, *Kant's Metaphysics of Experience* (New York: Macmillan, 1961), pp. 60–61.

15. Smith, *Kant's Critique,* A251–252.

16. See *Ibid.,* A252.

17. The relations of Whitehead and Kant are, indeed, quite intriguing. Though there has not been, as far as I am aware, any extensive comparative treatment of the two, several fine articles and papers have appeared. See, for example, Ivor Leclerc, "Kant's Second Antinomy, Leibniz, and Whitehead," *The Review of Metaphysics,* 20, No. 1 (September 1966), 25–41; Gottfried Martin, "Metaphysics as *Scientia Universalis* and as *Ontologia Generalis,*" *The Relevance of Whitehead,* ed. Ivor Leclerc (New York: Macmillan, 1961), pp. 219–234; Nathan Rotenstreich, "On Whitehead's Theory of Propositions," *The Review of Metaphysics,* 5, No. 3 (March 1952), 389–404, and "The Superject and Moral Responsibility," *Ibid.,* 10, No. 2 (December 1956), 201–206.

18. See PR 170–172 for the justification of this procedure.

PART TWO

THE SPECULATIVE CONSTRUCTION OF A THEORY

Chapter III

THE CONCEPT OF CULTURE

WHITEHEADIAN PHILOSOPHY faces the same challenge which every philosophy of process since Heraclitus has faced: how to account adequately for the seeming stabilities which we encounter in experience without sacrificing the basic philosophical intuition that "all things flow." The ongoing process of the world, which Whitehead characterizes as "Creativity," receives relatively permanent instantiations at the level of our ordinary experience. Ships, sails, sealing wax, cabbages, and kings—all possess a certain degree of permanence. Such permanences are not to be accounted for by recourse to the theory of concrescence *qua* immediate experience.

Because of his starting point, Whitehead is forced to take seriously the "ego-centric predicament." For if, as Whitehead contends, every being is a potential for every becoming, and "being" is necessarily the "being" of some actual occasion in the process of becoming, then the concrescent process seems to sum up the whole of past experience. There is no thing which is not prehended, positively or negatively. Perry's "ego-centric predicament" implied the impossibility of finding anything which is not known. The idealist claim, and the claim of some phenomenologists as well, that "all things are known" (the real is rational) is a result of capitulation to the structures defined by this predicament.[1] But as the American realist school long ago pointed out, such a capitulation is unnecessary since the conclusion is the result of arguing from the method of agreement without an instance of difference. That is, as no non-things are shown to be not-known, the conclusion that all things are known is unwarranted.[2]

Whitehead's attitude toward the ego-centric predicament is determined by his qualified acceptance of the subjectivist bias of modern epistemologies. The "reformed subjectivist principle" of Whitehead claims that analysis of experience yields not merely universals but objectified actual entities as well. The extension of perception to include physical as well as conceptual prehensions leads him to deny primacy to conscious experience. Whitehead recognized that the classical subjectivist doctrine coupled with a sensationalist principle holding that "the primary activity in the act of experience is the bare subjective entertainment of the datum, devoid of any subjective form of reception" (PR 239) led philosophy down a blind alley. Hume accepted the conclusion. Kant elaborated a solution to the problem while leaving the subjectivist principle unchanged. Even Hegel's critique of Kant did not alter the classical subjectivist doctrine. In contemporary philosophy, the Kantian and Hegelian traditions have resulted in exclusive emphasis on high-ordered conscious experience, at the cost of the more primitive perceptions.

The Humean tradition, expressed in logical atomism and ordinary language philosophy, is the result of epistemological affirmations grounded in sensationalist doctrines of perception. The failure of Russell's concept of logical constructions and the theory of descriptions which were aimed at overcoming the ontological poverty of linguistic empiricism led to the reaction of the later Wittgenstein, who produced a philosophy no longer interested in ontological issues, but concerned with the phenomenon of language use. This was a direct retreat again into the bosom of Hume, whose concept of "custom" provides the basis for ordinary language philosophy.

Equally characteristic of the contemporary traditions grounded upon sensationalist theories of perception has been the primary, if not exclusive, interest in *visual* experience as the basis of epistemological analysis and construction. A. O. Lovejoy has noted this fact with regard to Russell's concept of "a piece of matter," which is grounded wholly on an analysis of visual data.[3]

Whitehead's theory of perception, on the other hand, implies an actual experiencing of causal derivation as well as a presentationally immediate perception of the present world in its potentiality. Thus Whitehead avoids skepticism with regard to both the experience of causal connection and the unity of the self or ego: the former, because there is an actual experience of causal connection; the latter, because the sensationalist doctrine of passive entertainment of sense data which entailed no procedure for discovering the perceiving subject is supplemented by the subjective form of entertainment. The avoidance of Hume's skepticism, Kant's bifurcated world, and Hegel's overly intellectual philosophy provides Whitehead with an epistemological theory in terms of which the perceptual objects of ordinary experience can be adequately considered without having to accept sense data, and the constructions from sense data, as final realities.

Our present concern is with objects and relations existing within the context of human society. It will be necessary, therefore, to extend our discussion of Whiteheadian philosophy to include the types of order existing among actual occasions as encountered in the world of human experience. Our special concern will be to indicate the ontological status of human persons, societies, and cultures.

Theorists of human society often distinguish three perspectives from which a society may be viewed: the individual, the social, and the cultural. Thus Talcott Parsons, one of the most influential of contemporary theoretical sociologists, considers "personality systems," "social systems," and "culture systems" as the three related perspectives necessary for a complete characterization of social relations.[4] Social systems concern the interactions of human beings viewed as activities possessing a structure, but as abstracted from the norms or defining characteristics of this structure. Personality systems concern the needs and tendencies of individuals in such an interacting context. Culture systems deal with the "patterned or ordered systems of symbols which are objects of the orientation of action, internalized components of the personalities of individual actors and institutionalized patterns of social systems."[5]

1. SOCIETIES AND PERSONS

The ties which exist between actual occasions are their prehensions of one another. Sets of actual occasions considered in abstraction from their real connections with one another are termed "multiplicities." But multiplicities are not proper entities. The fundamental complex of actual entities is the "nexus." A nexus is a grouping of actual entities whose relatedness consists in their prehensions of one another. Nexūs are of two principal types: social and non-social. A social nexus is distinct from a non-social one in that it sustains a common element of form which is included in each of its members by virtue of its prehensions of some other member, while a non-social nexus does not. The social nexus contains a complex eternal object which expresses its internal order. This order is inherited by the other members of the nexus. The complex eternal object functions as the defining characteristic of the society.

The defining characteristic of a society is the key to the understanding of Whitehead's theory of the types of social order. The types of order extant in any cosmic epoch are expressions of the prehensions of the various complex eternal objects which constitute the defining characteristics of social order. Thus the laws of nature are descriptions of the behavior of actual entities. The relative permanence and statistical constancy of the laws of nature result from the fact that the initial aim of an actual occasion and, therefore, the relevant past which provides the initial data of concrescence for that occasion, are strongly influenced by the defining characteristics of the various societies of which it is a member. Such societies, which comprise the immediate, proximate, and remote environments of the actual occasions, are arranged in a hierarchical order from that in which the defining characteristics apply to every actual occasion and nexus of occasions to those nexūs which manifest a defining characteristic relevant only to the specific nexus in question.

The most general type of society is the "extensive continuum." This society, with its defining characteristic of extensive connection, "constitutes the whole environment within which our epoch is set" (PR 148). As the most generic determination of order, the defining characteristics of the extensive continuum are relevant to all actual occasions and nexūs. "Within" the extensive continuum there is contained the more specifically determined geometrical society. This society is dominated by the various types of geometrical order relevant to this epoch. Less general still is the electromagnetic society whose defining characteristics dominate the behavior of the actual entities which comprise the protonic and electronic forms of social order forming the fundamental entities of modern physics. More special societies, such as those which comprise stones, trees, animal bodies, etc., are compatible with, and informed by, the defining characteristics of the more general societies mentioned above.

The electromagnetic society which characterizes our cosmic epoch is the locus of yet more special types of order which promote or inhibit one another. The types of order relevant to the characterization of the ontological status of human beings and of the objects and institutions comprising human societies are: structured societies, corpuscular societies, and personally ordered societies.

A structured society is a type of order which "includes subordinate societies and nexūs with a definite pattern of structural inter-relations" (PR 151). The distinction between subordinate societies and subordinate nexūs is easily drawn: non-social nexūs are those which possess no defining characteristics capable of sustaining themselves apart from the stabilizing environment provided by a structured society (v. PR 151–152). A structured society may, therefore, contain both social and non-social nexūs, the latter being dependent upon the structured society for its genetic stability. Whitehead cites the living cell as an example of a structured society. The general molecular characteristics of the cell are independent of the cell structure, but the "life" of the cell is dependent upon the maintenance of that cell structure. The molecules comprising a living cell are, thus, subordinate social nexūs, while the life of the cell is expressed by a subordinate non-social nexus.

A nexus which is social but which has only a serial, i.e., non-spatial, order is an enduring object possessing personal order. A society analyzable into strands of such enduring objects is a "corpuscular" society. The difference between a structured society and a corpuscular society is that in a structured society there are both social and non-social nexūs present, and the defining characteristics of the entire nexus are relevant to the protection and maintenance of the non-social nexūs, while in a corpuscular society the relative autonomy of the subordinate parts is maintained since the subordinate societies (enduring objects) are capable of existing relatively unchanged outside the corpuscular society.

This distinction between structured and corpuscular societies is important in Whitehead's theory of the types of order. For we, in fact, find it necessary to distinguish between relative degrees of dependence of a "part" upon the "whole" which constitutes its immediately relevant larger context. Such distinctions are common to the natural sciences and the social sciences alike. For example, in embryology the distinction is made between "regulation" eggs in which the development of a part is determined more by its position in the whole than by its own internal constitution, and "mosaic" eggs in which the internal characteristics of each part determine its own development within the whole.[6] Regulation eggs are structured societies; mosaic eggs are corpuscular societies. An example from ordinary experience might be the distinction between types of political order. A federal union such as the United States of America may be contrasted with a political organization such as the United Nations which represents a confederation of autonomous nations. In Whiteheadian terms the former is an example of a structured society, and the latter, of a corpuscular society.

The structured society provides a favorable context within which the intrinsic aim of experience, the aim at balanced intensity, is possible of realization, since it allows for the maintenance of non-social nexūs. For novelty and social order are mutually inhibiting unless the social order provides a stable matrix within which otherwise unstable occasions are free to seek novel and intense satisfactions. Occasions characterized by novel prehensions are highly specialized forms which are only viable within a larger and more stable environment. The problem of achieving balanced intensity of experiencing revolves about the need to combine intensity with viability.

The best method of seeking balanced intensity is through the introduction of novelty into an otherwise stable context. Conceptual novelties are introduced in accordance with the category of conceptual reversion. Occasions in a society active in the introduction of novelty are termed "living." If these occasions dominate the structured society, i.e., if they are "regnant," then the society is termed a living structured society. Such a living society is one in which the structural pattern is such as to promote a stable environment for a living non-social nexus.

Now, consider a serial society of actual occasions with personal order. Assume that the members of this nexus are of a high conceptual character, i.e., that the occasions are dominated by the higher phases of experience. It is this temporal series of actual occasions which is the primary ingredient of the human self enduring through time. This personal order is part of an entirely living nexus which constitutes the life of the person in question. And although the entirely living nexus is, by definition, non-social, a personal order of occasions may be supported along the historical route of the nexus. The immediate environment of the personal order of a human self is a living, non-social nexus. This environment provides the novel data required by the personal order. The mutually contemporary occasions forming this nexus prehend data from the relevant past and provide a novel rendering of the data via the categoreal conditions operative in the higher phases of experience. The occasion of the personal order existing at any given moment of the self is the "presiding" occasion. This occasion is the locus of the final synthesis of the data from its immediate living environment. It is responsible for the intentions, anticipations, ideas, and ideals characteristic of the mental operations of a human person. But this self has as yet no survival power. It requires a still wider environment, composed of those subordinate societies and nexūs which give stability and protection to the entirely living nexus and its personally ordered series of presiding occasions. This is the animal body. It provides the stability which the occasions of higher conceptual order cannot provide because of their near-chaotic grasp for novelty.

The human self in its broadest sense is the interacting complex of societies and nexūs, living and non-living, ruled by the presiding occasions, which act as coordinating centers of the entire complex. In the narrow sense, however, the self may be said to have its locus in the presiding occasion which harmonizes and evaluates the data from the other high-grade occasions and from the animal body. The presiding occasion of the human self is the coordinator of the various centers of valuation within the societies comprising the mind-body complex. The unifying aspect of the personal order of actual occasions is "memory"—direct retention of the causally efficacious past. Prehensions of past data are added to the depth of reserve of the occasions of the present. Thus the various presiding occasions of a personal order, each a "self," constitute a unity by virtue of the fact of cumulative "memory." In this way the self is one through time. But there is still an important sense in which there are many selves. Each presiding occasion experiences its own individual concrescence, achieves its own satisfaction, and qualifies future occasions in its own particular way through its objective immortality. The unity manifest in cumulative memory is determinative only if a present self maintains essential agreement with the valuational patterns of past selves. Whitehead's theory takes account of the gradual, or radical, transformation of a present self away from its predecessors.

The discussion has concentrated thus far on two important characteristics of the human self—its capability of introducing and elaborating novel prehensions, and its transience. A third important characteristic must now be considered: the freedom of the self. The ninth categoreal obligation holds that "the concrescence of each individual actual entity is internally determined and is externally free" (PR 41). This is the category of freedom and determination. This category describes the balance of efficient and final causation in the growth of experience. "Causation is nothing else than one outcome of the principle that every actual entity has to house *its* actual world" (PR 124). *That* its actual world must be housed means that determination via efficient causation is a necessary characteristic of experience. But *the way in which* an occasion houses its past actual world is a function of its subjective aim. This implies final causation.

The subjective aim of an occasion is the result of that occasion's selection from the ordered possibilities open to it through the initial aim. "There is an order in the relevance of eternal objects to the process of creation" (PR 522). That there is an order in the *relevance* of possibilities seems to imply that the initial aim is non-specific. That is, although there is a single ideal possibility given to each set of circumstances involving a concrescence, there are other appropriate possibilities which, though not the best, would allow for the attainment of some order. Thus, in order to give any substantive meaning to Whitehead's insistence upon the free self-creating character of an actual occasion, it seems necessary to suppose that the specification of the initial aim on the part of a concrescing occasion involves a selection from a series of ordered possibilities, only one of which, in each case, is the best selection.[7] Here, "best" simply means that which will eventuate in the greatest degree of balanced intensity.

Four components which are relevant to the final determination of a subjective aim must be discriminated: (1) the concrete character of the past actual world functioning as efficient causation and limiting the possibilities open to an originating occasion; (2) the initial aim containing a graded envisagement of possibilities awaiting further specification and emphasis from the relevant actual occasion; (3) the persuasive lure toward the choice of the best among the relevant possibilities open to the actual occasion; and (4) the freedom of the occasion to complete its aim through self-determination.

Freedom, the freedom of an actual occasion, is a function of the relative degree of conceptual intensity possessed by the occasion. Actual occasions in which the conceptual pole is dominant can entertain complex ideals, and make comparative and negative judgments about these ideals and the concrete data relevant to them. Occasions in which the physical pole is almost wholly dominant, though in principle they are still possessed of some degree of freedom, are almost wholly determined by efficient causation.

Freedom varies also according to the context from which the process of becoming begins. There is no absolute freedom. The limits of the freedom of an actual entity are determined by the initial aim which is a function of its standpoint in the extensive continuum. The limits of freedom are given by the standpoint of the actual entity which provide it with its potentialities for becoming. "Freedom, givenness, potentiality, are notions which presuppose each other and limit each other" (PR 202).

The determinative "given" to which Whitehead is here alluding refers both to the given of the actual world of the causal past and to the specific subjective aim provided on the basis of this environment. Whitehead makes a crucial point when he says that freedom, givenness, and potentiality presuppose *each other* and limit *each other*. The actual world of any given entity functions causally with respect to it, but the efficient causation of the objectified past is, to a greater or lesser extent, the result of free choices of actual occasions seeking satisfaction, in accordance with the initial aims provided them, through utilization of their objectified data. And the initial aim given to the entity in question, provided in order to maximize the actualization of harmony, is itself a partial product of the same free choices in the entity's objectified past. In other words, at least part of the causal determination experienced by any given occasion is the product of free decisions in the past.

The idea of the self has been identified with the notion of a personal order of actual occasions which dwells within an environment containing a set of mutually contemporary occasions able to provide high-grade conceptual data. This latter environment itself dwells within the animal body composed of stabilizing societies possessed of a lower degree of conceptual intensity. Freedom is located, to some degree, within every one of the actual occasions of the human complex. But, for men to be truly free, the dominant presiding occasion, or occasions, must be free.

The human self is free, for the integrity of the self is a function of the integrating activity of a high-grade presiding occasion. The essence of an actual occasion of high conceptual order is the ability to decide between alternatives, to entertain alternate possibilities. Thus, although open possibilities are not unlimited, because of the fact that the presiding occasion must deal with the available data from its past and the past of the group of occasions of which it is a part, and must deal with this data in terms of its initial aim, still freedom of choice is a reality within limits.

Granted the existence of the mind-body complex of actual entities: what would the experience of human freedom be? The animal body will be the locus through which the data of sensation are given. These data together with the novel data provided by the occasions of high conceptual order will be processed by the coordinating activity of the presiding occasions which will aim, under ideal conditions, at the union of intensity and contrast in their satisfaction. But two main conditioning forces are present: those of the initial aim and of the causal past. The latter is equivalent, in high-grade organisms, to conscious and sub-conscious memory. We may call the former conditioning factor the disposition of the self, and the latter the predisposition of the self. Freedom may be meaningfully applied to the human person considered as permanent through time in three senses—two weak, one strong. In the strong sense, the human self is free insofar as its presiding occasion is able to produce and integrate novel data, deciding among a variety of possible alternatives. In the weak senses there is freedom insofar as the self is disposed to act by virtue of free decisions of the past occasions in the temporal sequence of which it is a part and insofar as it is *pre*disposed to act for the same reason. These two latter senses of freedom provide the foundation in Whiteheadian metaphysics for the approval of certain forms of routine, habit, discipline, custom, moral codes, introjected values, etc.

It is clear that these two weak senses of freedom presuppose a consciousness of the disposing and predisposing factors or, at least, the option at some point of altering the influence of these factors. If this option is not present, if the self is a slave of habit or custom, then he has become a victim of determination. Even the determined individual, however—one who is no longer free to act otherwise than he acts—may have had the freedom at some earlier point in his life.[8] There is a point at which a person on the way to becoming a drug addict can refuse the object of his addiction, and another point at which he is unable. The difference between a potential addict and the confirmed addict is a function of freedom as well as givenness. Freedom, givenness, potentiality, presuppose each other and limit each other.

I have briefly considered three qualities of the human self: freedom, transience, and novel purpose; in this consideration I have been able to give only the barest outline of the concept of the self. At present I am attempting to characterize the three principal perspectives from which human social relations may be viewed, having prepared the ground for distinguishing two of the three sociological perspectives with which we are concerned—human individuals and societies of such individuals.

The human mind-body complex is a living structured society dominated by a personal order of conceptually intense actual occasions whose aim is at balanced complexity of experiencing. The presiding occasions of the human self express the characteristics of freedom, transience, and novel purpose. The human structured society exists in order to promote the achievement of balanced complexity on the part of the presiding occasions of the self.

Human societies may illustrate either corpuscular or non-living structured types of order, depending upon the relative degree of autonomy of the subordinate nexūs. There is no means of determining a priori what type of order a human society illustrates. And if the forms of relationship existing among the various members of a society change, so the type of order may change. For example: at its inception, the Confederacy of Delos, formed in the fifth century B.C. by Athens and her maritime neighbors for mutual aid in the fight against Persia, was a union of autonomous states—i.e., a corpuscular society. When, under Pericles, the other members of the confederacy were subjugated and made part of an Athenian empire, the type of social order became a non-living structured type.

The same society may also manifest differing types of order depending upon the relative degree of generality of the defining characteristics chosen to describe the society. If we consider the United States of America as illustrating certain broad defining characteristics such as general patterns of language use, etc., we may find agreement through the entire society. If, on the other hand, we view the society from a less abstract viewpoint, in terms of its particular moral norms, aesthetic tastes, etc., the differences might overtake the generic commonalities. Thus, a society may illustrate both a structured and a corpuscular type of social order depending upon whether it is the common traits or the variegated aspects of the society which are selected as the defining characteristics of that social order.

The ontological distinction between a human individual and a society of such individuals is that implicit in the distinction between a "living" and a "non-living" society. The difference is that of the originative power of the individual and non-originative character of the institutions and events of a social complex abstracted from its individual members. That is, the introduction of relevant novelty into the social complex is accomplished only by the individual members. The institutions of a society are embodiments of creative or novel expressions, but are not, of themselves, living, self-perpetuating structures. The closest a society could come to manifesting a living social order is in the case of a totalitarian government with a highly rationalized bureaucracy headed by a single individual. This would constitute a structured society and the presiding occasion of the individual dictator might, in large measure, represent the presiding occasion of the entire social complex. A society such as this would, in Whiteheadian terms, be an organism analogous to that of a human organism. But because of the high degree of rationalized order necessary for such a society, it is doubtful if a clear-cut example of one could be given. Hitler's Third Reich at the height of its war-time efficiency would be the closest modern approximation to such a society.

In the main, Whitehead's philosophy seems to require one to steer a middle course between "organic" and "non-organic" conceptions of society. Organic conceptions associated with Plato, Hegel, or Spengler, for instance, are based upon the analogies existing between the human and the social organism. For example, the Hegelian conception of society is of an organism in which each individual citizen is an instrument with a purpose to be defined wholly in terms of the *telos* of the state.[9] On this view the state is the true individual, and the individuality of its members is a function of their membership in the state. Such a view is to be contrasted with the non-organic or contractual view of society illustrated by such thinkers as Hobbes or Locke. The philosophical rationale behind this view is a type of nominalism which sees all social or trans-individual phenomena as ultimately reducible to psychological facts relating to individual human beings.[10]

The Whiteheadian conception of society agrees with Hegel's organic view in that it holds that human society expresses a natural *telos,* but it conflicts with the Hegelian view in holding that this *telos* has its locus in the individual human beings of the society, not in the society itself. Whitehead is thus able to provide a strong individualistic emphasis most characteristic of the non-organic or analytic view of society. In so doing, he maintains a mediating position between the organic and analytic conceptions of society since he is able to provide, in the phylogenetic discussion of the types of order, the concept of a non-living structured society which is only a partial analogue of the living structured society comprising the human mind-body complex.

The discussion of types of social order has resolved the chief problem among those concerning the ontological status of the world of human social experience. Certain epistemological problems, however, are still outstanding, the most significant of which is this: "How does the human person come to know the world of social experience?" Part of the answer to this question has been supplied by a preliminary consideration of the concept of transmutation.

Whitehead's theory of transmutation aims to account for our perception of the world as continuous and extensive rather than as a plurality of discrete units. Transmutation functions as an explanation of ordinary human perceptual experience. But perceptual experience is obviously not sufficient to encompass human experience. We see extensive regions because of transmutation, but what allows us to *understand* what we see? When we see a school building, we "see" more than a colored, extensive region of space and time. We understand what we see when we look at a school building because we see that building as a symbol of certain aims related to the educational process and of certain human functions related to these aims. If we are to understand human cultural experience from a Whiteheadian perspective, we must understand how Whitehead's philosophy provides for such understanding.

Sense-perception in the mode of presentational immediacy involves a high degree of abstraction, as I have indicated. The translation from the "reality" of physical feelings in the initial datum of an occasion of experience to the "appearance" of conscious perceptions involves a de-emphasis of concrete, primitive experiences. Such abstractions, though obviously invaluable, must not lose their germaneness to the primitive experiences from which they derive. In this connection what Whitehead terms "rationalization" functions to preserve the connection between "primitive" and "abstract" experience. "Thus rationalization is the reverse of abstraction, so far as abstraction can be reversed within the area of consciousness" (MT 124).

Always accompanying the process of abstraction, there is a reverse drive toward recovery of the concrete experience. The conscious experience of some sensory detail leads one to seek a conception of the place of that detail within its larger sensory and conceptual context. This is a result of the recognition in consciousness of the realities lying behind the abstractions which arise from concrete experience. This intuition in consciousness of the substratum of concrete actualities upon which all concepts are based leads to an attempt to discriminate and articulate the nature and extent of the relevance of the analytic concepts to the synthetic ground of experience.

This process seeks to read backward from the concepts to the primitive experiences underlying them, and attempts to uncover the concrete reality partially obscured by the selective emphasis of consciousness. This process is an instance of symbolic reference between Appearance and Reality rather than the more common form of symbolic reference which proceeds in the opposite manner, from Reality to Appearance. This is not merely an attempt to undo what consciousness has accomplished; it is an attempt to utilize the analytic, selective character of conscious experience to enhance the value experiences which, without consciousness, would remain vague and undifferentiated. The concreteness of reality is both the starting-point of individual experience and the goal of the process of rationalization. "The prize at the goal is the enhancement of experience by consciousness and rationality" (MT 125). Whereas in sense-perception transmutation effects a transfer from reality to appearance, in rationalization there is re-introduction of the value experience of the causally efficacious world. The *significance* of a concept, its intension, is therefore grounded upon the process of rationalization.

With his notion of rationalization Whitehead is seen to lean very far toward the classical concept of the ontological foundation of reason. As Paul Tillich has so well pointed out, classical concepts of reason have tended to hold reason's fundamental nature to consist in its participation in being.[11] Over against, and along side, such a conception there has been the view of reason as "reasoning"—the concept of technical reason—which Tillich attributes to British empiricism. In the concept of "rationalization" Whitehead is stressing the ontological grounding of consciousness and concepts in the primitive world of concrete experience, and in so doing provides the basis for contrasting ontological reason with that type of technical reason which is concerned mainly with the interplay of concepts in the world of presentational immediacy.

Donald Sherburne in his *A Whiteheadian Aesthetic* has made a distinction between "horizontal" and "vertical" transmutation which parallels the distinction to which I have pointed between "transmutation" and "rationalization." "It is via vertical transmutation that the welter of actual occasions constitutive of a man are prehended as a unity, but it is in virtue of horizontal transmutation that significance is attached to the concept of 'man.'"[12] Distinguishing between types of transmutation to indicate the difference between abstraction and rationalization I think is quite helpful. I would propose, however, that the terms "vertical" and "horizontal" be replaced by "extensive" and "intensive." Extensive transmutation defines an extended region, and intensive transmutation as "intended" significance. This terminology is superior since, in addition, it calls attention to the relations between intensional and extensional meanings of concepts. If extensive transmutation provides an understanding of the perception of macrocosmic entities, intensive transmutation explains the understanding of the significance of perceptual objects.

In a revealing passage from *Adventures of Ideas,* Whitehead indicates the relationship between intensive and extensive transmutation:

> The human body is an instrument for the production of art in the life of the human soul. It concentrates upon those elements in human experience selected for conscious perception intensities of subjective form derived from components dismissed into shadow. . . . In this way the work of art is a message from the Unseen. It unlooses depths of feeling from behind the frontier where precision of consciousness fails [AI 349].

In conscious perception, extensive transmutation selects only certain components of experience for emphasis in presentational immediacy. The remaining components are "dismissed into shadow." Intensive transmutation, however, reintroduces "meaning" by concentrating intensities of subjective form derived from the dismissed components.

The data of ordinary experience—the perception of colors, sounds, smell, etc.—require extensive transmutation. Intensive transmutation is most dramatically evident in those experiences of "value" associated with moral, aesthetic, or religious experience. But in spite of the variant emphases of extensive and intensive transmutation, it should be made clear that both transmuting functions enter into almost every instance of conscious experience. For the terms "intensive" and "extensive," as I am using them, are borrowed from theories of language in which the "intension" of a statement is its "meaning" and its "extension" is the reality or realities to which the statement refers.[13] Thus, the extension of an empirical statement such as "I see the black pen" is the extensively transmuted percept of the colored object before me, while the intension of the statement is the *judgment* which grasps the significance of the percept.

Turning to the problem of culture: the contributions of Whitehead's concept of transmutation to the understanding of society can now be noted. Three varieties of data are available for analysis according to the epistemological theory described above. These are "atomic" facts, "social" facts, and "societal" facts.[14] Atomic facts are untransmuted perceptions; social facts are extensively transmuted perceptions; and societal facts are intensively transmuted perceptions. In discussing ordinary perceptual experience, one could ignore atomic facts since practically every perception is a transmuted one. Perceiving is almost exclusively the result of the two modes of transmutation.

If, however, we consider the analogies between this paradigm of perception and the special problems of perception in human societies with personality, social, and cultural systems, we may make the following application of the foregoing distinctions: atomic facts concern the actions and purposes of specific individual beings; social facts concern groups of individuals;

and societal facts, the forms of organization suggestive or determinative of types of behavior and interpretation. Such facts are what Whitehead terms "socially diffused habits of behavior and . . . interpretation" (AI 320). Atomic facts, therefore, deal with individuals *qua* individuals, social facts with groupings of individuals—"masses"—considered in abstraction from their specific forms of organization; societal facts concern the defining characteristics of social groupings. With these distinctions in mind it is possible now to come to an understanding of Whitehead's concept of "culture."

2. A DEFINITION OF CULTURE

No single discipline has a monopoly on the word "culture." It is used in a technical sense by anthropologists, sociologists, and social psychologists, as well as by philosophers,[15] and within each discipline, there are a variety of approaches to the topic. One may seek to define culture in its most generic sense as referring to any and all cultures, or one may consider the topic concretely and in terms of particular existing cultures. The theoretical approach tends to express certain normative considerations while an empirical or phenomenological approach emphasizes the descriptive rather than the normative dimension. In the characterization of a Whiteheadian definition of culture to be given in this section, the theoretical and normative approach will be utilized.

At the beginning of this chapter, Talcott Parsons' definition of culture was given. We shall now pursue Parsons' concept of culture further as a means of introducing the Whiteheadian view. According to Parsons, culture, theoretically considered, concerns the system of symbols which characterize the behavior and the products of human action.[16] Culture systems consist of "eternal objects," objects not involved in process. Parsons borrows directly from Whiteheadian philosophy the concept of non-spatial and atemporal objects with which to identify cultural systems.[17]

Both for Whitehead and for Parsons the culture of a society involves, mainly, the abstract forms of organization of the thoughts and actions of the individuals in that society. In Whiteheadian terms, the culture of a human society consists of the abstract defining characteristics relevant to the characterization of that society. A defining characteristic is a complex eternal object which expresses the internal order of a society. Therefore, from the theoretical point of view, a culture is an abstraction in a sense in which neither individuals nor societies are. Thus, while a human society is a group of people with distinctive ways of interaction, a culture is just these modes of interaction. Both an individual and a social group may be objects of perception, whereas a "culture," in this theoretical sense, may not.[18] If we are to describe a particular culture, therefore, we should have to find the principal defining characteristics descriptive of the organization of the thought and action of the individuals within that society. At the abstract level these would be the general aims describing the ethos of that society; at a more concrete level these would constitute the specific laws, customs, etc., which characterize the group.

The aim of all experience is at balanced intensity. And since structured societies, which comprise both individuals and human societies, are means of organizing experiencing occasions in order to promote the aim of experience, it would appear that the consideration of culture would lead to the question concerning the kind of society which would best promote the aim of experience. It is just this stress on the *aim* of experience which requires us to emphasize the normative aspect of the theory of culture. For, as will be evident in the chapters which follow, Whitehead's consideration of cultures or civilizations has as its purpose the characterization of those cultural aims which would best promote intensity of experience.

The normative character of Whitehead's approach to the theory of culture is evident from his terminology. Whitehead seldom uses the term "culture" in his later writings; he uses "civilization" instead to cover both the normative and descriptive characterizations of human social aims and interests. But the term always carries a certain normative connotation as Whitehead uses it. "Civilized beings are those who survey the world with some large generality of understanding" (MT 4). When Whitehead uses the term "civilization," therefore, he is thinking in terms of a standard or norm which may be used to discriminate civilized from uncivilized experience and expression.

I have found it helpful to make a distinction between "culture" and "civilization." For the most part I shall use the term "culture" in discussing the general concept of the normative dimension of distinctively human social activities, and "civilization" in considering the subject of cultural norms in terms of their relative degree of success or failure in achieving the aim at subjective intensity of experience. Thus, the concept "culture" will most often be discussed in terms of human activities as obedient to certain aims or norms, but in abstraction from the question of whether these aims or norms are the best or most ideal in promoting the attainment of the aim of experience. "Civilization" will refer to the same subject matter as culture, with the added concern for discovering aims and interests which will best promote intensity of experience. Such a distinction seems to be in line with Whitehead's intentions since, when he uses the term "culture," it is, most often, in this neutral sense which I have proposed (v. SMW ix).

Culture is the complex of aims and interests which define and organize human social activity and its products. That is, culture, in the abstract sense of the term, is constituted by the complex of defining characteristics of a society as well as by the cultural "interests" of art, science, religion, etc., which direct human energies toward the realization of these characteristics. A society is civilized to the degree that its cultural interests promote the general aim at intensity of experiencing. This abstract definition of culture requires further specification. In particular, we need to distinguish between the general aim of nature at specific types of order which promote balanced intensity of experiencing and the more specifically *human* actions directed to the same end. That is, we must see the way in which Whitehead would distinguish between "nature" and "culture." In the course of this discussion we will gain some insight, as well, into the meaning of "human social activity and its products."

The human mind-body complex, as a type of order, is a prime illustration of the way in which the processes of nature have conspired to achieve the aim at balanced intensity. But when we discuss human societies and the ideals or aims which help to define them, we must introduce a distinction between the general *telos* of experience at subjective intensity and the specific aims of finite, free human persons.

One of the purposes of this discussion of the concepts of person, society, and culture in the context of Whitehead's theory of the types of order has been to illustrate the radically naturalistic perspective of Whiteheadian philosophy. One implication of this naturalistic bias is that any distinction between man and nature must be qualified by the principle of the continuity of all forms of order implicit in Whitehead's interpretation of social experience. But Whitehead has provided the means for making this distinction, however qualified, in his ambiguous characterization of the term "nature." Consider, first, the meaning of "nature" to be found in his earlier writings in the philosophy of science:

> Nature is that which we observe in perception through the senses. In this sense-perception we are aware of something which is not thought and which is self-contained for thought. . . . nature can be thought of as a closed system whose mutual relations do not require the expression of the fact that they are thought about. . . . we can think about nature without thinking about thought. . . . then we are thinking "homogeneously" about nature [CN 3].[19]

The concern in the investigation of nature is with the objective data of perceptual experience abstracted from the experience of such data in an individual concrescence. The natural philosopher deals with objective data abstracted from the subjective form of any individual experience. Nature is the "assemblage of factors within fact" (*Prin. Rel.* 21), considered apart from the valuations of such factors by a concrescing subject. A provisional disjunction between "fact" and "value" is made by Whitehead in order to describe the specialized function of natural philosophy. But this distinction is not to be considered as having a *fundamentum in re* any more than does the hypothetical analysis of experience which disjoins objective datum and subjective form.

For Whitehead, "natural science is exclusively concerned with homogeneous thoughts about nature" (CN 4). That is to say, natural science considers perceptual objects *non-reflectively*. A thinking about nature which includes a consideration of nature-as-thought-about is a heterogeneous thinking about nature. A speculative philosopher who seeks to promote the most general systematization of civilized thought (PR 25–26) must think heterogeneously about nature. Whereas the scientist's subject matter is the object of perceptual experience *qua* object, the principal subject matter of the speculative philosopher considering nature would be the various theories and doctrines proposed by the scientists in order to explain perceptual objects.

In addition to this narrow view of nature, there is a broader concept characteristic of Whitehead's later, speculative writings and somewhat more germane to our topic. In the broader sense, nature is the whole of actuality in process. The natural philosopher deals with nature in a non-reflective sense only. The synthesis of the knower with the object known is not his concern. A thinking about nature which would consider the knower–known synthesis would constitute metaphysical reflection. Metaphysics is distinguished from natural science by the fact that whereas the former is concerned reflectively with nature—i.e., is concerned with a thinking about nature which includes nature-as-thought-about—the latter considers nature solely in terms of perceptual objects (v. PNK vii).

Whitehead elaborates this concept of nature explicitly in terms of an attempt to characterize the distinction between nature and culture, or civilization. This distinction is introduced in the following way: "Art is the education of nature. Thus, in its broadest sense, art is civilization. For civilization is nothing other than the unremitting aim at the major perfections of harmony" (AI 349). The identification of art and civilization as agencies aiming at the major perfections of harmony does not seem to provide a means for making a distinction between "civilization" and "nature" since the aim of *all* experience is at such harmony. But Whitehead does introduce such a distinction:

> The merit of Art in its service to civilization lies in its artificiality and its finiteness. It exhibits for consciousness a finite fragment of human effort achieving its own perfection within its own limits. . . . A million sunsets will not spur on men towards civilization. It requires Art to evoke into consciousness the finite perfections which lie ready for human achievement [AI 348].

Both nature, broadly considered, and human art seek "the major perfections of harmony." The difference is that whereas natural processes produce harmonious results as the outcome of a slow process, human art and, therefore, human civilization, achieve their aims through the "quick purposeful adaptation [of Appearance to Reality] originated by finite creatures" (AI 345).

These two meanings of "nature" must be kept in mind in the discussion which follows, for Whitehead's theory of culture and civilization presupposes both meanings of the term. Cultural experience and expression are defined in terms of the rapid adaptations of finite creatures, while "natural" experience is discussed in terms of the slow outcome of the unity of concrescent experiences. In this sense, cultural experience forms a part within the whole of nature, a part relevant to certain complex types of order (i.e., structured societies dominated by living personal orders of presiding occasions characterized by freedom, transience, and novel purpose). In the narrower sense of the term, "nature" is an abstraction from actuality which aims to elucidate the character of the objects of perceptual experience without reference to subjective considerations. This so-called "homogeneous" thinking about nature comprises the natural sciences which are a part of the subject matter with which the philosopher of culture is concerned. The philosopher of culture, however, thinks "heterogeneously," or indirectly, about nature since one of his functions is to reflect upon the doctrines of the special sciences and their mutual relations in order to provide an adequate systematization of civilized thought.

Both natural and cultural experience may be discussed analogically in terms of the structure of experience per se. The principal elements of experiencing, from the perspective of the actual occasion, are datum, process, and satisfaction. We may distinguish, at the macrocosmic level, therefore, objects, agencies, and aims of experience. Objects are the result of processes in the past; agencies constitute instantiating processes in the present; aims define the future-oriented drive toward goal-satisfaction.

A natural object, such as a tree, has its own internal *telos* in terms of which the processes of experiencing occasions act in order to maintain the internal order of the particular society which constitutes that tree. The satisfied occasions of the society become relevant objective data for the next emergent occasions of experience, and the internal *telos* is maintained by the provision of the relevant initial aim. Thus the "treeness" of the tree is maintained because the agencies of experience of each successive temporal epoch act upon the objects of the past in terms of an aim at the type of order which constitutes that tree.

An analysis of the relation of natural to cultural agents, objects, and aims should clarify the discussion of culture in which we are engaged. For we have said that, on Whiteheadian principles, the culture of a society is the complex of aims which define human social activity and its products. A consideration of culture in terms of human activity and its products entails a discussion of cultural aims in relation to particular types of agencies and objects.

The Whiteheadian distinction between natural and cultural objects, agents, and aims recalls the distinction made by Aristotle between natural objects in which internal, teleological causation is operative, and artificial objects which are the products of external causes.[20] The tree is a natural object; a table made from the tree is a product of art. In the first instance the final, formal, material and efficient causes are, in some sense, internal to the tree. In the second instance the tree is reduced to the status of material cause of the artificial object, the table, made from it. The formal, final, and efficient causes are now internal to the artificer.

Whitehead's distinction between the artificial and the natural is similar to Aristotle's. Human culture is artificial. Artificial, or cultural, objects are products of human agency acting in accordance with the aim at intensity of experience. The term "cultural agency" applies peculiarly to human persons who are capable of the introduction of novel and creative actions aimed at achieving subjective intensity. The cultural agent seeks to transform the natural environment in accordance with a purpose or an aim.

The difference between natural and cultural agency is to be found in the latter's emphasis upon the higher phases of experience. The cultural agent is capable of intensive transmutation—i.e., transmutation relevant to intuitive and derivative judgments. As such he is capable of consciously introducing meaning into the actual world as well as deriving meaning from it. The meanings thus introduced and derived are guides in the production and enjoyment of cultural objects. A selection of the most generic meanings provides a culture or civilization with its cultural aims.

Cultural agents are, properly speaking, human individuals. In discussing the ontological status of persons and societies, I noted Whitehead's position in relation to the so-called "organic" view of society. The originative, novelty-introducing capacities must ultimately be seen to reside in the presiding occasions of human personal order. For example, a dancing troupe qualified by the characteristic "precision" is not itself precise, but is a group of individuals each of whom is precise. In any grouping, "the composite group illustrates its qualities passively. The activity belongs to the individual actualities" (AI 274).

These comments suggest the relationship between Whitehead and the majority of recent British philosophers on the question of the ontological status of trans-individual states of affairs. The classic example from discussions in recent British philosophy is illustrated by the statement, "England declared war in 1939." It is the status of "England" which is in question. The dissatisfaction of discussions of this type of term relates to the seeming dilemma of the necessity of either hypostatizing "England" into some organic unity reminiscent of the Hegelian organic conception of the State, or of analyzing the term into Humean "simples," i.e., psychological facts relating to individual human beings. Neither solution seems quite to answer the problem. The organic conception is not acceptable because, to the analytic and anti-authoritarian strain of British philosophy, it gives an unrealistically large amount of efficacy to a trans-individual phenomenon. The Humean solution on the other hand lands one in skepticism with regard to the viability of any analysis which requires reference to unified activities such as seem to be experienced in a social context.

Whitehead's resolution of the issue of the ontological status of trans-individual states of affairs is an attempt to balance the organic and analytic tendencies. For Whitehead, the statement "England declared war in 1939" would be interpreted in terms of the actions of individual Englishmen in power, acting in accordance with aims or purposes, "defining characteristics" if you will, of the society of which they were members. England, a structured society with a complex sub-structure of enduring objects, corpuscular societies, etc., possessed of defining characteristics such as "individualism," "love of freedom," "colonialism," "imperialism," "self-preservative motivation," etc., declared war, in the sense that the individual members of the society acted in large part to maintain the viability of a society with the same defining characteristics as those having provided the individual motivations for declaring war. Only the individual gives active expression to these qualities. Social groups, or institutions, are not properly cultural agents in the Whiteheadian sense of that term, although the defining characteristics of an institution will affect the type of activities engaged in by individuals. Ultimately, however, the focus for the theoretical discussion of culture from the normative perspective is the human individual.[21]

Cultural aims are the eternal objects forming the predicates of cultural objects. They are the ideals or values which the cultural agents of a society affirm and seek to instantiate via the creation of cultural objects. Those ideals characterizing societies which promote the general aim at intensity of experience are the norms which define a civilized society. Cultural aims are those propositional lures which introduce the efficacy of final cause into the cultural process. They are the values which individuals and societies affirm and seek to instantiate through unique actions or through habit, law, or custom. Cultural aims are societal facts. Normatively speaking, cultural aims are those values in accordance with which a civilized society realizes its societal states of affairs.

Cultural objects are the artificial objects produced in society in accordance with the structure of meanings affirmed by that social grouping. Cultural objects are distinguishable from natural objects to the extent that the latter are the outcome of some wide purpose in nature, the former are the products of the quick purposeful adaptations achieved by finite structured societies with personal order—i.e., human beings. Cultural objects are propositional in character. That is, a cultural object is a proposition in which the contemporary enduring nexus comprising the object is the logical subject and the complex eternal object forming the defining characteristic is the logical predicate.

Consider the illustration of a simple artifact—a hand ax, for example. Some primitive hand axes are nothing more than pieces of stone, the natural shape of which may be relevant to the performance of simple cutting operations. The distinction between these stones as natural objects and as cultural objects is to be found in their altered significance when used by human agents. As cultural objects, they express a potentiality for being used to accomplish a delimited set of aims—e.g., the cutting of firewood, the making of dugout canoes, etc. These cultural objects, as propositions, have as their logical subjects the nexūs forming the particular physical objects comprising the stones, while the predicates are the complexes of aims which define the significance of the hand axes as tools for human use. Thus a cultural object may be viewed both as an objectified proposition and in terms of the defining characteristics which constitute the rule for the objectification of the proposition. Likewise, cultural agency may be construed both in terms of the processes of active centers of decision and in terms of the aims providing the criteria in accordance with which the decisions are made.

Our definition of culture as the complex of aims which define human social activity and its products obviously stresses the factor of cultural aims over those of cultural agency and objects. That is, "culture" is characterized as those aims which define cultural agency and objects. This one-sided characterization of the concept of culture is not purported to be wholly adequate to the full scope of the topic of culture, but is presented in order to indicate the perspective from which the remainder of this study will be undertaken. The consideration of cultural objects and agency, though important, will be subordinated to the analysis of the cultural aims which define a civilized society and the cultural interests which implement those aims. The primary reason for this stress is that it will allow us to make a relatively clear transition from the topic of culture per se to that of civilization or normative culture. Also it will provide the basis from the consideration of the cultural interests of art, morality, science, religion, and philosophy, and their relationships. And, as we shall see, a consideration of the mutual interaction of cultural aims and interests will yield provocative insights into the Whiteheadian concept of civilization which this study is trying to illumine.

NOTES

1. See Edmund Husserl, *Ideas* (New York: Collier, 1962), p. 19, and *Cartesian Meditations* (The Hague: Nijhoff, 1960).
2. See *Realism and the Backgrounds of Phenomenology,* ed. Roderick Chisholm (Glencoe, Ill.: Free Press, 1960), pp. 160–161.
3. Lovejoy, *The Revolt Against Dualism* (Lasalle, Ill.: Open Court, 1929), p. 266.
4. See Parsons' *The Social System* (Glencoe, Ill.: Free Press, 1951), pp. ix, 14–19, 539–541. For similar characterizations, see Ralph Linton, "Society, Culture, and the Individual," *The Tree of Culture* (New York: Knopf, 1955), pp. 29–40; and A. L. Kroeber and Clyde Kluckhohn, *Culture* (New York: Vintage, 1952), pp. 264–269.
5. Parsons, *System,* p. 327.
6. Cited in Kenneth Boulding, *The Image* (Ann Arbor: University of Michigan Press, 1959), p. 123.
7. For a discussion of this type of solution to the problem of freedom and determination, see John Cobb, *A Christian Natural Theology* (Philadelphia: Westminster, 1965), pp. 151–154; and Donald Sherburne, *A Whiteheadian Aesthetic* (New Haven: Yale University Press, 1961), pp. 41–46.

8. See Charles Hartshorne's essentially Whiteheadian discussion of this point in *Philosophical Interrogations,* edd. Sydney and Beatrice Rome (New York: Holt, Rinehart, 1964), pp. 338–340; and his *Beyond Humanism* (Lincoln: University of Nebraska Press, 1968), pp. 152–159.

9. See Hegel's *Philosophy of Right,* trans. T. M. Knox (Oxford: Clarendon, 1962), pp. 155–158; and W. T. Stace, *The Philosophy of Hegel* (New York: Dover, 1955), pp. 422–426.

10. For a discussion of such a non-organic approach to social theory, see Ernest Barker, *The Political Thought of Plato and Aristotle* (New York: Dover, 1947), pp. 130–132; J. O. Urmson, *Philosophical Analysis* (Oxford: Clarendon, 1956), pp. 151–154; and Maurice Mandelbaum, "Societal Facts," *The Structure of Scientific Thought,* ed. Edward H. Madden (Boston: Houghton Mifflin, 1960), pp. 166–176.

11. See Tillich's *Systematic Theology* (Chicago: University of Chicago Press, 1951), 171–75.

12. Sherburne, *Whiteheadian Aesthetic,* p. 163.

13. See Rudolph Carnap, *Meaning and Necessity* (Chicago: University of Chicago Press, 1956) and *Introduction to Symbolic Logic and its Applications* (New York: Dover, 1958), pp. 40ff.

14. See Mandelbaum, "Societal Facts."

15. For an account of the various disciplinary approaches to the subject of culture, see Kroeber and Kluckhohn, *Culture,* pp. 77–143.

16. See Parsons' *Essays in Sociological Theory* (Glencoe, Ill.: Free Press, 1949), pp. 8ff.

17. See Parsons' *The Structure of Social Action* (New York: McGraw-Hill, 1937), p. 762.

18. See Clyde Kluckhohn, *Culture and Behavior,* ed. Richard Kluckhohn (New York: Free Press, 1962), pp. 20–22.

19. See also *Prin. Rel.* 20–21; PNK vi–vii; PR 24; and Robert Palter, *Whitehead's Philosophy of Science* (Chicago: University of Chicago Press, 1960), 22–27.

20. See *Metaphysics* 1013a25–1014a25 and 1014b16–1015a19.

21. For discussions of the individual reference of theories of culture, see Clyde Kluckhohn, "The Concept of Culture," *Culture and Behavior,* ed. Kluckhohn p. 31; and Ruth Benedict, *Patterns of Culture* (London: Routledge & Kegan Paul, 1935), pp. 253ff.

Chapter IV

CULTURAL AIMS

I HAVE CHARACTERIZED "culture" in a Whiteheadian sense as the complex
of aims and interests which define and organize human social activity and
its products. In this chapter I shall discuss five specific aims which, according to Whitehead, define civilized societies. In the following chapter
I shall consider those cultural interests—art, morality, religion, science,
and philosophy—which organize cultural experience. An understanding
of these cultural aims and interests, and of their interrelations, is crucial
to a balanced assessment of Whitehead's theory of culture.

According to Whitehead, "a civilized society is exhibiting the five qualities of Truth, Beauty, Adventure, Art, Peace" (AI 353). With few exceptions, these qualities are discussed only in *Adventures of Ideas*. Therefore,
that work will provide the major source for the following discussion. I
shall find it helpful, however, to consider the metaphysical basis of some
of the relevant concepts in terms of the theories of "experience" and "culture" developed in the two preceding chapters.

1. ART AND CIVILIZATION

"Art is purposeful adaptation of Appearance to Reality" (AI 344). So
defined, Art is a generic feature of the process of experience. Concrescence
as a function of datum, process, and satisfaction involves Art in every
case. Each drop of experience is an aesthetic event in which the process of
growth involves an adaptation of the initial datum in accordance with an
initial aim. "Reality" for the given occasion becomes "Appearance," but
Appearance as adjusted and adapted in accordance with the given datum
constituting Reality for that occasion. The aim of Art is the same as the

aim of all experience—balanced complexity leading to intensity of experiencing. Balanced complexity is a function of two qualities attaching to experience: Truth and Beauty. The purpose of Art, therefore, is to achieve Truth and Beauty in experience, and "the perfection of Art . . . is Truthful Beauty" (AI 344).

Whitehead's concept of Art is generic in two senses. First, it has reference to activities which transcend the human. All experience is comprised of aesthetic events; all processes, therefore, involve Art. Secondly, Art as applied to strictly human activity encompasses a broader range of processes than are normally called "artistic." Our discussion of Whitehead's notion of Art as a quality of civilized societies must clarify both these aspects of the generality of Art. The first aspect has been touched upon in our discussion of cultural objects in Chapter III. We shall have occasion in this chapter to extend the rather sketchy comments found there. The second topic will lead to a discussion of Art in human experience and expression, and its relation to "art" as a cultural interest.

For Whitehead, as for Aristotle, "art" involves both a "feeling" and a "making." In Whiteheadian terms, the capacity of self-creativity which involves the intervention of consciousness and concepts in the higher phases of experiencing would be termed Art. Likewise, the expression of such a capacity in the adjustment of one's environment is Art. Art is the experience and the expression of the self-creativity inherent in all experience. "Human" art is self-creative expression resulting in the production of cultural objects. Cultural objects of a given society may be dominantly qualified by "Truth," "Beauty," or "Truthful Beauty." The aim of a civilized order is to coordinate its creation of cultural objects so as to achieve the quality of Truthful Beauty. Though Truthful Beauty is the perfection of Art, "some measure of success has been reached, when either Truth or Beauty is gained" (AI 344). The blunt Truth of sense-perception, which serves as the basis for scientific and technological control of the environment, is one product of Art; the Beauty of an abstract design is another. The former may contain little Beauty, the latter little in the way of Truth. Each, nonetheless, serves the wide purposes of a society. The harmonious coordination of the contributions of scientific and technological activities and the free expressions of the "fine" arts along with the other aesthetic activities can lead to a society's overall attainment of Truthful Beauty.

Truth is a characteristic of Appearance. When Appearance conforms to Reality, a truth-relation exists. In a truth-relation there must be some common element among the relata of Appearance and Reality. This common factor establishes a limited identity-relation, but carries no implication that the involved subjective forms are conformal, though they may be so. So characterized, the truth-relation admits of different degrees depending on the degree of identity involved and of differences in type, depending on whether or not the subjective forms concerned share any conformations and whether or not consciousness is involved.

The examples of truth with which human beings are most concerned are those which involve sense-perceptions and propositions. Sense-perceptions involve three types of truth: the direct, "blunt" truth in which there is some conformation of subjective forms as well as of objective data; the indirect truth expressing the relation of a percipient to the type of order which functions as its environment; and the indirect, "symbolic" truth involved in the more complex forms of symbolic reference.

"Blunt" truth is an example of symbolic reference in which there is a direct conformation of clear and distinct Appearance to Reality because of a conformation of subjective forms. In spring we feel the grass greenly. That is, we feel the grass with the subjective form characterizing the nexus prehended. This type of truth makes possible both artistic production and aesthetic enjoyment. Thus, it is the kind of truth presupposed by Art in the broad sense, and expresses the type of truth-relation which makes possible the attainment of the more subtle kinds of symbolic truth-relations sought by the sophisticated forms of human art.

The second type of truth-relation exemplified in perception results from the peculiar relation between the percipient occasion and its immediate environment—i.e., the animal body. For example, all healthy animals of the same species or type (which, therefore, have the same physiological make-up) have some features of perception in common. Given a set of circumstances uncomplicated by undue emotional or psychological stresses, all human beings will perceive in certain common ways. Each normal, healthy human has five prominent senses which differ widely in acuteness from those of certain other types of animals. Some animals have a more acute sense of smell, others of sight. The dog has greater auditory and olfactory sensitivity than has the human species. The Appearance in this case is a function of the complex and subtle physiological differences which define the perceptual differences between various types of immediate environments for the percipient occasions. In this type of truth-relation the perception expresses "a fact of nature, and the Appearance expresses the issue of a Law of Nature, belonging to that cosmic epoch and to those more special conditions within that epoch" (AI 317). This kind of truth-relation merely suggests that the normal, healthy animal body of a given physiological type will have certain a priori perceptual structures determining the kind of perception common to that type.

The third type of perceptive truth-relation is the most common in conscious, human experience. It is the symbolic, and in it there is direct causal connection between the Reality and the consequent Appearance. There is an initial arbitrariness about the birth of a symbol, but once a symbol is born the conditioning of the percipients sharing the symbol keeps it alive. In a natural language the words and their meanings have no necessary connection one to the other, but because a given set of contingent circumstances have conjoined the sounds or visual markings and the propositional meanings, a truth-relation does exist. Certain symbols—those used in dramatic and poetic literature, for example—convey subjective form as well as objective content. Language, music, ritual acts—all have symbolic significance and participate in this type of truth-relation. This truth-relation provides the locus for Whitehead's theory of symbols and of human art.

Consider an illustration of this truth-relation as it is manifest in the ritual acts of a given religion. The sentiments associated with an important event factually occurrent in a given community are evoked and re-presented by recourse to a prescribed ritual. In such an instance at least two important types of truth-relations are present. First, there is a truth-relation between the ritual actions and the elicited emotions. This relation is a function of the common subjective forms called forth by the ritual. Second, there may be a truth-relation between the emotions and the real concrete event celebrated by the ritual—i.e., the "justice," "love," or "power" of God. This second type of relation leads to a consideration of propositional truth.

The conscious entertainment of a proposition provides an example of a combination of truth-relations of the symbolic sort. A verbal sentence is capable of expressing a set of propositions which are its meanings. The symbolic significance of these sentences is grounded in arbitrariness and convention. Each word has significance, and the words comprising sentences convey significance. Symbolic truth merely requires that (in this instance) the language be used correctly—i.e., that the propositions assigned to the verbal sentences in the course of the natural growth of language and the more rapid character of conventions must be the criteria for symbolic truth.

In the conscious entertainment of a proposition, at least two truth-relations are present: the symbolic truth-relation between the oral or written sentence and its meaning in that instance, and the propositional truth-relation, a function of whether or not the proposition expressed by the sentence refers to a nexus exemplifying the pattern which is the predicate of the proposition. The truth-relation of a proposition is definitely concerned with objective content, whereas symbolic truth concerns subjective form. Thus, religious propositions are symbolically true if they call forth the desired subjective responses. There may be propositional truth as well, in which case the proposition which constitutes the meaning of the doctrine, ritual act, etc., has characterized, to some extent, the nature of things, as well as serving as a lure for feeling.[1]

The question of the relation between symbolic and propositional truth is of no little importance in theories of religion, for example, where symbols and propositions are in constant use. Religion cannot survive without its measure of propositional truth. Religion in its various expressions must be grounded in realities or lose its effectiveness. The reason a proposition—aesthetic, religious, etc.—cannot divorce itself arbitrarily from reality is that in its origin it is derived from physical experience. For Whitehead, ideas are born as *interpretations* of modes of activity. The initial data for any actual occasion beginning its concrescence are comprised by physical feelings. The derivation of conceptual feelings from these physical feelings takes place through conceptual valuation and reversion. Reversion does allow of some novel eternal objects' being introduced into the concrescence but only insofar as they are germane to the eternal objects in the initial data. Thus ideas, symbols, theories, etc., are interpretations of reality.

The second aim of Art is Beauty. "Beauty is the mutual adaptation of the several factors in an occasion of experience" (AI 324). As was the case with Truth, Whitehead delineates both *types* and *gradations* of Beauty. The end in terms of which the adaptation of the factors of experience takes place is the aim defined in terms of the category of subjective intensity. The aim is at both harmony and intensity. Beauty in a minor form exists when there is no mutual inhibition of the subjective forms derived from the objective contents. The major form of Beauty exists when, in addition to the lack of mutual inhibitions of subjective forms, there is the introduction of novel contrasts in the objective content which intensify the subsequent conformal feelings. The fact of Beauty in an occasion of experience recalls the aims of balance and complexity in the theory of concrescence.

Whitehead makes a useful distinction between "Beauty" per se and "the Beautiful." Beauty concerns the mutual adaptation of several factors as realized in the concrescent process. But one may term "beautiful" those parts of the objective content which contribute to the final harmonious synthesis of experience. Thus the primary sense of Beauty refers to the realization of a completed occasion; the secondary sense concerns the elements of an occasion discoverable by analysis. This secondary sense of Beauty presupposes the optimum objective environment and the optimum subjective response. Given these two presuppositions: a judgment concerning the contribution of that datum to concrescent unity may be made. This distinction bears implications beyond the analysis of individual experience. Any environment may be analyzed in order to discover its "beautiful" components.

> We may be thinking of artists, or of cultivated men of the modern world, or of the ruck of mankind in a given city at a given time. But in all its senses, "beautiful" means the inherent capability for the promotion of Beauty when functioning as a datum in a percipient occasion [AI 329].

Insofar as Beauty is a quality of civilization, it would have to be manifest in the harmonious relations among all men in a society as well as in the expressions of the creative artists of that social grouping. Thus, the sociological analysis of the subject of elites and differentials in a human society would, on Whiteheadian terms, have as its aim the determination of the potential for harmony of the various components within the social unity. The crucial point is that a genetic analysis of human social unity shares essentially the same methodological limitations as that of the genetic analysis of an individual concrescence.

The aim of beauty is the perfection of harmony, which is the perfection of subjective form. Perfection of subjective form is achieved when there is balanced complexity of experiencing (v. PR 424–425). The term "perfection," however, must not be construed in too broad a sense. The perfection of subjective form depends upon the absence of inhibiting factors which introduce discord into the final synthesis of experience. But this does not mean that inhibition must be totally absent. All perfection is perfection *of a certain kind*; all realization involves exclusion. The completely inhibited component in a given concrescence is not properly a part of that perfection. This meaning of inhibition, which Whitehead terms "anaesthesia," is a result of the normal functioning of negative prehensions in the process of concrescence.

In addition to "anaesthesia," there is a mode of inhibition which does derogate from perfection. The positive presence in a single occasion of experience of two mutually inhibiting components leads to the feeling of "aesthetic destruction." "This is the feeling of evil in the most general sense, namely physical pain or mental evil, such as sorrow, horror, dislike" (AI 330). The experience of such discordant feelings mitigates the perfection realized within experience.

The fact of "anaesthesia," a result of the finitude of experiencing occasions, provides for various *types* of perfection. "Aesthetic destruction," the positive feelings of discord, determines that there be varying degrees of perfection. Discord exists both within experiences realizing various degrees of perfection and between various types of perfections which are mutually discordant. Also, imperfect occasions aiming at a higher perfection are to be valued higher than a lower realized perfection. Discord as aesthetic destruction is what Whitehead means by "evil." Discord, however, though evil in itself, can serve individuals and societies by introducing disharmonies which require a transition to a higher perfection. In this way discordant feelings can supply the contrast between an outworn realization and a dynamic ideal which can initiate a move toward a new perfection. In this way "progress is founded upon the experience of discordant feelings" (AI 330). That is, progressive realization of perfections of varying types and degrees is dependent upon the intermingling of harmony and discord, of beauty and evil.

Truth, as a quality, applies to Appearance alone. Beauty characterizes Appearance, Reality, and the Appearance–Reality contrast. This being the case, there are some forms of Beauty which are not among the aims of art. For example, the Beauty qualifying Reality is that out of which an occasion arises; it cannot be a goal of experience.[2] Whereas Truth concerns conformation of Appearance to Reality, Beauty concerns the mutual adaptation of the several factors in experience. So it is that Truth presupposes a common element bridging the gap between Appearance and the contrasted element of its subsequent Reality. With regard to Beauty, however, a much less narrow type of conformation is required. Beauty requires only so much conformation as will produce maximum effectiveness or the harmonization of the various items, whereas Truth requires the actual presence of some factor in common between Appearance and Reality in a given instance. These variant types of conformation may be explained by recourse to Whitehead's categoreal notions. Consider the following categoreal obligations from the categoreal scheme of *Process and Reality*:

(i) *The Category of Subjective Unity.* The many feelings which belong to an incomplete phase in the process of an actual entity, though unintegrated by reason of the incompleteness of the phase, are compatible for integration by reason of the unity of their subject [PR 39].

(vii) *The Category of Subjective Harmony.* The valuations of conceptual feelings are mutually determined by the adaptation of those feelings to be contrasted elements congruent with the subjective aim [PR 40–41].

Truth is concerned with that conformation required by logical compatibility; Beauty is concerned with the much broader notion of aesthetic compatibility. Together these types of compatibility complete Whitehead's theory of harmony. The aim at Truthful Beauty is an aim at the fullness of harmony. Since the pre-established harmony of concrescence requires both a harmony of data and of subjective form, so the theory of harmony as here considered requires both a logical, or quantitative, and an aesthetic, or qualitative, harmony.

Truth is closely tied with the objective content of an occasion of experience, and gains its justification by the partial conformation of Appearance to Reality. Such a conformation carries no necessary implications for the type of subjective form with which it may be associated. Thus the type of subjective form requisite for the realization of Beauty may or may not be promoted by a given truth-relation. If it is, then the truth-relation is per se beautiful; if it is not, it may be either neutral or evil. Truth, therefore, gains its full justification when it is attuned to the *telos* of the universe which is the production of Beauty. Truth, though on the whole not essential to Beauty, is often important to its maintenance, and is directly relevant to the realization of Beauty of the highest type. "The Truth that for such extremity of Beauty is wanted is that truth-relation whereby Appearance summons up new resources of feeling from the depths of Reality" (AI 343).

The "evocation" of reality by recourse to valuation and reversion can bring about a selection from, and enhancement of, items of reality which in subsequent experiences have not been stressed. This involves the introduction of a novel perspective on the significance of remembered, perceived, or imagined data. The sudden realization of the profound beauty of the ordinary and the mundane provides an illustration of this type of Truthful Beauty. Factors in reality are brought forward to provide the truth-relation upon which significant beauty rests, but the factors are precisely those which have been omitted in the previous "editions" of reality provided by prior concrescent occasions.

When in the Appearance–Reality relation Truthful Beauty has been attained, there has been a perfection of Art. But the question of the type of agency involved is important, since only if it is due to "quick, purposeful adaptation originated by finite creatures" (AI 345) is art in the ordinary sense involved. If it is due to some wide universal purpose, the term art is applied only by extension. The principle is the same in both cases, however, since the natural *telos* toward promotion of harmony eventuates in the production of that type of Beauty grounded upon Truth. It is precisely the fact that the distinction between art and nature is not an absolute one which allows Whitehead to avoid any simple opposition of the products of art to the products of nature. The sense of continuity between art and nature is one basis for Whitehead's refusal to drive a wedge between man and his natural environment.

Two broad formal possibilities regarding the relation of man and nature have dominated philosophic literature. One may affirm a continuity between man and nature, in which man is a part of nature explainable in the same general terms as are all natural processes, or one may affirm a disjunction between man and the natural world such that he is something essentially distinct from nature. The former approach we may term *naturalistic,* the latter *dualistic.*

I have already stressed Whitehead's denial of any type of radical philosophic dualism.[3] It is clear, therefore, that he would not wish to affirm any view which would require an absolute disjunction between man and nature. If, therefore, we are to define Whitehead's view of the relations of man and nature more sharply, we must compare his view with other naturalistic theories. Whitehead himself notes the extremes of naturalistic interpretation when he says that

> Mankind has gradually developed from the lowliest forms of life, and must therefore be explained in terms applicable to all such forms. But why construe the later forms by analogy to the earlier forms. Why not reverse the process? It would seem to be more sensible, more truly empirical, to allow each living species to make its own contribution to the demonstration of factors inherent in living things [FR 15].

An apparent implication of Whitehead's words here is that there are two extremes of naturalistic interpretation of man's relation to nature as a whole:

the explanation of man in terms of those characteristics discoverable in more primitive natural forms, and the explanation of natural phenomena in terms of more complex forms. The former naturalism is reductionistic; the latter is teleological.

The reductionist type of naturalism may be illustrated by calling to mind the thesis of Freud's well-known work *Civilization and its Discontents*. The Freudian theory of civilization relies on concepts developed partly from speculation and partly from the investigation of the physiological functioning of organic beings.[4] Basal instincts are hypothesized as determinants of human actions. "The evolution of civilization . . . must present the struggle between Eros and Death, between the instinct of life and the instinct of destruction, as it works itself out in the human species."[5] These instincts are thought to exist throughout the biological species. In man the struggle between them works itself out in terms of a narrowly interpreted concept of sublimation. It is this concept which establishes the relation between man and the rest of nature. *Kultur,* or civilization, is the product of a repression and sublimation of natural, instinctual drives. Such sublimation is motivated by primal guilt feelings and by a victory of the reality principle over the pleasure principle. The continuity of man and nature on this view is a function of a theory of determination centering on a concept of ubiquitous material and efficient causation. That is, the explanation of human actions requires a look backward to more primitive historical, biological, and mythological circumstances for its source. In Whiteheadian terms, Freud has construed the later forms of human life and organization almost wholly by analogy to the earlier forms.

Contrasted with this reductionist type of naturalism is the teleological view of the relation of man and nature. An extreme example of such a teleological view is to be found in certain forms of romanticism. In such a view man is taken to be the unique embodiment of the aim of all nature. For example, according to Novalis, "The present heaven and the present earth are of a prosaic nature; this is the world-period of utility. The judgment of the world is the beginning of the new, formed poetical period. Man . . . is the Messiah of Nature."[6] On this view the advent of man brings with it a transformation of the very meaning of nature. This reverses the emphasis of the Freudian view by construing the earlier forms of nature in terms of the later. If the reductionistic theory views man primarily in terms derived from the lower forms of nature, the teleological view conceives him as the end in terms of which the contributions of more primitive natural forms are to be construed.

Whitehead's type of naturalism attempts to mediate the reductionistic and the teleological views. Whereas for Freud human art is a *sublimation* of nature, and for romanticism it is a *transformation* of nature, for Whitehead art is the *education* of nature. Thus, the function of culture or civilization is not merely to sublimate natural forces and objects, nor to give

vent to the unique subjectivity of man through aesthetic expression; the aim
is rather to "educate" nature. Thus, as we previously quoted, "Art is civilization. For civilization is nothing other than the unremitting aim at the major
perfections of harmony" (AI 349). The Latin verb *educere* from which
the English verb "to educate" derives has the meaning of "to lead forth,"
"to draw out." The art of civilization is to draw out of nature whatever
within it is capable of higher harmonies. Nature and culture are correlatives.
And nature itself may be "educated" quite apart from specific human actions.

Whitehead's concept of art is a key to the understanding of his theory
of civilization. This concept may be understood by grasping the relation
between what I shall call the "aesthetic principle," operative in the concrescence of an actual entity, and the definition of "Art" given in *Adventures of Ideas*. The aesthetic principle is to be expressed as follows: "An
actual fact is a fact of aesthetic experience. All aesthetic experience is feeling
arising out of the realization of contrast under identity" (RM 111). The
generality of Art is here explicitly affirmed. The discussion of the vibratory
character of enduring objects and of the cycles of the seasons in nature provide examples of the pervasiveness of aesthetic experience and expression.

Art is an "interweaving of absoluteness upon relativity" (AI 339). The
relativity of a work of art is the harmony of the whole; the absoluteness is
the brute individuality of the components. The importance of Truth to Art
and the production of Beauty lies in the fact that Truth requires the factor
of absolute individuality. The physical prehensions which provide the initial
data, the objective content, are prehensions of individual actual occasions.
The maintenance of a truth-relation between the individualities of Reality
and the consequent Appearance means that the transmuted Appearance
is enhanced by the realization of an apparent unity undergirded by real
individuals. Important Beauty requires this foundation of real, relevant individuals, which the truth-relation supplies.

In the concepts of "absoluteness" and "relativity," we have the two basic
requirements for the realization of the aim of Art at that balanced complexity of experience which Whitehead terms "Truthful Beauty." That
Whitehead wishes this characterization of the activity of Art to be applied
beyond the level of individual experience can easily be shown by noting his
discussion of the development of those ideas which are relevant to the civilization of human social experience.

> One of the most general philosophic notions to be used in the analysis of
> civilized activities is to consider the effect on social life due to the varia-
> tions of emphasis between Individual Absoluteness and Individual Rela-
> tivity. Here "absoluteness" means the notion of release from essential de-
> pendence on other members of the community in respect to modes of
> activity, while relativity means the converse fact of essential relatedness
> [AI 54].

Part I of *Adventures of Ideas,* which considers "that group of ideas that most directly contributed to the civilization of the behaviour-systems of human beings in their intercourse with each other" (AI 127), has as one of its principal themes the development of the idea of freedom and the transition from the dominance of compulsion toward social relationships founded upon persuasive agencies. The themes of the growth of "freedom" and of the transition from "force" to "persuasion" are both interpreted in terms of the relationship of individual absoluteness and individual relativity. Thus the same doctrines which interpret experience at the level of individual concrescence also interpret the sociological experiences of human societies.

Human art is distinguished from the generic concept of Art by three specific characteristics: artificiality, finiteness, and consciousness. Human art is characterized by a high degree of artificiality. That is to say, the adaptation of Appearance to Reality is such that, through the introduction of selective valuations, reversions, and propositional feelings, the Appearance is more distinct from the initial Reality than is the case in lower forms of experience. The artificiality should not, however, be such as to neglect entirely the foundation in reality from which the aesthetic experience emerges.

The finiteness of a work of art is, also, an important consideration. It insures the distinction between the work and its environment. That is to say, human art is not only distinct from the experiences which gave rise to it, but is, or should be, distinct and even unique among the other objects of Appearance. "The work of Art is a fragment of nature with the mark on it of a finite creative effort, so that it stands alone, an individual thing detailed from the vague infinity of its background" (AI 348). It is these two characteristics—finiteness and artificiality—which determine the importance of human art to civilization. The stimulus of the possibilities inherent in finite creative effort influence men in the achievement of high-level cultures.

The final and determinant characteristic of human art is *consciousness.* Conscious experience per se is a product of Art in the generic sense. The art which arises in conscious experience is a specialization of the generic type of Art. This is human art. Consciousness emphasizes the element of appearance in an experience, thereby increasing its artificiality. Since in conscious experience appearance is clear and distinct and the reality of the causally efficacious world may be only dimly distinguished by consciousness, the problem of the relation of the product of human art to the causally efficacious world from which it derived is an acute one. The essence of art is artificiality, but that the perfection of art is measured in terms of its germaneness to the world of its origin may be seen by considering the question of the genetic origin of human art.

> The starting-point for the highly developed human art is . . . to be sought amid the cravings generated by the physiological functionings of the body. The origin of art lies in the craving for re-enaction. . . . The arts of civi-

lization now spring from many origins. . . . But they are all sublimations, and sublimations of sublimations, of the simple craving to enjoy freely the vividness of life which first arises in moments of necessity [AI 349–350].

Several important aspects of Whitehead's concept of human art may be noted here. First, by relating the origin of art to the desire for re-enaction Whitehead has made perfectly clear the basis of his naturalistic theory of civilization. The vibratory character of elementary particles, the cycles of renewal of the seasons, and the repetition of vivid human experience are aspects of the same basic desire for the achievement of aesthetic balance in experience. Second, by specifying the origin of the desire for re-enaction as the physiological functionings of the body, Whitehead has noted a concrete example of what was mentioned earlier in connection with the analysis of the ontology of the human self—viz., the environing occasions of the presiding personal order are of such a nature that they provide high-grade intensities of experience and a stabilizing structure. A third important point is that the craving for repetition or re-enaction involves a free enjoyment of the re-enacted experience which implies a freedom from the necessity of exact or complete repetition. Freedom is of the essence of human art, since it allows for a selection of the important or desirable aspects of experience to be repeated. The unduly dangerous, the inconvenient, or the trivial aspects of an adventurous experience may be suppressed or altered with the result of increased aesthetic enjoyment. "If Odysseus among the shades could hear Homer chanting his Odyssey, he then re-enacted with free enjoyment the perils of his wanderings" (AI 350).

The importance of the selective emphasis of art is to be found in the fact that experiences recollected or re-created without the obscuring character of trivial details, and without the immediate physical hardships which may have been distracting in the original experience, often have the power of expressing significant truths. Here Whitehead seems to indicate that most of our learning by experience is, in fact, a learning by the *reflection upon* experience, and such reflection usually involves an artistic reproduction of the past experience.

A fourth point to be made concerns the sublimatory character of art. Whitehead's assertion that higher forms of art are sublimations of the craving for re-enaction of vivid experiences, and his claim that art could be viewed as "a psychopathic reaction of the race to the stresses of existence" (AI 350), leads one to reflect upon the proximity of Whiteheadian concepts of art and civilization to the Freudian type of naturalism discussed above. The vocabulary suggests a direct connection between Whitehead and Freud at this point. The seemingly Freudian character of Whitehead's theory of art caused Donald Sherburne to criticize Whitehead's aesthetics as a "backward looking" theory.[7] Sherburne concentrates upon the possibilities inherent in the theory of propositions and the category of transmutation for the construction of an aesthetic theory, but has de-emphasized

Whitehead's theory of the origin of art. Such a lack of emphasis upon the physical basis of aesthetic experience distorts Whitehead's theory by emphasizing the idealist over the realist elements in the Whiteheadian philosophy. Had Sherburne given sufficient consideration to the differences between the two principal types of naturalism, his reservations concerning Whitehead's naturalism may have been lessened, and his otherwise excellent interpretation of Whitehead's philosophy of art thereby improved. For Whitehead's theory is certainly not backward-looking, as Sherburne seems to think. To accept the physical basis of human experience is not to affirm that man is, essentially, comprised by his physiological drives and instincts. The fact that art involves sublimation of natural cravings and a repetition of past experience does not negate the fact that it also involves the education of nature. Nothing is more forward-looking than the Whiteheadian view that, through the emergence of novelty in art, "the adventure of mentality gains upon the physical basis of existence" (AI 350).

Part of the difficulty which Sherburne, and others, have in accepting Whitehead's unapologetic naturalistic bias results from a misconstruing of the delicate balance Whitehead seeks to maintain between idealist and realist elements in his philosophy. To read Whitehead as if he were reducing the higher functions of experience to the status of physical feelings simply because the former are sublimations of the latter is to misconstrue the character and status of the physical and the mental in the philosophy of organism. Such a reading of Whitehead in regard to the theory of art results in a blatant commission of the genetic fallacy. On the other hand, what I have termed reductionistic naturalisms are open to the kind of charge which Sherburne is making, since they explicitly affirm the implications about the pre-eminence of the role of the physical over the conceptual in human experience.

This discussion of the origin of art should clarify the difficulty involved in maintaining the balance between artificiality and germaneness to Reality in Whitehead's theory of art. The problem is easily stated though not so easily solved. The problem is an expression of the same tendency which gives rise to what Whitehead terms the fallacies of misplaced concreteness and simple location, viz., that of accepting the presentationally immediate world of sense-perception, and judgments based upon the presentationally immediate world, as an adequate foundation upon which to base an understanding of the nature of things. The specific problem inherent in the arts of a civilized society is that there must be sufficient artificiality in aesthetic expressions in order that Appearance may transcend the physical basis of existence, but sufficient germaneness to Reality such that the actual world of atomic valuational process is not swallowed by the presentationally immediate world of passive potentiality. Without a sense of the causally efficacious world from which derive the higher phases of conscious perceptions and judgments, there will be a bifurcation of the world of value experience and the structures of conscious experience, and a consequent disconnection between Reality and Appearance. Thus, according to Whitehead, "it is the essence of art to be artificial. But it is its perfection to return to nature, remaining art" (AI 349).

The proper balance between germaneness and artificiality in cultural expressions is the key to a civilized society. Too much artificiality involves a society in a mere play of ideas, images, and objects which inadequately express their derivation from the causal past. Without regard for the dim, massive causal feelings from which any experience derives, an individual or a society can actually lose its *fundamentum in re* and be set adrift in the shallow pursuit of shallow aims. Cultures and civilizations at their height have learned that though art, in essence, is artificial, the perfection of art requires a "return to nature"—i.e., a sense of germaneness to the world of concrete experience. Such civilizations have achieved a balance of artificiality and germaneness by aiming their aesthetic expressions at the attainment of Truthful Beauty.

2. ADVENTURE

The discussion of the meaning of civilization has thus far emphasized the role of Art in the attainment of Truth and Beauty. But the concept of civilization is much broader than the attainment of any single type of perfection. Two fundamental inadequacies of most theories of civilization, according to Whitehead, relate to the assumption of the possibility of the maintenance of static perfection. In the first place it has been the tendency in the West to associate ideas of culture and civilization much too closely with the static ideals embodied in Greek and Roman civilizations. Secondly, our concepts of what constitutes a civilized society are, too often, based upon an exaggeration of the importance of the fine arts: painting, sculpture, music and the dance, literature, architecture, etc. This second inadequacy seems to be a direct implication of the first since the historically-minded tendency toward an acceptance of past civilizations as models for current civilizing activities must lead to an over-emphasis upon those functions of a culture which most concretely represent that culture in surviving cultural objects.

Whitehead's theory of civilization is aimed at counteracting these tendencies. His theory of Art applies the concept of art beyond the narrow area of the fine arts. The acceptance of a past civilization as an ideal for future realization is challenged by Whitehead's concept of "Adventure." Without an adequate conception of Art, we tend to overrate the specifically fine arts; without the concept of Adventure, we tend to be backward-looking or blindly conservative in our notions of the meaning and purpose of civilized experience and expression; i.e., we tend to think of "civilization" as a substantive rather than a gerundative concept.

The concept of Adventure is based upon the axiom of the impossibility of the static maintenance of perfection. This axiom is considered in terms of three important principles fundamental to Whitehead's metaphysics: the principle of process, the principle of finitude, and the priniciple of individuality. The first principle states that "the very essence of real actuality . . . is *process*" (AI 354); the second claims that "every occasion of actuality is in its own nature finite" (AI 356); and the third, the principle of individuality, maintains that "the individual, real facts of the past lie at the base of our immediate experience in the present [and] are the reality from which the occasion springs" (AI 361).

The principle of process is the most basic challenge to the notion of static perfection. The conception of static actuality derives, according to Whitehead, from both the Platonic and Aristotelian philosophies. The eternalistic elements of Plato's thought (centered in his theory of Ideas), though partially repudiated in his later writings, provided a strong bias toward static notions of perfection and provided, as well, a lure away from the world of phenomenal flux. The Aristotelian notion of primary substance is a second foundation for theories of static actuality. The concept of primary substances as the static subject of qualification led eventually to Locke's sensationalism in which the mind is passive to the reception of ideas, making reality inhere "not in the process, but in the static recipient of the process" (AI 355–356). Both ontologically and epistemologically strong tendencies toward viewing the world in terms of static actuality are present here.

The principles of finitude and individuality are closely related since it is the origin of each actual occasion in *physical* feeling which determines its radical finitude. This relation and its implications may be noted by recalling the fact that in the history of philosophy the principle of finitude has often been denied on the grounds of the pre-eminence of conceptual or intellectual feelings. Whereas for Whitehead history is to be viewed as "the theatre of diverse groups of idealists respectively urging ideals incompatible for conjoint realization" (AI 356–357), for Hegelian philosophy diversity and incompatibility are overcome through the self-mediation of *Geist*. As the *conceptual* entertainment of incompatibles is possible, proponents of the infinitude of realized perfection often tend toward an over-intellectualized view of the world. For only through mentality could there be conjoint realization of incompatibles excluded from conjoint physical realization. The contemplative bias of Plato's *Republic*; the intellectualism of the Augustinian and Thomistic concepts of the beatific vision; Spinoza's intellectual love of God, and the Hegelian Absolute—all these express philosophical attempts to overcome the incurably finite character of individual existence.

These three metaphysical principles directly imply the importance of the concept of Adventure in Whitehead's philosophy by illustrating the unavoidable fact of process as a translation from one finite perfection to another. The aim of experience at balanced complexity is achieved *temporally* and, therefore, *temporarily*. The examination of macrocosmic experience shows it to be comprised of a series of transitions from one instance of harmony to another.

All but one type of translation from harmony involves some *dis*harmony. Harmonious translation is possible only when a stabilized perfection admits of variations in detail within the general pattern. A school of art or of philosophy, *qua* aesthetic fact, may have an energetic life as long as novel perspectives within the broad presuppositions of the school are possible. When all such variations are exhausted, a translation to a different type of order must be made if decay is to be prevented. A quick period of transition brings about a new direction. A new direction is the result of previous imaginative entertainment of alternative modes of thought and action. But any such translation from one type of harmony to another, no matter how quick, must involve a period of disharmony.

Two important corollaries of the priniciple of finitude have emerged in this discussion. The first is that finitude involves the exclusion of alternatives. The categoreal conditions of subjective harmony and subjective unity are important determinants of that fact; the second, that conceptual valuations and reversions, primal activities of the mental pole of an occasion, insure that subjective forms appropriate to relevant alternatives excluded from physical realization will be retained in the concrescence. This preservation of the subjective forms appropriate to excluded alternatives is the ground both of the introduction of disharmony and of the possible transcendence of the present type of order through the realization of alternative harmonies. Such inherent novelty, though a source of disharmony, provides experience with a way of transcending the mere cyclical repetition of a given set of possibilities.

Here the notion of discord and disharmony is introduced on a positive note. And though all forms of disharmony are expressions of positive states of actual occasions, not all disharmony is desirable. As we noted earlier in the chapter, the undesirable type of disorder is termed "evil." Evil is present when destruction is the dominant fact in an occasion of experience. Three principal types of disharmonious situations are considered by Whitehead: (1) the decay of order due to the exclusion of relevant possibilities; (2) the decay due to mutually destructive alternatives; and (3) the disharmony resulting from the translation to an alternative type of order. Negative prehensions of potentially disharmonious elements signal the inability of the occasion of experience to harmonize the elements introducing disharmony at the level of physical data. Negative prehensions provide the way in which Whitehead deals with the concept of evil as non-being. Also, since even a negative prehension has a subjective form and, therefore, leaves its mark upon the experience of the actual occasion, Whitehead seems to agree with the Platonic insight that non-being has a kind of being.[8]

There are three positive ways of dealing with threatened disharmony. The first, and most primitive, is merely the way of conformal feelings. This method provides the occasion with a positive feeling of discordance which eliminates the bare incompatibility by a transference of the disruption to the subjective form of the feelings. In this instance, there is no real reduction of disharmony; rather, an acceptance of the qualitative character of disharmonious experience and an elimination of the quantitative incompatibility. A more creative means of meeting disharmony is through the introduction of conceptual valuations in order to increase or decrease the relative intensities of incompatible feelings. Through aversion there is a "reduction to a background" of certain incompatible elements and the "raising to a foreground" of other selected elements.

Both the way of conformal feelings and the way of conceptual valuations are, in the higher types of experiences, merely introductory to the principal means of bringing harmony into an occasion of experience. This is the way of the introduction of Appearance. The use of the higher phases of experience—the comparative feelings—to introduce a mediating set of prehensions which are relevant to each of two incompatible sets brings about an alteration of the significance and intensity of each in the final phase of experience. This way utilizes the function of transmutation to combine massiveness with intensity through the unification of the diverse individuals into a single transmuted feeling. Such an introduction of appearance into experience is creative of stable harmonies only if the prior utilization of conformal feelings and conceptual valuations has been such as to insure that the transmuted feeling is grounded upon the reality of the given world.

The components of experience *qua* objective data constitute a nexus of occasions related one to the other by the requirements of the categoreal conditions of concrescence and the content of the individual subjective aim. A strong doctrine of individuality requires, however, that there be a prehension of individual components each for its own sake. At the level of macroscopic experience, the prehension of individuality consists in the extraction of the individual objects of perception from the qualitative factors involved in a particular perception. The emotional characteristics of an object are retained and the sensory elements are ignored. Often, repeated experience of an object is required for this realization of individuality to take place.

> The successive immanence of occasion after occasion in the life of the soul will in the present occasion of that life include the cumulation of the successive prehensions of some particular object. In the various prehensions of it new qualities secure prominence, original qualities are present with some difference. There is thus a gradual elimination of the more special types of quality, which vary and fluctuate, from conformal effectiveness in the tone of the final prehensions [AI 337].

Thus the prehension of individuality is a prehension of permanent factors in experience which derive from antecedent reality, and which qualify consequent appearance.

This theory of individuality provides cogent expression of Whitehead's fundamental criticism of sensationalist epistemologies. Since such theories presuppose the fundamental character of the qualitative aspects of experience, there is a denial of individual details as derived from immediate experience. Presentationally immediate experience is emphasized at the expense of causally efficacious reality. The doctrine of causal efficacy, combined with the principle of individuality, provides Whitehead with theoretical justification for affirming that the actualities of the past form the real foundation of our immediate present experience. The enduring objects of human experience, which combine in themselves the intensities of emotions derived from their individual component occasions, constitute the individualities of ordinary human experience.

> A complex experience which includes conscious attention to . . . enduring individualities at once unlooses a wealth of feeling far beyond anything derived from patterns of sensa, merely as such. The great Harmony is the harmony of enduring individualities, connected in the unity of a background. It is for this reason that the notion of freedom haunts the higher civilizations. For freedom, in any one of its many senses, is the claim for vigorous self-assertion [AI 362].

This mention of freedom is significant since it points up the continuity of implication between the metaphysical structure in terms of which Whitehead's theory of perception is expounded and the social and cultural correlates in the life of human societies. But it is not only the element of freedom which finds its fundamental expression in the theory of individuality; anticipation and purpose, as well, derive from this notion. For if a truth-relation exists between apparent and real individuality, the appearance will indicate a past actual world which is relevant to the prediction and control of the future. Aims which seek the prediction and control of future experience must depend upon the fact of the direct derivation of a given present from its past actual world.

The three principles of process, finitude, and individuality determine the impossibility of the maintenance of any attained perfection at a constant level of intensity for a long period of time. Such an impossibility implies that no civilized society can get along without the search for novel perfections. The perfection of Art is always a perfection within limits; its Beauty is but one instance among a variety of possible instances of harmony, given that particular past actual world; its Truth is based upon a finite selection from among the welter of individual past experiences. Perfection and limitation are correlates. The concept of Adventure provides theoretical justification for the creative restlessness which always follows upon the establishment of tradition in aesthetic experience and expression. The complementary functions of Art and Adventure as cultural aims seek to insure that, though no *static* maintenance of perfection is possible, a *dynamic* maintenance of perfections may be attained by any given society.

In *The Function of Reason* (pp. 20–21), Whitehead distinguishes three ways of attempting to achieve balanced complexity, the aim of experience. These he terms: the Way of Rhythm, the Way of Blindness, the Way of Transience. "Blindness" is the acceptance of "mere life" after the exhaustion of novelties introduced through rhythmic variations. It is relapse and reintegration at a less intense level of experience. Rhythm initiates "a round of experiences, forming a determinate sequence of contrasts . . . codified so that the end of one such cycle is the proper antecedent stage for the beginning of another such cycle" (FR 21). Fatigue arising from the repetition of cycles requires "a high level coordination of stretches of past experience" (FR 22). For example, in human experience a strong remembrance of past experiences leads to boredom when those experiences are repeated. Repetition is more likely to bore the highly intelligent person than the moron. Indeed, the mentally retarded often enjoy interminable repetition of sounds, movements, etc., because rhythmic repetition substitutes for retention and remembrance. Among the highly intelligent, mere repetition within a given cycle must give way to the elaboration of cycles of cycles.

In his famous essay "The Rhythm of Education," Whitehead provides an important illustration of the use of rhythm in avoiding life-tedium. The fundamental rhythm of intellectual progress is comprised by the three successive stages of "romance," "precision," and "generalisation." These stages, identified with Hegel's concepts of thesis, antithesis, and synthesis,[9] establish the pattern which pervades the intellectual life of an educated man. The stage of romance is dominated by unsystematic entertainment of novel fact. "The stage of romance . . . holds within itself unexplored connexions with possibilities half-disclosed by glimpses and half-concealed by the wealth of material" (AE 17). In the stage of precision "width of relationship is subordinated to exactness of formulation" (AE 18). This is the stage which allows for a precise analysis of the romantic subject-matter previously encountered. The stage of generalization is "a return to romanticism with added advantage of classified ideas and relevant technique" (AE 19). It is the period which begins with general ideas and notes their application to concrete circumstances.

The cyclical process of romance, precision, and generalization forms the fundamental structure allowing for the adventure of learning. But the cycle itself is repeated with variation of temporal intensity throughout the life of the individual. Infancy, the period prior to the beginning of formal education, establishes one life-stage within which the cycle may be present. A child's first perceptual awareness of the presence of objects and their connectedness is romance. The mastery of spoken language as an instrument for cognitive and emotional expression constitutes a period of precision. Generalization is first experienced when language is employed to classify and increase the enjoyment of objects.

But this cycle itself is a part of a larger cycle which includes the periods of infancy, adolescence, and manhood. The first twelve years of life constitute a natural stage of romance. This stage of precision is constituted roughly by the period of secondary education. The period of entrance into manhood, ideally within a university context, forms the stage of generalization within this cycle. Whitehead's point is that "the development of mentality exhibits itself as a rhythm involving an interweaving of cycles, the whole process being dominated by a greater cycle of the same general character as its minor eddies" (AE 27).

There are instances in which the introduction of novelty into experience via rhythmic cycles may be impossible. Limitations of insight, or lack of technical competence, may lead to the loss of balance and intensity in experience. When such a situation arises and the Way of Blindness is unacceptable, the Way of Transience may be employed. But "transience is really a way of blindness: it procures novel individuals to face blindly the old round of experience" (FR 21). The boring individual who finds it impossible to alter the subject matter upon which he dwells interminably may enhance his experience by changing his friends rather than his topics of conversation. The myth of the ephemerality of youth is based upon the bias that the life of intense interest cannot be sustained amid ordinary social circumstances. By making youth a period of brief duration we defend ourselves against the destructive boredom which comes from the continued expectation of novelty. After all, "youth is not defined by years but by the creative impulse to make something" (AE 119). The Way of Transience insures that there will be a new generation of intense, idealistic young to enjoy the old round of experience. "The Way of Transience means the substitution of short-lived individuals by way of protecting the species from the fatigue of the individual" (FR 21).

The striking aspect of this concept of "transience" is that the term has been employed in a rather unusual way. The Way of Transience must not be confused with the rhythmic transition from one kind of novelty to a novelty of a totally different type. Such a confusion renders inexplicable the fundamental progressivism of Whiteheadian theory. There is no adventure which does not involve the introduction of new rhythmic patterns. But there are two types of rhythmic novelties: the intra-experiential and the inter-experiential. There is, first, novelty as introduced within the limits of a created pattern. This involves the playing out of the permutations within a given system. But when these permutations are exhausted a new pattern must emerge. That new pattern, however, is not seen to be discontinuous with the old. The new pattern serves to incorporate or complement the previous patterning. Whitehead's faith in the historical progress of such patterning is illustrated vividly by these words:

> When in the distant future [Symbolic Logic] has expanded, so as to examine patterns depending on connections other than those of space, number, and quantity . . . the symbolic examination of pattern with the use of real

variables will become the foundation of aesthetics. From that stage it will
proceed to conquer ethics and theology [ESP 99].

Whitehead's concept of Adventure is the principal novelty in his understanding of civilization. For Whitehead the term "civilization" has a meaning which transcends any given civilized society. Civilization is a process, a
civilizing. The civilization of man is the civilizing of experience seen in
terms of the pursuit of balanced complexity, i.e., aesthetic intensity and
contrast, within the single actual occasion as well as within nexūs and
societies.

As I indicated previously, most theories of civilization are model theories,
theories which determine the quality of a present order by appeal to some
former model culture such as Periclean Athens or Renaissance Italy. Most
concepts of civilization, therefore, are backward-looking. Whitehead, on
the other hand, shares the bias of the eighteenth-century idea of progress
and that of the Emergent Evolutionists of the nineteenth and early twentieth centuries. Though hardly as optimistic as Teilhard de Chardin, for example, who views the evolutionary movement as an increasing "hominiza-
tion" in terms of which the creation of a noösphere, or sphere of intellectual
culture, will provide man with a new emergent being,[10] Whitehead nonetheless is biased in favor of the progressive concept of development. In fact,
Whitehead's evolutionary vision closely parallels Max Weber's concept of
"rationalization" as applied to the evolution of human societies—the notion
that, historically, social institutions have been marked by an increase in immanent order and rational efficiency.[11] Thus, there is a "slow drift of mankind towards civilization" (AI vii). And contrary to the slow physical decay
of nature in obedience to the second law of thermodynamics, there is a
counter-tendency illustrated by the rhythmic alteration of wave phenomena,
the cycles of the seasons, and the originative quality of human reason.

The second law of thermodynamics entails the consequence that any
finite transformation of energy involves a loss of available energy for future
transformations. That is to say, the total amount of energy available for any
transformation is less than that available for any previous transformation.
This loss of overall energy-availability is expressed as an increase in *entropy*.
The availability of energy is a measure of the order of a given system. The
greater the amount of order the more types of energy-transformations are
possible utilizing that system. On the other hand, the more disorderly the
system the less available energy is present. Increase in entropy in accordance
with the second law of thermodynamics is a measure of the decrease in regularity and an increase in randomness. So stated, the law of increasing entropy points to a seemingly inexorable movement in the universe from a
higher to a lower energy state—i.e., from order to disorder.

Whitehead's most succinct response to this challenge to the progressive
naturalism which he affirms forms the central thesis of *The Function of
Reason.*

History discloses two main tendencies in the course of events. One tendency is exemplified in the slow decay of physical nature. With stealthy inevitableness, there is degradation of energy. The sources of activity sink downward and downward. Their very matter wastes. The other tendency is exemplified by the yearly renewal of nature in the spring, and by the upward course of biological evolution [FR "Introductory Summary"].

In this statement the acceptance of general entropy-increase is balanced by an observation of a countertrend in nature which expresses itself in entropy-consumption. This countertrend is manifest in the activities of "life." Though the general trend of nature toward an entropy-increase is accepted, Whitehead points to a local trend within the natural world which succeeds in reversing the tendency toward disorder within that local environment. The validity of the second law is not challenged by the existence of this countertrend since, for example, the ordered complexity of a living cell, though eventuating in entropy-consumption, may result in entropy-increase elsewhere. The important consideration is simply that life, *via* its originative and reproductive capacities, can be an entropy-consumer within its local environment.

Whitehead calls attention to two types of entropy-consumption in nature: first, the cycles of the seasons eventuating in the renewal of nature in the spring; and second, the progressive, upward trend of biological evolution. The first instance is an elaborate example of the rhythmic processes of nature illustrated by the vibratory character of elementary particles. Recalling the discussion of physical purposes in Chapter II: in the indirect physical purpose the inclusion of a reverted conceptual feeling allowed for the alternation of the form of the feeling, issuing in a rhythmic or vibratory character in the occasions of the enduring object under consideration. This basic vibratory character realizes the principle of contrast under identity which is the basis of both nature and art. Cycles in macrocosmic nature are exemplifications of this same fundamental urge for novelty expressing itself in the realization of contrast under the form of identity.[12]

The second form of entropy-consumption mentioned by Whitehead is that of the upward course of biological evolution. Here the mere cyclical character of renewal associated with the reproductive activities of plant and animal life is transcended. The introduction of emphasis upon the higher phases of experience in an occasion of experience (i.e., those associated with conceptual activity) brings about an increased ability of the occasion to synthesize complex contrasts. Reverted feelings are no longer felt "immanently"; rather, they are transcendently felt in their functions as the predicates of propositions. Cyclical repetition has been transcended in favor of the emergence of novelty. For complex contrasts are not merely aggregations of contrasts—"This doctrine that a multiple contrast cannot be conceived as a mere disjunction of dual contrasts is the basis of the doctrine of emergent evolution" (PR 349).

Entropy-consumption through biological reproduction is mainly unconscious and determined. The emergence of man and his translation of his natural environment into the artificial environment of culture suggests, however, the possibilities of conscious attempts to decrease entropy. Cultural objects are manifestations of this ordering capacity. Language, social habits, laws, customs, and institutions are all expressions of a conscious counteragency seeking to move from disorder to order and thereby to consume entropy.[13] The possibility of civilization is bound up, on Whitehead's view, with the achievement and maintenance of types of order capable of a balanced complexity of experience. Thus, the history of man is the history of the civilizing of human experience. This civilizing of man is the adventure of ideas from which Whitehead derives the title of his work on philosophy of civilization. Adventure is the transcendence of achieved perfections in accordance with the demand that such transcendence improve present experience.

Adventure is grounded upon the fact that progress is possible, and necessary, because of the finitude of perfections. The intermingling of beauty and evil is a fact of all existence. The evil resulting from discord can promote a higher harmony. Harmony and Discord are necessarily correlatives because of the principle of finitude and the fact that "mental functioning introduces into realization subjective forms conformal to relevant alternatives excluded from the completeness of physical realization" (AI 333). Thus, in every experience there is the fact of finite realization along with the possibility of the conceptual entertainment of significant alternatives.

Adventure depends, in human beings, upon the predominance of the higher phases of experience. The introduction of consciousness leads beyond the primitive mental functionings associated with physical purposes which, as we saw in Chapter II, are the primary feelings providing for the introduction of rhythmic pattern into physical nature. The introduction of Appearance in the form of consciousness prevents the simplification of qualitative variety of the primary phase of experience through negative prehensions. Consciousness is a form of simplification, to be sure, but a form which preserves the reality of experience. Transmutation, as employed in conscious experience, is a form of simplification, but it nonetheless maintains Reality in the background "as explanatory of the procedures by which its rich variety has been saved" (AI 335).

Adventure must be viewed from two perspectives. It is the actual transcendence of achieved perfections which adds significant new patterns of novelty aiding in the civilization of experience, or it is the unsuccessful *attempt* to meet in a novel way the threat of collapse of a type of order. Not every adventure is successful. Nor is every adventure so timed as to have significant consequences in regard to any upward trend. Some epochs are doomed to patchwork efforts, finding novel ways to decline. To "go out with a flourish" is to adventure while declining. Satire is an example of such adventure. "Satire is the last flicker of originality in a passing epoch as it faces the onroad of staleness and boredom" (AI 358). Nonetheless, the satirists may experience the intensity and harmony of significant experiences while satirizing the outworn aspects of their society. According to Whitehead, Lucian in the second century, Voltaire and Edward Gibbon in the eighteenth, Lytton Strachey and Sinclair Lewis in the twentieth, are examples of satirists in epochs of decline. Yet each of these lives unquestionably possesses the excellence of personal adventure. It is also true that the prophet of a new order, the artist or dreamer, who achieves in thought what his society is unwilling or unable to achieve in practice is experiencing adventure, in spite of the fact that the fruits of his imaginings are not to be realized in his lifetime.

Whitehead is committed to the view that ideas arise as interpretations of actions. "Practice" precedes "theory"; action is prior to thought. The slow drift of man toward civilization is characterized by an increasing realization of ideas from various modes of action. The adventure of ideas is the story of "the emergence of ideas from activities, and the effect of ideas in modifying the activities from which they emerge" (AI 127). The theme of this movement is the slow development of the dominance of persuasion over force in man's self-understanding. This story Whitehead tells in terms of the emergence of the ideas of individuality and freedom.

Progress toward civilization must be accompanied by an increasing sense of "individual absoluteness," a sense of the importance of the autonomy of the individual person vis-à-vis society and the state. To the degree that the compulsion of nature and circumstance is overcome, and individual absoluteness is balanced with relativity, freedom is realized. Compulsion has two basic modalities: the "iron compulsion of nature" and the compulsion of the ruler–ruled relationships among men (v. AI 108–109). There is no complete transcendence of these compulsions, but the growth of persuasive agencies leads to cooperative efforts to coordinate activities so as to achieve a conquest over the compulsion of nature. The development of technologies, primitive and modern, decrease the compulsory dominion of nature over man, and the rise of democratic and communal ideals decreases the arbitrary exercise of power by man over man.[14] The upward surge of human civilization is a function of the realization of rhythm within a novel pattern. The new pattern must surpass the old. The history of civilization is the story, if it be told from a grand perspective, of self-surpassing perfections serving as the goal for the civilizational process.

Whitehead's progressivism is not as naïve as it might seem; for the slow advance of man in the upward adventure toward civilization is punctuated by many barren periods of existence. The progressivism of Whitehead is *metaphysically* significant and is, of course, of some significance to the individual contemplating the entire span of human existence. But there is no guarantee that one's life can possess the intensity and harmony of civilized experience. Only on the grand-scale view do we see this upward movement. "But such broad views obscure the details on which rests our whole understanding of the process" (SMW 1).

The category of conceptual reversion discussed in Chapter II is relevant to Whitehead's theory of adventure. Though ideas initially emerge from antecedent actions, it is not the case that the ideas of a given historical epoch are totally determined by the modes of activity of that epoch. If this were the case, every adventure would have its origin in blind contingencies, and history would move by accidents which could only later be rationalized. But Whitehead believes that intellectual ferment can produce new ideas which will serve as lures for new forms of activity. "The world dreams of things to come, and then in due season arouses itself to their realization" (AI 359). This seems to contradict Whitehead's basic pragmatic orientation. Thought arises from antecedent modes of activity, but new ideas may be entertained as contrasts to ideas originally arising from practice. Primarily action precedes thought, but the category of conceptual reversion, we may recall, allows for the emergence of ideas distinct from antecedent actions. The possibility of reverted feelings prevents Whitehead from holding every adventure to be blind in its beginnings. It is often true that the ideas which serve as motivating factors in adventures beyond a set of given circumstances are unrealized. As Whitehead notes, for example: "Columbus never reached China. But he discovered America" (AI 359). Transitions between epochs or types of civilization do not constitute radical discontinuities. If it is the case that the "quick transitions to new types of civilization are only possible when thought has run ahead of realization" (AI 359), then it will always be possible ex post facto to discover the threads which tie one epoch to another.

3. PEACE

As we have seen, the quest for Truthful Beauty entails a certain degree of egoism giving to the realizations of the aims of Art, Truth, Beauty, and Adventure subjective forms productive of disharmony in experience. How may one expect any important harmony in individuals or societies if existence is seen as an unending struggle against the decay of finite perfections? But human societies do sometimes attain social climates indicative of a non-egoistic, non-despairing state of mind. We may think of the familiar "models" of civilization: Periclean Athens; the early sixteenth-century humanist culture of England, or mid-eighteenth-century Europe. Whitehead seeks to provide an explanation for this conquest of cynicism and despair by delineating a fifth quality or cultural aim which can rectify the weaknesses inherent in the other four considered by themselves. This quality is termed "Peace."

In the discussion of the theory of concrescence in Chapter II, distinctions were drawn between the datum, process, and satisfaction of an actual occasion. In Chapter III, the distinction was made between cultural objects, agency, and aims. The analogy between the three elements of culture and the theory of experience was drawn upon, implicitly, to provide the abstract foundations of a Whiteheadian theory of culture. Cultural objects are the "data" of a culture; cultural agencies are "processes" creative and expressive of culture; cultural aims, the qualities of "satisfactions" in a civilized society. At a somewhat more abstract level it is possible to understand the five cultural aims as differentially relevant to the three elements of concrescence. Truth and Beauty, as regulative properties of experience, are characterizations of the data of experience; Art and Adventure, as regulating functions, characterize the *process* of concrescence; Peace is that quality expressive of the ideal *satisfaction* of experience. Such an attempt to note analogies between cultural aims and the elements of concrescence serves an important purpose in that it claims that, *qua* aims or qualities, all five cultural aims are relevant to the satisfaction of experience, but that Peace is expressive of the unity of satisfaction in a way which presupposes the relevance of Truth and Beauty to the datum, and of Art and Adventure to the process, of experience.

The satisfaction of an actual occasion is the attainment of its objective unity. The formal reality of an occasion belongs to it only as concrescent process; with the attainment of satisfaction the occasion passes to its objective existence in which it may be considered only in regard to its consequences for subsequent occasions. The passage to satisfaction signals the loss of subjectivity. Thus, in one sense, satisfaction is never fully experienced, except by anticipation, by the satisfied entity. "[Satisfaction] cannot be construed as a component contributing to its own concrescence; it is the ultimate fact, individual to the entity" (PR 129).

Actual entities must be viewed in both their subjective and superjective characters. As subjective they are processes of integration enjoying subjective immediacy; as superjective they are objective creatures possessing efficacy for future concrescences. The objectively immortal actual entity, the entity having attained its satisfaction, "is the pragmatic value of its specific satisfaction qualifying the transcendent creativity" (PR 134).

The most significant fact about the relation of the satisfaction to any individual concrescence is that the attainment of satisfaction is not open to the reflective experience of the concrescing occasion, but is rather a result of such experiencing. That is, the full determinate satisfaction of an occasion is not consciously experienced by that occasion except insofar as the experience of the subjective aim as a lure toward a particular experience of its satisfaction prior to its actual attainment. The realization of objective immortality *qua* subjective experience can only be a realization by anticipation. Such realization carries with it an insight into the radical limitation of individual experience. The finitude of becoming involves the consequences that the attainment of a given harmony of experience necessarily entails the rejection of viable alternatives, and that no static maintenance of a given attainment is possible. There is also the implication that no single occasion can have full conscious experience of any achieved perfection except those existing in the past. All experience is an ever-not-quite, for "completion is the perishing of immediacy: 'It never really is' " (PR 130).

It is this final implication of the finitude of experience which drives one to the realization of the tragic contingency of becoming. Here we have reached a point in Whitehead's philosophy which finds echoes in every major modern existentialist philosophy. The problem of the way in which to accept the fact of the finitude of experiencing and to overcome the anxiety engendered by such an acceptance is, in twentieth-century philosophy, the result of the refusal to exempt any element of existence—not even reason itself—from the flux of passing fact. It is this characteristic which Whitehead shares with the modern existentialists and with the philosophies of Peirce, James, and Dewey. But the problem which Whitehead faces here is at once more subtle and poignant than that encountered by most philosophers of finitude. For existentialist philosophers death expresses the inexorable self-limitation of human existence, causing every human act to fall under the cloud of final annihilation; for Whitehead human finitude is an expression of the character of *each drop of human experience* (as well as every drop of experience per se). Whitehead's is a much more radical eschatology than is to be found in any contemporary existentialist system. Whitehead's concept of man is imbued with greater poignancy and tragedy. The crucial fact is not that, soon or late, death will put an end to an individual's achievements; it is rather that no present achievement is fully open to conscious enjoyment. Existence is an ever-not-quite.

The fact that an actual entity is closed to the conscious experience of its own satisfaction is the reason why the mere pursuit of Truthful Beauty is not ultimately satisfying. By definition, *nothing* can be ultimately *satisfying*. What is sought, therefore, is a species of anticipation which will bring a sense of inner justification for a striving whose end will never be fully realized. This leads, in Whitehead's philosophy, to the intuition of Peace.

Peace is never defined by Whitehead; rather, it is discussed from alternate points of view in order to evoke some factors implicit in its intuition. Some clarity may be brought to the discussion of the topic of Peace if we introduce a general metaphysical distinction. Whitehead's philosophy of organism attempts to mediate between nominalist and idealist approaches to problems of ontology. The particularistic emphasis of nominalism is expressed for Whitehead by the fact that, according to the ontological principle, actuality must be discussed in terms of the internal constitutions of individual actual entities; the idealist impulse toward organic wholes is stressed by the principle of relativity which emphasizes the intrinsic interrelations of actual entities. It is this attempt to take seriously both the connectedness and the particularity of things which provides an insight into the function and significance of the aim at Peace.

The fact of the finitude of personality, expressing itself in the ever-not-quite character of all human experiences, drives individuals to the need for a transcendence of individuality in an attempt to find greater fulfillment in societies existing beyond the present, momentary self. This transcendence can be no mere absorption of the self by some supra-individual organism, but must be such as to preserve the integrity of the individual experiencer. Whitehead's problem is that of the proper relations of the One and the Many, of universality and particularity, of the social and individual.

In attempting to clarify the function of Peace as a cultural aim, White-head takes a phenomenological approach, seeking to illumine this general notion from several perspectives. For example, he attempts to show how the intuition of Peace may be evoked by the experience of tragedy. The principles of finitude, of process, and of individuality are central to this discussion. Tragedy presupposes a realization of the finite and passing character of things. The sense of loss entailed in such a realization threatens to bring despair, unless an intuition of endurance beyond the flux of passing fact is attained. For conscious beings, "the enjoyment of existence is en-twined with pain, frustration, loss, tragedy. Amid the passing of so much beauty, so much heroism, so much daring, Peace is then the intuition of permanence" (AI 369).

The experience of the sense of Peace requires a certain transcendence of one's individuality. The transcendence required for the realization of Peace is motivated by the realization of the finitude of existence. This finitude is a result of the incomplete subjective realization of one's own satisfactions and the necessity of the objectification of one's experiences as efficacious elements for future process. Peace is the ideal subjective form according to which one affirms as worthwhile individual creative effort in the face of the seeming transience of all achieved perfections. Transcendence of the actu-ality of immediate experience is achieved, in human beings, by the passing on of experiences to the subsequent members of the personal order com-prising the self through time. Acts, decisions, and aims of the momentary self are offered to the succeeding self for its appraisal and acceptance or re-jection. Faith in the efficacy of personal experience of selves beyond the im-mediate experiencing self is the primary instance of transcendence.

The quality of Peace provides the basis for the maximal development of one's aim at intensity of experience. The experience of Peace is grounded upon two intuitions which, when seen in their intrinsic relatedness, issue into the experience of that Peace which forms the apex of civilized experi-ence. These two intuitions have been noted, implicitly, in the foregoing dis-cussion, but must be explicitly delineated at this time. The first is the sense of the "Eros" character of experience.

Nothing intrinsic to an occasion of experience can provide assurance of that measure of conformation of Appearance sufficient for the attainment of balanced complexity of experience. Whitehead, therefore, seeks beyond individual experiences for the basis for a belief in, and a hope for, a tendency in nature which urges toward a creative conformation of Reality and Appearance. This tendency he terms "Eros," the urge toward ideal strength of beauty.[15] Whitehead conceives such an Eros, which is extrinsic to any single temporal actual entity, as "the active entertainment of all ideals, with the urge to their finite realization, each in its due season" (AI 357).

The issue at stake in the intuition of Peace is the need for adequate transcendence. Actuality is incurably atomic; therefore, individual centers of experience express the nature of things. How to transcend individual experience so as to take account of the world below and beyond one's own experience is the fundamental problem inherent in Whitehead's account of experience. The world "below" enters into the experience of each occasion via the provision of the initial subjective aim. The initial aim, through the provision of the standpoint in the extensive continuum, indicates those actual entities which shall be in the past actual world of the given occasion. The character of the aim is decided by virtue of the possibilities of harmony inherent in that past actual world. The aim determines the best for that occasion, given its standpoint in the continuum. Such transcendence, however, which merely indicates a taking into account of the world from which the occasion derives, is transcendence only in one direction. There must be transcendence "beyond" the individual occasion as well. The Eros, by itself, cannot provide for such transcendence.

The autonomy of each actual occasion entails the possibility of deviation from its initial aim such that the final satisfaction expresses a distinct variation from the initial aim. Satisfactions are, therefore, more than mere actualizations of the propositional lures toward ideal perfections which are the subjective aims. The fate of an actual entity considered by itself is, therefore, uncertain. The realization that there is an Eros urging toward ideal perfections is not sufficient to provide a meaningful context for creative action. There needs to be, in addition, the knowledge that the actual satisfactions achieved in each individual case will be met with the same loving care as is manifest in the provision of the ideal aim. The feeling of transcendence beyond individual experience "requires for its understanding that we supplement the notion of the Eros by including it in the concept of an Adventure in the Universe as One" (AI 380). That is, in addition to a lure toward ideal perfection, there must be some sense of actualized harmony. This second type of transcendence is involved in the first, for the Eros can supply relevant initial aims to the occasion of the temporal world only if it responds to the actual state of the past actual worlds of all contemporary occasions. Such responsiveness can only come from actual physical prehensions of the state of each successive temporal world. Such prehensions are feelings of the objectively satisfied occasions, occasions in their objective immortality.

The sense of Peace deriving from a faith in the primordial Eros and the consequent Unity of Adventure is the capstone of civilized experience. That such a sense of peace is necessary is a belief which Whitehead derives from reflection upon cultural history. Whitehead's reading of history, as well as his reflections upon the meaning of human experience, led him to the conclusions that man does seek to create beauty, that beauty does fade and pass away, that such passing is experienced as tragedy, and that there must be some antidote to tragedy, other than stoic endurance, if civilizations are to be created. Peace, the intuition of the transcendent permanence of beautiful things, is life's reply to inevitable tragedy. And, as we shall have occasion to see in a later chapter, that reply is the origin of the religious vision which has always been a fundamental element in the development and maintenance of civilized cultures.

Whitehead's theory of civilization requires that a civilized society exhibit the five qualities of Art, Adventure, Truth, Beauty, Peace. These cultural aims, however, can be made a part of a social order only if the theoretical and practical energies are directed toward their realization. In Western culture human energies have been so directed in accordance with a set of dominant cultural interests—art, morality, science, religion, philosophy. The next step in developing a Whiteheadian theory of culture, therefore, is to investigate these dominant interests which, properly exercised, give rise to the requisite qualities defining a civilized society.

1. In this connection, see Peter Munz, *Problems of Religious Knowledge* (London: scm Press, 1959), Chapters IV and V, for a discussion, from the perspective of a broad-based language philosophy, of the factual and symbolic realms of truth. The similarity to the Whiteheadian theory of symbolic and propositional truth-relations is to be noted, even though Munz finds he must affirm an ultimate disjunction between the two types of truth.

2. It is for this reason, also, that "goodness" cannot be an aim of art. For "good and evil lie in the depths and distances below and beyond appearance. They solely concern inter-relations within the real world" (AI 345). Goodness (and evil) refer only to Reality. The settled world of actual entities constituting the reality of the past on one side of the occasion is complemented by the anticipation of a given concrescence. Quite obviously, then, goodness cannot be an aim of art. It is this fact which renders so complex the relations between art and morality, as we shall see in Chapter VII.

3. But see AI 244ff. Here, in replying to criticisms of A. O. Lovejoy in *The Revolt Against Dualism* (Lasalle, Ill.: Open Court, 1929), pp. 193–234, Whitehead clarifies the place of dualistic concepts in his philosophy.

4. Freud, *Civilization and its Discontents* (London: Hogarth, 1961), p. 118.

5. *Ibid.*, p. 123.

6. Novalis' *Hymns and Thoughts on Religion*, trans. W. Hastie (Edinburgh: Clark, 1888), p. 123.

7. Donald Sherburne, *A Whiteheadian Aesthetic* (New Haven: Yale University Press, 1961), pp. 193–195.

8. See Plato, *Sophist*, 257ff.

9. The dialectical pattern of these three stages suggests the importance of dialectical thinking as a rhythmic process allowing for the discovery of novel alternatives within a given set of entertained concepts. The contrast of p and p̄ arises from the entertainment of p. The coordination of both p and p̄ at a more general conceptual level provides a new set of relationships which maintains the same abstract cyclical pattern while introducing novel content. The dialectical pattern derives from the fundamental aesthetic experience of the concrescence. For "all aesthetic experience is feeling arising out of the realization of contrast under identity" (PR 427).

10. See Teilhard's *The Phenomenon of Man* (New York: Harper Torchbook, 1959).

11. See Weber's *Sociology of Religion*, trans. Ephraim Fischoft (Glencoe: Free Press, 1961), for a discussion of religious institutions based on this hypothesis.

12. This rather neat tying-together of the realms of art and science should not be assumed to be completely in accord with the physicist's current conceptions of the fundamental character of things. Some demurrers to Whitehead's concept of the vibratory character of atomic particles have been issued on the grounds of the "new" quantum theory. See, for example: Abner Shimony, "Quantum Physics and the Philosophy of Whitehead," *Philosophy in America*, ed. Max Black (Ithaca: Cornell University Press, 1965), pp. 240–261; Harold N. Lee, "Causal Efficacy and Continuity in Whitehead's Philosophy," *Studies in Whitehead's Philosophy*, ed. Alfred Landé (New Orleans: Tulane University, 1961), pp. 59–70; Alfred Landé, *Foundations of Quantum Theory: A Study in Continuity* (New Haven: Yale University Press, 1955), especially "Are There Quantum Jumps?" The criticisms of Whitehead contained in these articles do not suggest the need for any *radical* revision of Whitehead's theories at this point, however.

13. For discussions, in addition to those provided by *The Function of Reason*, of some of the philosophical implications of the second law, see: R. B. Lindsay, *The Role of Science in Civilization* (New York: Harper & Row, 1963), pp. 153–165, 290–298; S. Polgar, "Evolution and the Thermodynamic Imperative," *Human Biology*, 33, No. 2 (1961), 99–109; Erwin Schrodinger, *What is Life?* (New York: Macmillan, 1955), pp. 68–75; H. S. Seifert, "Can We Decrease our Entropy?" *American Scientist*, 49 (1961); Kenneth Boulding, "The Entropy Trap," *The Meaning of the Twentieth Century* (New York: Harper & Row, 1965), pp. 137–155; T. A. Burkill, *God and Reality in Modern Thought* (Englewood Cliffs: Prentice-Hall, 1963), pp. 180–184.

14. The effect of technologies upon personality systems has been considered, mainly from a Freudian perspective, by such theorists as Herbert Marcuse (*Eros and Civilization: A Philosophical Inquiry into Freud* [New York: Random House, 1955] and *One-Dimensional Man* [Boston: Beacon, 1964]) and Philip Rieff (*The Triumph of the Therapeutic* [New York: Harper & Row, 1965]).

15. The term, of course, is borrowed from Plato. See Socrates' discourse on Love in *Symposium*, 202–212.

Chapter V

CULTURAL INTERESTS

IN THE PRECEDING CHAPTER we investigated those cultural aims which according to Whitehead define a civilized society. In the following pages we shall consider the subject of "cultural interests," those generic interests which, in human societies, give substance and direction to the attempt to achieve cultural aims. These interests exist at a somewhat lower level of generality than cultural aims, defining as they do the specific disciplinary modalities of intellectual culture. The distinction between cultural aims and interests is, however, more than merely one of degrees of generality. Cultural aims have the characteristics of something *aimed at*: cultural interests are concerned with the ways in which human beings direct their energies in order to achieve the aims or ideals which define their society.

Complexity of social organization is a function of an organized set of multivalently relative actions and interests. Civilization is possible only when there is sufficient conceptual clarity regarding the pursuit of these interests and activities so that a harmonious balance is attained in human social experience and expression. Insofar as thinkers have troubled themselves over the role of philosophy as a civilizing agency, the question of the proper relations of the various human interests in society has been considered an eminently *philosophical* issue. The history of philosophy, in one of its principal parts, is the story of the variety of ways in which philosophers have sought to provide a rational organization of cultural interests.

1. CULTURAL-INTEREST THEORIES

The aim of the Platonic scheme of education in Books II through VII of *The Republic* is to produce the philosopher capable of entertaining the vision of the Good, that Form of Forms which is the principle of all knowledge and the ultimate ground of all practice. The key concept in this scheme is dialectical unity. "Practice," the exercise of right opinion, is subordinated to the "theory" of first principles. "Doing" is a secondary mode of "knowledge," and to know the truth is to do the truth. The contemplative philosopher, not the artist or the man of action, is the ideal embodiment of Platonic thought. Thus Plato's classification of cultural interests is formal and synthetic and expresses a conviction that thought and action are ultimately unified in the highest type of knowledge, the knowledge of the Good.

Aristotle, accepting Plato's basic scheme, radically altered the relations between theoretical and practical reason. This alteration expressed itself in a threefold classification of cultural interests and activities into theoretical, practical, and productive enterprises.[1] Aristotle's classification of cultural interests is directed against the idealist reduction of Plato, which issued in a unified system of the sciences. Where Plato was synthetic in his provision of a hierarchy of disciplines, Aristotle was analytic. His classification of the sciences shows a bias toward a distinct set of disciplines which derive from the three separate activities of men: knowing, doing, and making. In this way, metaphysics, as a theoretical science, considers a distinctly different subject matter and requires a distinctly different method of inquiry than does, for example, either ethics or politics, which relate to the practical activities of man. Where Plato saw a unified hierarchy of the sciences moving in a continuous manner from the modes of practice to the formal theoretical disciplines, Aristotle provided a vision of separate sciences of theory and practice with only a provisional priority given to the theoretical over the practical disciplines.[2] Much of the intellectual history of Western culture has been determined, directly or indirectly, by the alternation and interplay of these two different conceptions of the proper organization of cultural interests. Since Plato and Aristotle, concepts of the scope of reason and the relative unity or distinctness of its theoretical and practical modes have been primary in the construction of the organization of cultural-interest theories.

Since the post-Renaissance period, theories of cultural interests have shifted away from humanistic pursuits. The dominance of the humanities in the cultural realm came to an end with the explosion of the natural sciences after Newton. Descartes had prepared the way through the construction of a philosophical system which affirmed an extreme subject–object disjunction, implying a mind-body dualism which took mental functioning and, to a degree, all "purified" affective states, outside of nature. This view destroys the Platonic vision of the ultimate unity of intellectual and practical interests. The sciences of psychology and physiology, on the Cartesian scheme, are ever-distinct examinations of essentially disjoined substances.

The essential impact of Descartes upon subsequent philosophy, as Whitehead has noted, is that his philosophical scheme entailed "the inevitability of Hume" (v. MT 113). The search for a criterion by which to determine necessary truth leads, on Cartesian principles, to the doctrine of clear and distinct ideas as the fundamental basis upon which an adequate and certain philosophy can be constructed. Hume's philosophy was the logical consequence of the combination of the Cartesian type of skepticism, the rationalist criterion of clear and distinct ideas, and the rejection of the appeal to the mediation of God as the ultimate guarantor of knowledge.

Hume's skepticism rests upon his affirmation that all demonstrated knowledge is limited to the comparison of clear and distinct ideas and his subsequent assertion that, on rational or empirical grounds, sense-perceptions provide no warrant for inferences beyond themselves. Perceptions are the basis for matters of fact and for existence based on experience, which constitute merely probable knowledge. It was this conclusion which led to his famous classification of cultural interests with which he closes *An Enquiry Concerning Human Understanding*.

> If we take in our hand any volume; of divinity or school metaphysics, for instance; let us ask, *Does it contain any abstract reasoning concerning quantity or number?* No. *Does it contain any experimental reasoning concerning matter of fact and existence?* No. Commit it then to the flames: for it can contain nothing but sophistry and illusion.[3]

Only that reasoning which proceeds abstractly in terms of quantity or number, or that which proceeds experimentally in terms of matters of fact, is valid. Matters of general or particular facts are to be established in experience and by experimental reasoning. Morals and criticism are based on "taste and sentiment"; beauty is "felt more properly than perceived," and the foundation of theology is faith and divine revelation. Hume has accepted the distinction between theoretical and practical interests and, in rejecting logical proof as establishing matters of fact and existence, has denied that practice, or "custom" as he calls it, is rationally defensible in any important sense.

Accepting Hume's skeptical conclusion, Kant sought to expand the boundaries of theoretical reason somewhat and to revitalize reason in its practical mode. On the Kantian view, cultural interests may be discussed in terms of the principal modes of science, morality, aesthetics, and religion.[4] The first, second, and third critiques and *Religion Within the Limits of Reason Alone* provide the discussions of the nature and limits of these various enterprises. If Hume erred in his supposition of the ultimacy of clearly presented sense-experience, then Kant's philosophy must be examined with some care in order to determine to what extent that specific error of Hume placed Kant in a compromising position. The skeptical element in both philosophies radically affects the autonomy of individual interests in culture.

Hegel's philosophy, viewed from a Whiteheadian perspective, shared the same principal error as the Humean and Kantian schemes and perpetuated this error into contemporary philosophy. If the immediate starting-point for Kant's critical philosophizing was Hume's skeptical reduction, the immediate impetus for much of Hegel's thought was the Kantian philosophy. Kant's bifurcated world, itself a product of the attempt to answer Hume's challenge, seemed a principal weakness to the mind of Hegel. But Kant could not be ignored. Hegel's reaction to Kant was similar to Kant's reaction to Hume. All three shared an important assumption: skepticism with regard to the interpretation of sense-perception.

In Hegel's *Phenomenology of Mind*, it is the critique of "sense certainty" which provides the basis for a number of dialectical transitions which end, ultimately, in the systematic unity of the Absolute.[5] The Hegelian philosophy stresses the higher phases of conscious, intellectual experience in its solution to the problems involved in the Humean and Kantian positions. Hegel has swallowed Kant's bifurcated world; theoretical and practical reason have found their union at the highest speculative level.

The theory of cultural interests which emerges from the Hegelian philosophy is complex and detailed, based as it is upon the three dialectical moments of the self-reflective movement of the Idea. The ways of knowing are arranged hierarchically and synthetically from the bare ideas of logic and metaphysics, through the mediated ideas of nature and the natural sciences, to the sciences of the spirit, or *Geisteswissenschaften,* which include the social sciences, ethics, and politics, and, finally, aesthetics, and religion —all of which find their unity in Philosophy, or Absolute Knowledge. Clearly, we have in Hegel one logical consequence of the Kantian attempt to meet Hume's skeptical challenge by introducing a radical cleavage between the worlds of fact and value. An idealist reduction similar to Platonic philosophy (but by no means identical in form or implication) is perpetuated by Hegel and, once more, the unity of all forms of knowledge is affirmed at the cost of the autonomy of the various cultural interests.

In this century the dominant strains of philosophy have shown little enthusiasm for the development of cultural-interest theories, primarily because of the strong reaction which contemporary philosophers have been conditioned to express against the Hegelianisms of the last century. The broad existentialist tradition and the positivist and analytic traditions of Great Britain, as well as the pragmatic philosophies developed in this country, have shared to a lesser or greater extent an antipathy to the kind of systematization of the cultural interests which was the issue of Hegel's philosophy. This century has been faced at the extremes with either the positivist reduction of cultural interests to the language and concepts of the physical sciences, as was the case with the *Encyclopaedia of Unified Sciences,* or the contrary dominance of the *Lebenswelt* which gives preference to the subjective world of human experience over the world of empirical science in the organization of the sciences of culture.

A partial resolution of the conflict implied by these extremes can be noted in the later developments of linguistic analysis. Ordinary language philosophy has expressed its genius by rejecting all such partial reductions as are evidenced in the positivist or existentialist traditions in favor of an impartial reduction of all cultural interests to issues of language rules and their use. Disclaiming this synoptic function completely, the later Wittgenstein proposed that each discipline be left to develop its own principles, methods, and ways of intending the world. Such an approach prevents the partial reductions which occur whenever a cultural-interest theory is developed from too close an association with the data of a single interest.

But the weakness of the ordinary language approach, from the point of view of those who are interested in the organization of cultural interests, is that the assurance of the autonomy of each interest is provided only at the expense of any significant understanding of their mutual relations. Several philosophers who stand near the ordinary language tradition have voiced their disapproval of this implication over the past twenty years. H. H. Price's well-known essay "Clarity Is Not Enough" [6] contains a plea for a return to a stress upon the synoptic function of philosophy. In acknowledging the need for the synoptic vision of the speculative philosopher, there is a recognition that in addition to providing a means for insuring the autonomy of human interests, philosophers must aim at the construction of theories which will give to the practitioners of the various theoretical interests some concepts illumining the viable relations with other human disciplines.

The current growing reaction against the non-speculative aspect of contemporary forms of philosophy derives from a dissatisfaction with the excessive cost which must be paid for the provision of individual autonomy to cultural interests. Judging from the history of philosophy: the dilemma seems to be this—either we have a metaphysical theory which provides a synoptic vision of the whole of human thought and action at the cost of giving dominance to but one of several modes of human interest; or else the various interests are given autonomy, but at the cost of the loss of a synoptic vision. The problem set for anyone who would forward a cultural-interest theory is the attempt to balance the demands of each perspective. Thus the two basic criteria of a cultural-interest theory are: (1) that the theory provide some synoptic vision of the viable connections of disciplines and (2) that the theory insure a significant autonomy for each discipline vis-à-vis the others.

The first criterion requires that a cultural-interest theory give an account of the pragmatic relations between the various individual interests, so that sound judgments are possible concerning the practical questions involved in the cooperation of intellectual interests in a society. The second criterion involves the requirement that the syntactical and semantic relations of concepts and theories within a given interest shall not be determined by the cultural-interest theory but shall emerge from the practice of the methods intrinsic to that interest. In order to meet these criteria, a cultural-interest theory must provide an explanation of the various human interests in terms and concepts which are not primarily or uniquely dependent in their construction or operation upon any specific interest or set of interests. Only in this manner may a harmful type of reduction be avoided. The aim of such a theory is not to avoid reduction per se, but only the partial kind of reduction which results in bringing into question the methods or results of certain human interests.

All explanations are reductions, for to explain usually means to characterize in alternative language that which is to be explained. Such alternative language, when used to characterize a problematic entity or concept may be taken as a substitute for the entity or concept. Thus the psychologist may "explain" a work of art, a set of ethical actions, or a religious belief in terms of psychological principles, but seldom to the satisfaction of the artist, the ethical man, or the religionist. The psychologist, partial to his own methods and principles, cannot provide an adequate explanation of interests other than his own. What is needed, therefore, is an *im*partial reduction or explanation such as that attempted by the ordinary language philosophers, but one which at least approaches the ideal of synoptic clarity. Only so may we hope to satisfy the demand for both intrinsic unity and autonomy of the various human interests. In what follows I intend to show that just such a theory is to be found in Whiteheadian metaphysics.

2. ABSTRACTION

In his writings Whitehead expressed a concern for the development of a synoptic understanding of the principal cultural interests of civilized societies. This concern is clearly revealed in the following statements taken from *Science and the Modern World* and *Process and Reality*: "It must be one of the motives of a complete cosmology, to construct a system of ideas which bring the aesthetic, moral, and religious interests into relation with those concepts of the world which have their origin in natural science" (PR vi). "The various human interests which suggest cosmologies, and also are influenced by them, are science, aesthetics, ethics, religion" (SMW ix).

Each of these statements contains reference to five separate human interests. Why Whitehead selects these particular interests for emphasis is a question with which I shall deal in the following pages. For the answer to this question will provide information about the type of theory which Whitehead wishes to put forward. Thus, if we are to understand Whitehead's approach to the construction of a theory of cultural interests, the following questions should be answered: (1) According to what principle does Whitehead select for emphasis the five above-mentioned cultural interests? and (2) What are the resources in Whitehead's philosophy for the construction of a general theory of cultural interests? To discover the rationale behind Whitehead's emphasis upon *religion, art, morality (ethics)*, and *sci-*

ence as those interests which suggest *cosmologies*, we shall first have to take a look at Whitehead's concept of abstraction.

Contrasting affirmations about the status of abstractions found in the history of philosophy most often result from a confusion of two prominent senses of the term. The two extremes taken by philosophers in the past may be illustrated by contrasting Bergson with Plato. For Bergson, reason (through the use of formal abstraction) distorts reality, which is available in its true sense only to immediate intuition. "There is no form, since form is immobile and the reality is movement. What is real is the continual *change of* form: *form is only a snapshot view of a transition*." [7] A formal abstraction is a "snapshot" which captures a mere hint of the reality subjected to abstractive processes. Platonic philosophies, on the other hand, hold that the permanent and fixed character of mathematical and philosophical abstractions expresses the true nature of the world. These two philosophies differ concerning the relative status of formal and selective abstractions.

Whitehead distinguishes two types of abstraction. There is abstraction from possibility and abstraction from actuality: "The simple eternal objects represent the extreme of abstraction from an actual occasion; whereas simple eternal objects represent the minimum of abstraction from the realm of possibility" (SMW 246). Abstraction from possibility entails increasingly complex eternal objects and, therefore, increasing specificity. "Red" is more abstract than "color" in this sense of the term. The second sense of abstraction involves a high degree of generality. In this sense of the term, therefore, the concept "color" is more abstract than that of "red."

For the sake of clarity we may label these two types of abstractions "formal" and "selective." The formal type is an abstraction from actuality; the selective type is an abstraction from possibility. Metaphysical concepts claim the highest degree of formal abstraction and the lowest degree of selectivity. Poetic expressions and religious parables provide examples of high degree of selective abstraction, but possess only a slightly formal character. One main contribution of Whitehead's philosophy is his mediation between these extreme views of the status of abstractions by his denial of a sharp dichotomy between Appearance and Reality, and his refusal to assign unqualified priority to the one over the other.

Formal abstraction provides, by the introduction of appearance, a general characterization of common aspects of particular experiences. Selective abstraction is concerned with the concrete particularities of experience selected from the welter of primary experiences. Artists and poets do not try to generalize upon experience via the process of transmutation, but to evoke fundamental experiences through the use of images and symbols. Whitehead attempts to combine these alternative approaches into a complete characterization of experience in which the formal and selective types of abstractions will complement one another and each will be germane to our primitive and unitary experience of the world:

> Philosophy is the critic of abstractions. Its function is the double one, first of harmonising them by assigning to them their right relative status as abstractions, and secondly of completing them by direct comparison with more concrete intuitions of the universe, and thereby promoting the formation of more complete schemes of thought [SMW 126].

Concrete experience, reality, provides the criterion in terms of which the validity and correct relative status of abstractions are to be judged. Abstraction, in both its formal and its selective senses, characterizes concrete experience. One implication of Whitehead's concept of abstraction is that formal abstraction seeks in concrete experience those universal characterizations common to experiences of that same type or, in the case of metaphysical concepts, to *all* experience. Selective abstraction provides a perspective upon experience which discriminates only selected components for emphasis. One may abstract any given "part" from a "whole," or may view any given whole from a perspective from which its wholeness is entirely without parts, or in which the parts are seen to be constitutive of the whole. (Here "part" has the qualitative connotation of "aspect" as well as its more primitive quantitative significance.)

In point of fact these two types of abstraction always occur together. The only exception to this is the ideal case of a metaphysical concept which applies to every item of experience, thus maintaining a formal but non-selective character. Selective abstraction must always involve formal abstraction for the reason that an eternal object is required to objectify any data for prehension by an occasion of experience (v. PR 93, 249). Still it is possible to indicate varying emphasis as to type of abstraction utilized in the various human interests operating in culture. The fact that this may be done provides a key to understanding the Whiteheadian approach to the problem of cultural interests.

Utilizing the concept of abstraction illumined above, I intend to show that the bases of the five cultural interests given such stress by Whitehead in his writings on the philosophy of civilization are to be found in the primary types of abstraction from experience. Three of the interests, the aesthetic, the moral, and the religious, are grounded upon selective abstractions from Whitehead's phenomenological account of concrete human experience. Science is based upon a peculiar balance between formal and selective abstraction from human sense-perception. Philosophy, in its speculative character, expresses the formal emphasis at its extreme.

3. THE VALUE-INTERESTS

For Whitehead, the most fundamental human experience is the sense of existence for its own sake, the sense of "worth." This experience is not merely a sense of personal worth, of the value of one's self. For like William James, Whitehead does not believe that the distinction between Self and non-Self is a primitive experience.[8] The value-experience which lies at the basis of all experience is the mere sense of worth, apart from any discrimination as to type or kind. The fundamental distinctions between types of value-experience are grounded in the threefold division entailed by the finitude of individual actualities. This division is that of the experience of the Whole, that Other, and this-Myself. "There is the feeling of the ego, the others, the totality" (MT 110). Actual experiencing is a unity which occurs within the context of many actualities, and the many actualities and the one actuality are members of a final unity expressed by the totality. Value-experience, therefore, is an experience of intrinsic unity, extrinsic plurality, and extrinsic unity or totality.

Individual value-experience has intrinsic value and extrinsic value, and the extrinsic value is either a value for others *qua* definite others, or a value for the totality *qua* unified whole. But no absolute disjunction need be implied by this differentiation, for extrinsic experiencing of either sort may provide the occasion for increased intrinsic value. The basic experience is the realization of worth; only after discrimination of the right selective emphasis does the experience divide into intrinsic and extrinsic aspects. Discrimination is discrimination of an experienced world. The fundamental qualifications of the world are expressions of this threefold discrimination of experience into the ego, the other, the totality.

This way of discriminating types of experience derives from the fact that Whitehead's general account of experience entails the concept of individual *occasions* of experience whose context is a nexus of other experiences, past and future. The value of an experience derives from the relation it bears to its context. It may relate primarily to itself, or to a finite part of its context, or to the totality of experience. Thus the conceptual schema utilized by Whitehead concerns the relations of whole and part. This part–whole model is by no means expressive of any necessary facet of experience, but seems to be used by Whitehead on the pragmatic ground that by such a means we actually discover a foundation for the aesthetic, moral, and religious interests.

The primary qualifications of experience are in terms of types of value-experience. The types of value-experience discriminated from the perspective of a finite actuality are related analogically to cultural interests which express value-experiences. This correlation is possible since, on Whiteheadian terms, there can be no essential difference between types of value-experiences throughout the complex orders of nature. The experience of a human being may be more complex, more subtle, and self-conscious, when the experience of a more primitive actuality is simple, crude, and unconscious; but, at base, the value-situation of every actuality may equally be seen as a manifestation of the unity-plurality-totality matrix of experiencing.

According to Whitehead, actuality is essentially composite. The compulsion of composition, which is the essence of experiencing, is identified with the Platonic and Lockian notion of "power." "The essence of power is the drive toward aesthetic worth for its own sake" (MT 119). The fundamental experience of *intrinsic* worth is aesthetic experience. From this perspective, "actuality is the self-enjoyment of importance" (MT 117). It is the intrinsic character of aesthetic experience which is crucial for the understanding of the aesthetic interest. Aesthetics concentrates upon "the closed fact" (MT 62). It "neglects the safety of the future for the gain of the present" (AI 346). Aesthetic experience demands "fruition, here and now" (AI 346). Art provides, in aesthetic experience, the enjoyment of "vivid, but transient, values" (SMW 290).

Aesthetic experience concerns the intrinsic value-experience of an actual entity. The finite immediacy of the individual experience is the subject of aesthetic experience. But aesthetic experience, as the experience of finite immediacy, points beyond itself. The composition comprising the finite actuality, when analyzed, discloses factors in experience with their own self-enjoyment. The question of the meaning of the intrinsic value of mere factors in one's own experience leads beyond aesthetic experience to a realization of the instrumental, extrinsic aspects of experiencing.

Two types of extrinsic factors enter individual experience. The first type of externality is encountered in the experiences of the component factors from which the self-completing character of experience derives. In this experience there is disclosed the "others" from which a finite experience derives, and the sum of which is increased by the completed experience of every actual entity. "They are factors in the new composition which in its completion is one of themselves" (MT 119). This realization of the fact of the importance of others in the attainment of one's own satisfaction carries with it the realization of the importance *to* others (in the future) of one's own experiencing. It is here that we find the basis for Whitehead's account of moral experience.

The relation between the aesthetic and the moral interests is based upon the contrast between immediate and proximate, present and future, experiencing. This distinction has been embodied in Whitehead's category of subjective intensity. "The subjective aim, whereby there is origination of conceptual feeling, is at intensity of feeling (α) in the immediate subject and (β) in the *relevant* future" (PR 41). The aim of experience has two dimensions, the immediate present and the relevant future. This first aspect of this aim is directly related to aesthetic experience, the second to moral experience. "Art neglects the safety of the future for the gain of the present . . . [for] the effect of the present on the future is the business of morals" (AI 346).

The aesthetic and the moral interests together represent the two dimensions of the aim at subjective intensity. Aesthetic experience, which aims at intensity here and now, is balanced by moral aims which emphasize the relevance of present experiencing for the future.

> The canons of art are merely the expression, in specialized forms, of the requisites for depth of experience. The principles of morality are allied to the canons of art, in that they also express, in another connection, the same requisites [PR 483].

The "other connection" is the relevant future. The relation between aesthetic and moral experience and expression inheres in their shared character as modes of achieving depth of experience. Morality is "control of process so as to maximize importance. . . . Our action is moral if we have . . . safeguarded the importance of experience so far as it depends upon that concrete instance in the world's history" (MT 13-14). Moral responsibility is thus a function of the freedom of each occasion to shape its own satisfaction.

Moral responsibility has two dimensions: it is the subject's responsibility for being what it is, and it is its responsibility for the future consequences of its existence. Moral experience is the aim at depth of experience, both for one's self beyond the present and for other future selves, which recognizes the specific effects of the past actual world upon present experience and the probable consequences of present upon future experiencing.

In addition to morality, there is a second extrinsic mode of value-experience. This mode is dependent upon the experience of the value "of the totality of historic fact in respect to its essential unity" (MT 119). The religious mode of experiencing is based upon the realization of the importance of the totality of individual details for the unity of any given pulse of experience. Religious experience has an extrinsic aspect since, like moral experience, it is based upon a sense of value *for*. But unlike moral experience there is no limitation concerning the relevant context in terms of which an experience is to be judged religious. The religious context is the totality of historic fact. Moral experience is concerned with the maintenance of importance insofar as it depends on that single experience; religion is concerned with the unity inherent in the totality of historic fact. "Morality emphasizes the detailed occasion; while religion emphasizes the unity of ideal inherent in the universe" (MT 28).

Value-experience, at this level of abstraction, is determined by these modes of experiencing: the experiences of totality, externality, and internality. But no ultimate separation can be made of these experiences one from the other. Prior to discrimination, they are one experience—the sense of *worth*. Even after discrimination there is really only one experience.

> These three divisions are on a level. No one in any sense precedes the other. There is the whole fact containing within itself my fact and the other facts. Also the dim meaning of fact—or actuality—is intrinsic importance for itself, for the others, and for the whole [MT 117].

Morality, aesthetics, and religion are found to be based upon discriminations of a single value-experience. These discriminations realize the possibilities

of selective emphasis in relation to the three aspects of an actuality's relatedness to the totality of other actualities: as a unity, as a plurality, or as a mere
relatedness to itself. To understand how these discriminated experiences become culturally significant, we must note the role played by *concepts* in
the rationalization of experience.

Concepts arise when eternal objects are abstracted from physical feelings,
either by valuation or reversion, and used to analyze and discriminate selected aspects or elements within the physical data provided. Concepts are
tools of consciousness which allow it to discriminate and to select for emphasis relevant factors with the synthesis of initial data forming the physical
pole of a concrescent occasion. As such they provide the limiting example of
the abstract morphological schemes which Whitehead considers so important to intellectual progress. "Concepts meet blind experience with an
analytic force. Their synthesis with physical occasion, as ground, is the perceptive analysis of the blind physical occasion in respect to its degree of
relevance to the concepts" (RM 113).

The importance of concepts cannot be overrated. Truth as the conformation of Appearance and Reality is safeguarded, in conscious experience, by
the framing of concepts appropriate to the distinct and various modes of
experiencing. In aesthetics the concepts largely concern canons of art and
the symbols and metaphors utilized in artistic production. In morality, concepts of "justice," "right," and "good" are paramount. In religion, where
concepts are largely woven into dogmatic form, the concepts relate to the
distinctly religious modality of experience which concerns man's response to
the element of deity in and transcending the world.

Concepts are results of the growth of the importance of abstractions in
human conscious experience. The desire and need for analytic clarity over
against the primitive synthetic unity of fundamental experience leads to an
increase in the number and qualitative subtlety of the concepts derived from
physical experience. In the construction of concepts a selection is made from
originally undiscriminated totality of primitive experience. Provided concepts maintain their relevance to the concrete value-experience from which
they derive, consciousness can add depth and intensity to the entire occasion
of experience through its selection and emphasis of certain details of the
whole. The loss of germaneness to primitive experience spells the dislocation of Appearance and Reality, the effect of which has been discussed in
Chapter IV.

Whitehead has an essentially Platonic view of concepts or universals since
they may be said to transcend any given temporal state of affairs. Abstraction does result in the realization of a relevant description of certain generic
features of a phenomenon or set of phenomena. But the application of the
ontological principle to the Platonic universals emphasizes the significance
of eternal objects as constitutive of processes of actualization in the phenomenal world, which processes comprise what is really real. Formal abstrac-

tion, the dislocation of an eternal object from an actual occasion or nexus of occasions, does not provide one with more complete experience of the fundamental character of things. Abstractions, in a sense, distort reality. But, at the same time, they can provide a relevant description of generic features of experience which render them justifiable in spite of the distortion involved. Whitehead's aim is, as John Smith has said of Hegel and Dewey in this regard, "to save reason from its own abstractions." [9] Whitehead has characterized philosophy as the critic of abstractions, and has argued forcefully against the wholesale commission of the Fallacy of Misplaced Concreteness in modern philosophy. He well recognizes that, though abstractions are necessary, one should be prepared to take up a critical stance toward them.

Given the fact of the necessity of abstraction: the question arises as to the criteria of abstractive processes. On what grounds do we abstract from concrete experience? Here the Whiteheadian concept of "importance" discussed briefly in Chapter I becomes relevant.

Abstractions are performed for a purpose. That purpose is to satisfy an interest. The interest and the aim, like all the elements of experiences of actualities, are partly determined by the initial aim and are partly an expression of the freedom of the individual actual occasions. Importance is to be understood as the expression of perspective emphases which in a given situation allow for the attainment of the purpose of balanced intensity of experience. Three species of importance, of crucial significance in achieving intensity of experience, have been considered thus far. These three species are perspective abstractions from the unity of experience, the fundamental sense of worth. As abstractions they do, taken singly, tend to distort the concrete unity of actual experience. But the abstractive process, allowing for the discrimination of three modes of value-experience, provides a means whereby at the conceptual level much richer and more complex types of experience are possible. To understand how these discriminations can issue into three more or less distinct types of cultural interests of religion, morality, and art, it is necessary to complicate the exposition somewhat by introducing the issue of consciousness and its influence upon value-experiences. This introduction of consciousness is a way of introducing, once more, the topic of Appearance.

Value-experience, at the human level, is inherently vague. Here, "vague" means relatively undiscriminated in conscious experience. This vagueness does not imply, however, that value-experience is less important than the clear and distinct deliverances of sense-experience. The twofold character of sense-perception, its discriminations into causal and presentational modes, explains why the primary feelings are only vaguely realized in the initial deliverances of conscious experience. The primary physical feelings, which comprise the basis of the three modes of value-experience, are simplified in consciousness through transmutation, and concentrated attention is given to the qualitative details abstracted from these physical feelings.

Consciousness is narrower than experience, being but a specialized form of it. The fundamental sense of reality is a sense of effectiveness. This sense of effectiveness "is the drive towards the satisfaction of appetition" (MT 122). The sense of efficacy, which is the sense of the "facticity" of reality, can be abstracted from consciousness in the narrowest sense of the term. But there is never a complete abstraction from subjective form of feeling except in the case of abstract mathematical concepts. The fact that a concept bears the mark of its derivation from the causal past is the basis upon which the provisional distinction between types of concepts in conscious experience is affirmed. Moral, aesthetic, and religious concepts are distinguishable since they are rationalizations of separate modes of value-experience.

Some clarity may be gained if this discussion of concept-formation is illustrated by a particular example. An outline of the procedure of rationalization of a given value-experience will support the arguments given above for the unity and autonomy of the value-interests. We will examine the concept of "the holy." The principles of concept-construction revealed in this analysis may be applied *mutatis mutandis* to the experiences which ground the other cultural interests.

> When we survey nature and think however flitting and superficial has been the animal enjoyment of its wonders, and when we realize how incapable the separate cells and pulsations of each flower are of enjoying the total effect—then our sense of the value of the details for the totality dawns upon our consciousness. This is the intuition of holiness, . . . which is at the foundation of all religion. In every advancing civilization this sense of sacredness has found vigorous expression. It tends to retire into a recessive factor in experience, as each phase of civilization enters upon its decay [MT 120].

Surveying nature need not result, of course, in an intuition of holiness. It is possible for the philosopher, at least the British philosopher, to see in nature only colored patches, though such a perspective is a difficult one to maintain for any length of time. The important point is that the intuition of holiness is based, in this illustration, upon a presentation via the senses of a scene which carries within it the implication of the value of finite details for the unified complexity of the totality. Concentrating our attention upon the value of the details for the whole leads us to an intuition of the sacred character of things. A concentration upon the intrinsic value of the details exclusive of their value for the totality of existence might lead to an intuition of beauty.

The experience of religious value, like the experience of aesthetic and moral values, is an implicate of every experience. "Our intuitions of righteousness disclose an absoluteness in the nature of things, and so does the taste of a *lump of sugar*" (MT 121). Reactions to our experience of the holy vary greatly. Feelings of holiness may be dismissed as irrelevant to one's particular interests at the time, perhaps attributed to a state of temporary melancholy; they may be enjoyed immediately and not rationalized in any way; they may serve as the impetus of a poem or painting. The theologian may wish to use such an intuition as evidence of natural knowledge of God and may proceed to characterize what may be discovered of the nature of God from such an experience. Those responses which seek, in the broad sense of the term, to rationalize (or intensively to transmute) the experience will do so through the construction of concepts. Indeed, this is one essential task which allows the various modalities of experience to have a civilizing effect upon culture. Without these types of expression the publicity of experience could not be guaranteed. For this reason Whitehead maintains that "expression is the one fundamental sacrament. It is the outward and visible sign of an inward and spiritual grace" (RM 127).

Concepts developed from the intuition of holiness would have as their ground the intuitive judgment concerning the value-relations of the finite actualities to the Unity of Experiencing. An intuitive judgment, we remember, expresses a contrast between the initial physical feeling and the proposition involved in the imaginative feeling. The imaginative feeling is formed by the contrast between the physical nexus and a predicative pattern, which has been reverted or derived from the physical nexus via valuation. An intuitive judgment provides a detailed comparison of the proposition and the physical datum. Such a comparison assures the correctness of the judgment. A concept derived from the intuition of holiness as described by Whitehead would consist of the following elements: (1) the physical datum, a nexus of entities expressing the physical and extensive characteristics of the perceived or imagined region; (2) the predicative pattern discriminated in accordance with the eternal objects "totality" and "individuality"; (3) the propositional feeling, a feeling of the germaneness of a relation of part to whole to the physical nexus prehended, where "whole" signifies the totality implied by the realization of the extension of the finite ground beyond itself. The intuitive judgment comprised by the contrast of the propositional feeling with the physical datum would have the subjective form of holiness. This subjective form—an emotional feeling—can be abstracted from in the formation of the concept, and a mere logical concept of the whole-to-part relation, or the relation of the one to the many, would remain. But the feeling of the physical nexus will conform to the feelings felt in that nexus, so that prehensions of the self-valuation of the details and the valuations of their relation to the whole are part of the physical datum. The concept derived from such an experience will be clothed with the subjective form of its origin. The future prehensions of that concept will receive this emotional content in the conformal phase of experiencing.

In an intuition of holiness derived from a particular perceptual situation, the concept constructed, or the concept which is evaluated in terms of such an intuition, may have little direct relevance to that particular scene. The fact of the common structure of experience has allowed for such an evocation of a religious intuition. The content of the concept may concern the immanence of God, or the love of God, or more specifically, His particular providence. Or it may concern the finite detail rather than the totality itself, in which case the concept may contain as its substance the concept of the value of each finite being, the concept of mutability of existence, or the finitude of all perfections.

Cultural interests born of the differing modalities of human experiencing must be adequate in their *expression* of the concepts which derive from the principal modes of human experiencing. This is the aim of Whitehead's theory of cultural interests and the meaning of his terms "rational religion," "rational morality," etc. Cultural interests are those areas of funded experience which evoke a continuing interest in the criticism and revision of concepts based upon novel experiences and more subtle rationalizations.

The process of rationalization is the process of the civilization of experience. It is the characteristic which best allows for progress in all cultural interests. Rationalization is the criticism of conscious experience. "Progress in truth . . . is mainly a progress in the framing of concepts, in discarding artificial abstractions or partial metaphors, and in evolving notions which strike more deeply into the root of reality" (RM 127). Both value-concepts and scientific concepts aim at striking into the root of reality. The construction of a concept is a function which aims from the perspective of a given cultural interest, or even from the perspective of a certain novel individual interest, to justify the selective emphasis of the perspective observation of conscious experience by calling forth the primitive causal feelings derived from the past actual world. The criticism of concepts proceeds by discarding artificial abstractions and false metaphors resulting from a disjunctive relation between Reality and Appearance.

The difference between moral, religious, and aesthetic *intuitions,* and the concepts based upon such intuitions, is the difference between *experience* and *expression*. Cultural interests define the areas of human cultural expression; they are repositories of conceptual data which constitute reflections upon, and direct expressions of, the differing modalities of experience. Conceptual feelings in concrescent experience are products of a contrast which indicates what might be or what might have been. The entertainment of concepts, therefore, involves the entertainment of ideals. Concepts are the products of selective emphasis and, therefore, are products of a sense of importance which drives the occasion to construct them.

4. SCIENCE AND PHILOSOPHY

In discussing the value-interests of art, morality, and religion, we have been concerned with those human interests which have their origins in selective abstraction from the unity of primitive experience—the sense of "worth." Our introduction of consciousness and concepts suggested the subject of formal abstraction in relation to these three modes of value-experience. There is an important type of human interest which is based upon the principle of formal abstraction, that of science. Whereas the value-interests have their origin in abstraction from primitive, emotional experience, science (i.e., natural science) has its origin, according to Whitehead, in conscious perceptual experience.

Natural science has "nature" as its subject matter. Nature, in its narrower sense, is the terminus of sense-perceptions. As such, it is "an abstraction from something more concrete than itself which must also include imagination, thought, and emotion" (*Prin. Rel.* 63). The type of abstraction made from the data of experience determines the type of science which will be developed. Natural sciences as a whole must concern themselves with the coherence of our sense-perceptions—i.e., must harmonize rational thought with the percepts of our experience.

The mode of presentational immediacy does not contain any direct reference to subjective forms of experiencing. It is empty of any emotional tone expressing derivation from the past. The nexus objectified in presentational immediacy manifests the general mathematical relations constituted by that nexus—principally those relations expressed by straight lines (v. PR 461–471).

Presentational immediacy is achieved via the transmutation of *sensa* from their role in causal feelings of derivation into characteristics of the presented duration of the contemporary world. The mathematical relations revealed in presentational perception are the geometric laws immanent in the objectified nexūs dominating the present cosmic epoch. Presentational objectification reveals "systematic relations which dominate the environment . . . by reason of the experiences of the individual occasions constituting the societies" (PR 499). These systematic relations form the basis of all the sciences. Such relations constitute a framework for measurement to which the various sciences may make common appeal. The utilization of such a common frame of reference is the key step in the development of accurate sciences.

The most abstract of natural sciences are the mathematical sciences which are concerned with the mere character of relations as manifest in presentational objectification. Geometry expresses the general and necessary relatedness of nature as revealed in sense-perception. The subject matter of geometry is arrived at by virtue of Whitehead's method of extensive abstraction. The aim of this method is to demonstrate the foundation in sense-perception of the geometrical forms, thus avoiding the merely operational view of the relation of geometric processes to the world of experience (v. PR 499–508).

The various natural sciences are to be seen as variant modes of abstraction from the world of nature as presented through the senses. But two modes of abstraction are utilized in science: formal and selective. In regard to formal abstraction, the various sciences would be ordered in terms of a hierarchy of degrees of abstraction from the concrete world. In terms of selective abstraction, the sciences would be divided according to their choice of specific subject matters.

Whitehead is concerned to avoid any absolute divisions among the various sciences. His reason for doing so is the theory of the actual occasion. The various degrees of complexity of order throughout nature are all comprised by actual occasions which express categoreal conditions applying to all other occasions. The continuity throughout nature is the continuity implied by the common categoreal structure of all actual entities. "The different modes of natural existence shade off into each other" (MT 157).

The classification of the sciences is a matter of relative indifference to Whitehead. But he considers the proper attitude of the scientist toward the specific limitations of his subject matter and his method of investigation to be of crucial importance. There are as many sciences as there are selectable and formalizable aspects of reality. But each selection and each formalization involves abstraction from the concrete continuity of experience. And each abstraction entails a specific set of limitations of the applicability and adequacy of that abstraction to the real world.

Take, for example, the distinction between the natural and the social sciences. On Whiteheadian principles this distinction is grounded in the qualitative differences in the subject matters of the two types of science. In the social sciences the issue of value-experience becomes important. "All explanations of the sociological functionings of mankind include 'aim' as an essential factor in explanation" (MT 155). In the sociological sciences, this approach to questions of value is the reason for a provisional distinction between social and natural sciences. The social sciences, on Whiteheadian terms, should include attention to the potentialities for freedom and novelty inherent in the human mind-body complex and in human societies. The natural sciences could safely abstract from such characteristics, so long as the abstractions are recognized for what they are, a set of partial perspectives on concrete actuality.

Scientific concepts, like value-concepts, are analytic tools for the discrimination of aspects of concrete experience. As such, they are helpful in achieving the aim of experience. For without the construction of adequate concepts (appearances), the more concrete experiences (realities) might be lost to conscious experience and reflection. The relevant data of the sciences derive from only certain aspects of the data of concrete experience. There is a twofold selective process determining the data with which science deals. There is the selectivity implied in the reliance upon sense-perception. Conscious perception is selective by its very nature. But beyond this, a further selective process is involved in the specializations of the various sciences. Whereas the astronomer may use a spectroscope to analyze light emitted from a given locus in the heavens to determine the position and relative velocity of a star, the physicist may use the same instrument to discover the composition of a star. But each expects the objects he is examining to illustrate *laws,* laws of motion or laws of chemical combination. It is through such concern with the laws of nature that Whitehead thinks science best serves the cause of truth.

We may consider briefly the relation between scientific and value-concepts as a means of clarifying the status of science as a cultural interest. Value-concepts are expressions in appearance of concrete value-experience in one or more of its principal modes. Scientific concepts, on the other hand, are precise formulations of the data of sense-perceptions which are then tested by symbolic reference to the world of past experience. Value-concepts require a movement from reality to appearance for construction, and then a counter-move from appearance to reality for their application and validation. But science starts with sense-perception. Science, therefore, constructs its concepts from the appearance and then symbolically refers the constructions back to those selected aspects of experience which the concepts seek to emphasize. For this reason the theories and concepts of the sciences are not directly founded upon concrete experience (reality). This conclusion is truer of the so-called "non-empirical" sciences such as mathematics and logic, and of the natural sciences, than of the social sciences which, by virtue of their human subject-matter, must concern themselves with questions of value.

So far we have considered four specific cultural interests: the aesthetic, the moral, the religious, and the scientific. The first three of these have been shown to be based upon selective abstractions from the unity of the concrete experience of "worth." These three value-interests are thus grounded in reality, though, as conceptualized, they are aspects of appearance. The scientific interest, on the other hand, has its ground in presentationally immediate experience—i.e., in appearance. We are now ready to discuss the final cultural interest emphasized by Whitehead: philosophy. In this discussion we shall see that philosophy, like science, is based upon formal abstractions; but, unlike science, it seeks ultimately to avoid selectivity in order to arrive at non-selective concepts applicable to all experience.

> Philosophy is the self-correction by consciousness of its own initial excess of subjectivity. Each actual occasion . . . has attained its individual depth of being by a selective emphasis limited to its own purposes. The task of philosophy is to recover the totality obscured by the selection. It replaces in rational experience what has been submerged in the higher sensitive ex-

perience and has been sunk yet deeper by the initial operations of consciousness itself [PR 22].

In the transition from reality to appearance, the objective data of an occasion of experience undergo valuations, reversions, transmutation, etc. In
human beings the sense-experience, or consciousness per se, resulting from
such processes is a simplification of the welter of concrete experience. The
task of philosophy is to recover the sense of the totality of concrete fact from
the selective and simplified character of conscious experience.

The generic concepts of speculative philosophy, as examples of extreme
formal concepts, can (in principle) be non-selective in character; that is,
they can apply to every item of experience. Philosophy's task, therefore, is to
construct those general concepts which may be used analytically over against
the synthetic ground of concrete experience in order to discriminate and
account for every item of experience. Philosophy as a cultural interest is
primarily aimed at constructing concepts which adequately express germaneness to the reality of concrete experience in its entirety. The underlying
principle of this concept of philosophy is that of the unity and continuity
of experiencing.

The canons of art, moral codes and theories, religious practices and dogmas, scientific theories and hypotheses, together form a complex repository
of human experience and expression, and define, moreover, the principal
ways of experiencing and expressing which are current in a civilized society.
But each of these cultural interests is in itself partial and limited. It is the
task of philosophy to expose, and to define the extent of, these limitations.
No single value-interest, or specialized science, or group of sciences, is adequate to encompass the entire meaning of things. Each of the individual
interests is partial and limited, and it is the business of philosophy to construct a classification of these various interests, exposing their limitations.

We must not mistake Whitehead's meaning here. There is a world of
difference between this view of the function of philosophy and the standard
idealist approach to the relations of the cultural interests. Aesthetics, ethics,
religion, and science are not mere partial approximations of an absolute
knowledge or experience which is reserved for a philosophical elite. Only
the most cursory reading of Whitehead could lead one to such a conclusion.
The emphasis, in the formal concepts of philosophy, upon the higher phases
of experience to the exclusion of the primitive, emotional feelings of derivation, has no defense unless the formal abstractness of the scheme is such as
to safeguard the autonomy of the principal cultural interests which are
conceptually included within it. Whitehead is as much concerned as was
William James with insuring that abstract concepts have real "cash value"
in concrete, perceptual currency. Thus philosophy is, in one sense, the most
impotent of all disciplines. Without its aim at defining the limits of, and
of helping to bring harmony into and among, the various cultural interests,
it would have little real value.

The rational scheme of thought which is the product of philosophy's effort to relate the other cultural interests is not a substitute for the experience, knowledge, and practice of these interests. The philosopher's experience of art is a reflective experience. Only *qua* artist or aesthete is aesthetic experience and expression realized. Likewise with regard to the moral and religious experiences. And, too, a knowledge of the implicit ontology undergirding the special sciences is no substitute for the knowledge and practices of the scientists themselves. Both the contrasted characters of conscious experience—reality and appearance—are necessary for a complete characterization of experience. And each of these characteristics, concrete experiences as well as abstract concepts, is necessary for the full realization of the aim of experience.

In some ways the relation between science and philosophy is analogous to the relation between morality and religion. The context within which moral value is achieved is finite and relative, while the context of religious value is the totality of fact. A somewhat similar situation exists in the relations of science to philosophy.

> It is the task of philosophy to work at the concordance of ideas conceived as illustrated in the concrete facts of the real world. It seeks those generalities which characterize the complete reality of fact, and apart from which any fact must sink into an abstraction. But science makes the abstraction, and is content to understand the complete fact in respect to only some of its essential aspects [AI 187].

Science emphasizes: (1) observation of particular occurrences, (2) inductive generalization, and (3) classifications of entities according to the laws of nature which they illustrate (cf. AI 183). Philosophy emphasizes generalizations "which almost fail to classify by reason of their universal application" (AI 183). Science and philosophy are both concerned with generalizations. The distinction between them is that science is concerned with selective or specialized abstractions while philosophy seeks the most generic notions possible. Science grounds itself in certain basic assumptions "which for its immediate purposes and for its immediate methods it need not analyze any further" (AI 184). These notions are specialized philosophic intuitions which are but vaguely defined in ordinary language. In spite of this distinction between science and philosophy, the similarities are great. Both are "concerned with the understanding of individual facts as illustrations of general principles" (AI 179).

Abstraction, as practiced by *both* science and philosophy, has the meaning of formal description of certain generic features. Such abstraction is the attempt to discover general characteristics of the subjects abstracted from. The contrast relevant to this type of abstraction is that between the general and the particular. In this sense both science and philosophy are abstract, but philosophy, aiming at the larger generalities, is more abstract.

The second sense of abstraction applies, properly, only to science. The sciences select certain aspects from a complete fact and consider these in relative isolation. Science aims at such selective emphases, while philosophy "seeks those generalities which characterize the complete reality of fact" (AI 187). Science is abstract in both the formal and selective senses, but philosophy is abstract in only the formal sense. As long as scientists and philosophers remain aware of the type and degree of their abstractive procedures, there can be no lasting conflict between philosophy and science.

So far we have considered Whitehead's theory of abstraction in terms of which he delineates various cultural interests, and we have utilized Whitehead's concept of abstraction in order to point out the bases in experience of each of five cultural interests—art, morality, science, religion, and philosophy. There is one remaining question concerning Whitehead's cultural-interest theory which should be answered: Does Whitehead's philosophy imply that these five principal interests in any way provide an exhaustive enumeration of cultural interests?

I have tried to show that Whitehead's frequent mention of just these five interests was no accident. It has been my contention that these interests illustrate the principal types of abstractions from the unity of an occasion of experience. The value-interests are based on selective abstractions from "reality." Science and philosophy derive from formal abstraction from "appearance." Science is concerned with formal abstraction from a specific selected subject matter; philosophy, in its speculative role, attains a formal, relatively non-selective, character. Utilizing the principle of abstraction in its formal and selective modes, these three types of emphases—the formal, the selective, and the combination of formal and selective—exhaust the principal types of abstraction from concrete experience. But there are at least three reasons why we should not take the five interests which we have been discussing as the only types of cultural interests.

The first reason is that, though Whitehead has sought to outline five kinds of ways of abstracting from the unity of experience, he has not attempted to delineate the various kinds of distinctions which might arise within each specific interest. Thus the variety of subject matters and methods which are evident within science per se, for example, is a function of internal developments within that interest, not the result of discrimination made necessary by Whitehead's philosophic principles. Even if Whitehead had sought to provide an exhaustive list of the principal types of cultural interests, there still would be a great deal of room for expansion and differentiation within each interest.

The second important point concerning the relative comprehensiveness of Whitehead's theory of interests concerns the criterion of selectivity from reality which determines the modes of value-interests. The model employed in the distinguishing of value-interests into three modes is that of the part–whole relation. The elements of individuality, plurality, and totality define this relation from the perspective of a single occasion of experience. There is no reason, intrinsic to Whitehead's philosophy, why this criterion of selection must be the only one employed for noting variant perspectives in concrete experience.

Finally, one must remember that cultural interests are based upon abstractions from an actual occasion of experience. But we experience more than just actual entities. We have experience of nexūs, societies of actual entities, as well. If we extend our discussion of the derivation of cultural interests via abstractions from concrete experience to include abstractions from nexūs, we might expand the relevant types of cultural interests discovered. For example, a concern for temporal nexūs would no doubt require the discrimination of history as a cultural interest.

The conclusion I draw from these brief comments is simply that the five interests emphasized by Whitehead are to be taken as important illustrations of cultural interests, but must not be taken as exhaustive of the relevant interests and activities of human beings in societies. New interests may be introduced in at least three ways: (1) by choosing different criteria of abstraction, (2) by making more subtle discriminations within a given interest, and (3) by introducing more complex subject matters (such as nexūs, etc.) as the ground from which abstractions are to be made.

Now that the main outlines of a Whiteheadian theory of cultural interests have been introduced, can we say that Whitehead has met the two primary criteria cited at the beginning of the chapter? Does this theory provide the various cultural interests of a civilized society with the basis for synoptic unity of a non-reductive type? This question may only be adequately answered by men who seek in their various specialized pursuits to test pragmatically this means of understanding the whole of a culture complex. But we may here at least indicate the way in which there is prima facie support of our two positive criteria.

In the first place, the unity provided by the theory is a function of the kind of meaningful relations which may be discriminated between the various cultural interests. The above consideration of the relations between art and morality, morality and religion, science and philosophy, etc., have demonstrated the resources in Whiteheadian theory for the affirmation of the unity of a culture complex.

Secondly, the autonomy of cultural interests is assured by the fact that an impartial reduction of all interests in terms of the general theory of experience allows for the basing of each interest in a perspective abstraction from occasions of experience. No single interest or group of interests is given priority. The reason for this is found in Whitehead's theory of abstraction. In addition to the traditional concrete–abstract contrast, Whitehead has introduced a part–whole contrast which complements the traditional theory of abstraction by providing a selective as well as a formal abstractive emphasis in experience, while refusing to give unqualified priority to either formal or selective abstraction.

NOTES

1. Cf. Aristotle, *Metaphysics*, 1025B25–1026A33; *Parts of Animals*, 639–640; *Nicomachean Ethics*, Book VI, Chapters 3–8; *Politics*, Book VIII. Also, see the Introduction to Richard McKeon's edition of *The Basic Works of Aristotle* (New York: Random House, 1941), pp. xviii–xxii.

2. Cf. *Metaphysics*, 1026A18.

3. Hume, *An Essay Concerning Human Understanding* (LaSalle, Ill.: Open Court, 1949), p. 184.

4. See "Architectonic of Pure Reason," in *Critique of Pure Reason* (London: Macmillan, 1941), pp. 653–655. Theodore Greene, in *Moral, Aesthetic and Religious Insight* (Chicago: University of Chicago Press, 1957), provides a theory of cultural interests constructed on this type of interpretation of Kant.

5. Hegel, *The Phenomenology of Mind*, trans. J. B. Baillie (London: Humanities Press, 1964), pp. 149–160.

6. H. D. Lewis, ed. *Clarity is Not Enough* (London: Allen & Unwin, 1963), pp. 13–41.

7. Henri Bergson, *Creative Evolution*, trans. Arthur Mitchell (New York: Random House, 1951), p. 328.

8. See James's *Principles of Psychology* (New York: Dover, 1950), I 272–273.

9. John E. Smith, "The Critique of Abstractions and the Scope of Reason," in *Process and Divinity*, edd. William L. Reese and Eugene Freeman (LaSalle, Ill.: Open Court, 1964), p. 26.

Chapter VI

PEACE AND RELIGION

WE HAVE BEEN FOLLOWING several strands of inquiry into the complexities of Whiteheadian philosophy. The time has come to begin tying some of these strands together. The theory of culture developed thus far includes three fundamental suppositions: first, that the goal of experience, at both the individual and cultural level, is "balanced intensity"; second, that when balanced intensity is achieved at the level of human culture, the cultural aims of Art, Adventure, Truth, Beauty, Peace will be in evidence; and third, that these primary cultural aims are efficacious when exercised in relation to the dominant cultural interests characterizing human societies—viz., art, science, morality, philosophy, and religion. The next logical step in developing Whitehead's theory of culture is to examine the relationship between cultural aims and cultural interests. A detailed examination would involve an extremely complicated set of analyses in which the civilizing effect of each of the five cultural aims would be considered in relation to each of five dominant cultural interests. Fortunately, there is a method of organizing our investigation of the relation of cultural aims and interests in such a way as to provide access to the import and principal implications of Whiteheadian philosophy on this subject without the necessity of rehearsing all the theoretical permutations. For, as we shall see, the cultural aim of "Peace," and the cultural interest of religion, are subject matters the relation of which will provide direct access to the most profound implications of Whiteheadian philosophy on the subject of civilized culture.

Whitehead's concern for the importance of religion as a cultural interest is one of the most significant aspects of his philosophy of culture. His life-long interest in problems of religion and theology manifested itself in the classic analyses of the relations of science and religion in *Science and the*

Modern World, in his highly original consideration of religious experience and expression in *Religion in the Making*, as well as in his re-evaluation of the Judaeo-Christian concept of God in *Process and Reality*. Whitehead's interest in religion is more than just a significant bit of biographical data. The fact that he should choose to discuss the problems of religion in such detail, despite his lack of expertise in the field, is strong indication of the importance of the topic to his general philosophic vision.

We remember that, according to Whitehead, the cultural aims of Truth, Beauty, Art, and Adventure could all be present without insuring a civilized society. Peace is the sine qua non of a civilized society. If a society possesses the quality of Peace, it is civilized since it will *ipso facto* manifest each of the other four cultural aims. An examination of the relation of Peace as a cultural aim to each of the five cultural interests, therefore, will provide a method of insuring the presentation of the fundamental aspects of White-headian theory on this point. But before I begin such an examination, let us note the important relation between Peace as a cultural aim and the cultural interest of religion. As we shall soon see, religion is the cultural interest insuring the possibility of the attainment of Peace, the sine qua non of civilization. Therefore, my strategy in the remaining chapters will be this: I shall characterize the relation between Peace and religion and outline what Whitehead has termed "the religious problem." In the final chapters I shall consider the way in which the religious problem is expressed, more broadly, as "the cultural problem" and examine the civilizing effect of religion (and Peace) upon the cultural interests of art, morality, science, and philosophy. In this way I shall have provided the main outlines of a Whiteheadian theory of culture and civilization.

1. THREE RELIGIOUS INTUITIONS

Whitehead achieves three distinct purposes in his developed theory of religion. He analyzes those factors in human experience which lead to the formation of a religion. He demonstrates that the transition of religion from its primitive to its rational forms parallels the historical transformations of human knowledge. And, finally, he gives a metaphysical account of those permanent formative elements which allow for stability amid change in the world, the intuition of which, and the intellectual conception of which, provide the very foundation of religions, primitive and rational.

The three aims of Whitehead's theory of religion may be recognized as three interrelated strands of inquiry into the nature and function of religion. Whitehead contrasts a general phenomenological approach to the subject of religion with a speculative or metaphysical approach. But there are two levels of phenomenological description in this work, though they are so intertwined as to make a sharp distinction impossible. One phenomenological level considers general historical experiences and affirmations regarding

138   SPECULATIVE CONSTRUCTION

fundamental religious concepts. At this level there is a genetic or historical account of the development of religion together with a survey of some common affirmations of contemporary rational religions. A second level of phenomenological description provides an account of the basic factors in individual religious experience in both its individual and historical modes. Plumbing the depths of Whitehead's concept of religion, therefore, involves us in the investigation of the analyses of fundamental religious intuitions, the question of the genetic development of religion, and, finally, the metaphysical elaboration of the fundamental religious insight.

Whitehead delineates the principal approaches to the structure of religious experience in terms of three characterizations of the fundamental intuition which grounds religion. One of these intuitions we have already considered in terms of the quality of Peace. That quality took its specific character from its context within Whitehead's discussion of the cultural aims which define a civilized society. An analysis of the other two characterizations of the fundamental intuition grounding religion will illustrate both the depth of insight of Whitehead's phenomenology of religion and the intrinsic relation between religious experience and the civilizing function of the quality of Peace.

The first characterization, the intuition of "holiness," derives from a discussion of the fundamental matrix of value-experiencing in *Modes of Thought*. We have considered that discussion in our analysis of the grounding in experience of the three value-interests. This intuition is evoked by a sense of the contrast between the individual and the totality of experiencing, a contrast which Whitehead claims to be presupposed in any realization of religious value. The sense of the value of a finite detail of experience for the totality of experiencing provides the experiential matrix within which the intuition of holiness is evoked. According to Whitehead, "religion is what the individual does with his own solitariness" (RM 16). The solitariness in terms of which Whitehead characterizes rational religion is the felt contrast of individuality with the totality of experienced fact. The extreme of solitude comes from a feeling of the contrast of self and non-self. To be "lost in a crowd" is to be lonely; to be amid the totality of existing things is to be solitary. Rational religion concerns man's solitariness—i.e., what he does with the experienced contrast of individuality and totality.

Seen in this way, the intuition of holiness may be understood as an alternative expression of the sense of Peace. The intuition of Peace, as we have seen, is the full realization that the individual is valued by transcendent actuality, valued both in its ideal possibilities and in its actual satisfaction. Peace, like the sense of holiness, derives from a felt contrast of the finitude of existence with the totality of experiencing.

In *Religion in the Making*, the primary intuition upon which religion is said to be based is "the intuition of immediate occasions as failing or succeeding in reference to the ideal relevant to them" (RM 59). The sense of

an ideal is basic to the intuition which founds religion. And a sense of "rightness" obtains when this ideal is conformed to. "There is a rightness attained
or missed, with more or less completeness of attainment or omission" (RM
59). This sense of rightness is of more than a merely transitory nature; "it
is an apprehension of character permanently inherent in the nature of
things" (RM 60).

Religious experience, so described, contains three essential aspects: (1)
a sense of rightness to be attained; (2) a sense of success or failure in the attainment of this ideal rightness; and (3) an intuition of *permanent* rightness in the nature of things transcending any successes or failures achieved
by finite occasions. The experience of evil derives from the recognition of
the contrast between the ideal of possible attainment of value and the failure
of such attainment. This is a contrast between harmony and disharmony,
good and evil, etc. The intuition of permanent rightness promotes the sense
of harmony and the final victory over evil.

Peace is considered by Whitehead within the context of a discussion of the
qualities of civilization in *Adventures of Ideas*. Here the fundamental contrast between individuality and the totality of experience is further specified
by the addition of an intuition of the contrast between the sense of permanence and the flux of passing fact. Like the sense of Peace, the intuition of
permanent rightness presupposes the fundamental contrast between individuality and totality in experience. "In its solitariness the spirit asks, What,
in the way of value, is the attainment of life? And it can find no such value
till it has merged its individual claim with that of the objective universe"
(RM 59). In addition to this contrast, two others are evident in the intuition of permanent rightness. The qualifier "permanent" implies a concern
for the contrast involved in the sense of Peace—i.e., the contrast between
permanence and flux. And the sense of "rightness," as I indicated above, contrasts harmony and disharmony, good and evil.

The relevance of these experienced contrasts to the understanding of a
developed theory of religion is touched upon in Whitehead's discussion of
"The Ideal Opposites" in *Process and Reality* (PR 512–518). Here Whitehead is interested in discriminating the fundamental contrasts which characterize what he calls "the cosmological problem," the problem which, as
we shall see, his theory of religion is meant to solve. These contrasts are:
joy and sorrow, greatness and triviality, freedom and necessity, conjunction
and disjunction (one and many), permanence and flux, good and evil. It
is the last three which form the components of holiness, peace, and permanent rightness. Presumably, any of these contrasts may be the subject of a
religious intuition, as long as it is placed within the context provided by
reference to the totality of experiencing.

The distinctions among the three religious intuitions are now clear. The
sense of holiness is the foundation of religious experience as it is evoked by
the general contrast of individuality and totality. The sense of Peace speci-

fies the intuition of holiness by the addition of a sense of the contrast between permanence and the flux of passing fact. The intuition of permanent rightness includes in one experience the contrasts of individuality and totality, permanence and flux, and good and evil. Because of its complexity, we may assume it to be the more adequate intuition for characterizing fundamental religious experience. Thus its employment in Whitehead's most systematic treatment of religion, *Religion in the Making*. Also, the specification of the intuition of Peace, and its employment as a cultural aim qualifying civilized societies, allow us to conclude both that religion as a cultural interest, insofar as it promotes the intuition of Peace, is of unique importance to the quest for civilized order and that the specific manner in which religion will serve is in providing grounds for hope that the despair consequent upon the realization of the inexorable fact of decay and passing away is transcendently overcome. The importance of the topic of religion becomes clear upon the recognition of the fact that the sense of Peace, a fundamental religious intuition, is an essential factor in the promotion of civilized order. "The essential truth that Peace demands is the conformation of Appearance to Reality. . . . A feeling of dislocation of Appearance from Reality . . . spells the decadence of civilization, by stripping from it the very reason for its existence" (AI 377, 378).

Individuals and societies which seek to uphold the cultural aims productive of civilization have in the intuition of Peace the guarantee of a tendency in the nature of things which lures toward the realization of Truthful Beauty, and which accepts the differential realizations of actual entities, harmonizing whatever it can. The final answer to the problem of combining novelty and germaneness in the transition from Reality to Appearance, is to be found by recourse to the intuition of Peace, a distinctly religious vision. And the briefest and most relevant characterization of an uncivilized society is that it is one in which the intuition of Peace is lacking, for such an intuition is the only guarantee against an individual's or a culture's losing the sense of being grounded in Reality.

2. A GENETIC ACCOUNT OF RELIGION

A second way of noting the relation between the cultural aim of Peace and the cultural interest of religion is to discuss the genetic or historical development of religion as Whitehead conceived it in his *Religion in the Making*. The "making" of religion is its development from a "primitive" social and moralistic interest to a "rational" religion in which the extreme generality of concern allows for a transcendence of any particular society or circumstance. In exposing Whitehead's theory of the development of religion, I shall be able to emphasize the specific function of the sense of Peace in a civilized society possessed of a rational religion. Whitehead's general theory of experience emphasizes the fact that the experiencing derives from physical, emotional data, and from actions and intentions in accordance with those data. Such a stress can only mean that, in considering the genesis of religion as a cultural interest, attention must be directed to its origin in actions and intentions which form the primary modes of human experience. This is precisely what Whitehead does in the historical segment of his *Religion in the Making*. Consonant with his type of naturalism, however, he does not attempt to discover the essence of religion in the primitive experiences from which it was born. He is concerned to discover the *terminus a quo* of primitive religious experience and expression in order to contrast it with the *terminus ad quem* expressed by the theory of rational religion implied in his philosophy.

Religious expression has its primary origin in the desire for re-enactment which is the ground of ritualistic impulses in human beings. Ritual, as "the habitual performance of definite actions which have no direct relevance to the preservation of the physical organisms of the actors" (RM 20), allows for the eliciting of emotions, primarily associated with paradigmatic events in the life of an individual or social group, without the necessity of an exact repetition of those events. In this way emotions are dissociated from their origin and artificially recalled through ritual. The aim of the ritual is to elicit a certain kind of emotion.

Insofar as ritual predominates, religion must be essentially a social phenomenon. For the eliciting of emotion is easier and more efficacious when a social grouping is involved in the ritual. And in primitive societies religious ritual provides the principal emotional bonds which join individuals to one another. An important incidental effect of ritual and other artificial forms of the stimulation of emotions is that the individuals who partake of these activities gain an increased range of emotional sensitivity. The emotions elicited by primitive ritual are, initially, closely associated with originally necessary activities. With increased free elaboration and variation of the original ritual forms, the individuals are allowed to perform actions and to experience emotions less closely bound to the narrow limits of the original experiences. Such deviations provide for an increasing subtlety and variety of emotional response.

Shifting to the speculative plane: one cannot fail to note here the importance of Whitehead's category of conceptual reversion as an explanatory device. This category, as was noted in Chapter II, allows for a consistent application of the principle that all conceptual feelings are derived from physical feelings. Yet it is able to explain the way in which the sublimations of physical feelings, such as those which take place in the development of religious ritual, can allow for novel experiences which are relatively detached from their primitive source. Whitehead's theory of conceptual reversion allows him to avoid, in his genetic investigations of cultural interests, the type of reductive analysis so common in naturalistic explanations.

According to Whitehead, the first approach to rationality in religion is to be found in the mythical elements inspired by a need to interpret the religious rituals and their connections with the elicited emotions. Myth approaches rationality since it serves to interpret experiences and actions, and, as such, is open to characterization as to its truth and falsity. "An idea arises from the antecedent establishment of modes of human functioning which are germane to it" (AI 320). In the case of religious ideas, modes of human functioning such as ritual activities stimulate conceptual valuations and/or reversions which result in the emergence into consciousness of concepts abstracted from religious practices and emotions which possess an analytic and interpretative power. Once the interpretation is constructed, there is a mutual relationship between the interpretative construct and the activities interpreted. In the case of religion, the myths constructed as explanations of the ritual and ritually educed emotions interpret the activities and emotions, and the activities and emotions express the myths.

> Two behaviour patterns mutually interpret each other, only when some common factor of experience is realized in the enactment of either pattern. The common factor constitutes the reason for the transition from one pattern to the other pattern. Each pattern interprets the other as expressive of that common factor [AI 320–321].

The common factor which serves as the reason for the transition between the patterns is the emotions. The myth interprets the ritual and its accompanying emotions and thus serves to explain the purpose of the ritual and the emotion; likewise, after the birth of the myth, the ritual interprets the myth as expressive of these same emotions.

Whiteheadian philosophy appears to give priority to ritual over myth in the development of religion. Anthropologists, on the other hand, generally tend toward a theory of the functional interdependence of myth and ritual, giving priority to neither. Thus Clyde Kluckhohn, after a general survey of the subject of myth and ritual, has said that "the factual record is perfectly straightforward in one respect: neither myth nor ritual can be postulated as 'primary.' " [1] Whitehead, on the other hand, seems to accept the view that ritual is primary and that myth functions as an explanation of ritual activities. But the category of reversion allows for exceptions to the theory that ideas emerge from actions. Thus, myths may precede their associated rituals on the Whiteheadian view. The category of reversion saves Whitehead's theory from a serious conflict with current anthropological theories concerning the relations of ritual and myths. But we are justified in making such an application of the category of reversion only in human experience. For Whitehead suggests the existence of ritualistic behavior even among animals, where myths would, of course, be absent (v. RM 25). Fundamentally, therefore, ritual precedes myth; but in human experience the category of conceptual reversion allows for the interdependence of myth and ritual.

Rituals, as has been indicated, set emotions free from their bondage to practical necessity. Myths function, in a similar fashion, to free thoughts from such necessity. Thus, whereas ritual inspires emotional sensitiveness, myths encourage the growth of imaginative feelings. Myths and rituals do not seem, at first, to allow for any relevant application of the questions of truth or falsity to non-rational religions. But truth-relations are entailed by ritualistic activities and mythical constructs. The discussion of symbols and propositional truth in regard to religious propositions given in Chapter IV may be consulted to clarify this particular aspect of Whitehead's theory of religion.

In ritual there is a dislocation, followed by elaboration and sublimation, of emotions from their original locus in practical necessity. In myth, thought transcends the immediate objects of perception. Imaginative feelings are evoked by the construction and entertainment of myths. At this stage religion is still lacking in sufficient rational organization to allow for private intellectual and emotional enjoyment. Beliefs are as yet uncoordinated, and the lack of coordination of basic beliefs entails the fact that religion is still, essentially, a social phenomenon. The social character of this type of religion necessarily follows from its lack of a coherently organized myth-structure since without such organization it is difficult for individuals to grasp the mutual relevance of the various factors of religion with sufficient completeness to allow for an enjoyment of religious experience apart from the social group. Under such conditions functions are specialized, and in a real sense the religion has no existence apart from the entire cult-group's performing its rituals, entertaining its myths, and experiencing the elicited emotions as a united complex.

A myth is entertained with the subjective form of belief. Belief in a myth is a belief in its efficacy in producing intended effects—be it the promotion of good or the avoidance of evil. Such belief is reinforced by the performance of the associated ritual, and, similarly, serves as a stimulus toward ritual activity. This more or less closed circle of ritual, emotion, myth, and belief is likely to be challenged only when a critical attitude is taken toward it by someone outside the circle.

Rational criticism of tribal religions is associated with the movement of individuals beyond the confines of their own tribal unity and their consequent subjection to novel ideas and practices. "Individuals were disengaged from their immediate social setting in ways which promoted thought" (RM 39). Such a movement promoted the transition of primitives from mere social consciousness to a world consciousness. When an individual's ideas and ethical intuitions are disengaged from a single finite social context, there is a transformation of the whole concept of religion. Social-consciousness concerns loyalty to one's immediate society, while world-consciousness "rises to the conception of an essential rightness of things" (RM 40). "Religion is world-loyalty" (RM 59).

The broadening of religion to the verge of rationality is a function of the transcendence of the particular limited contexts to which religious ideas are thought to be relevant. Whitehead's discussion of the Roman and Judaic religions in this regard makes this point clear. In the case of the former, a degree of rationality was obtained by maintaining the widest possible vision of geographical and social inclusion; in the latter case, the Jews sought to express the religious ideas in the broadest possible terms, though maintaining their direct relevance only to the Jewish nation. Each of these examples, in different ways, points to tendencies toward increased rationality through extended generality.

Religion which has overcome the provincialities consequent upon finite loyalties, Whitehead terms "rational religion." It is "religion whose beliefs and rituals have been reorganized with the aim of making it the central element in a coherent ordering of life" (RM 30). Rational religion aims to be adequate both to man's thought and to his conduct. The development of a rational religion must presuppose the progressive acquisition of general ideas and ethical intuitions relevant to the common religious experience of man. The acquisition of such ideas and intuitions of religions is expressed in a primitive, tribal form. For this reason, among others, the development of religion in the direction of greater coherence and adequacy most often comes from critical minorities, mystical or prophetic. The mystic and the prophet appeal to standards which transcend the limited moral or political context within which a particular religion finds its locus.

In the course of his genetic account of religion, Whitehead delineates three types of religious expressions. These may be termed: the tribal, the social, and the universal. The tribal religion accepts uncritically the myths and rituals as expressions of its own narrow social unity. The social type illustrates communal religion, partly rationalized and extending its area of concern intellectually, and/or geographically, and culturally, to ever-wider areas. The universal religions express a world-consciousness which entails both the universal applicability of their religious ideas and the particular relevance of their religious practices. The great religions of the world, such as Buddhism and Christianity, are examples of this last type.

Whitehead's emphasis upon the element of solitariness in religion seems to be a direct implication of the universal relevance of religion's rational forms. Tribal or social religions concern the relation of a selected finite social grouping to the object of religious experience. Recalling our discussion of morality in Chapter V: this simply means that primitive religion is more concerned with moral than with specifically religious value. The universalizing of religion entails the individual's disconnection from any finite surrounding, with the accompanying increase in the importance of solitariness. As long as the religion must be concerned with the ethical and political considerations stemming from ideas and intuitions relevant only to a finite selection of individuals, the religion will be essentially a social phenomenon.

With the growth of a self-consciously affirmed universality, world-consciousness takes precedence over social-consciousness, with the result that religious truths take the universal rather than the social or tribal form. In primitive religions, spiritual problems were danced out; in rational religion they are prayed out or thought out. In rational religion loyalty to a finite group is replaced by loyalty to the totality of individuals. Thus world-consciousness is a disengaged consciousness. "The individuals are indifferent, because unknown" (RM 40). It is this indifference which precludes such a consciousness from serving as the basis for moral reasonings.

This genetic account of religion suggests the significance of the relationship between the rationalization of religion and the increasing importance of individuality and universal experience in Whitehead's theory of religion. The universalizing of religion through the development of generally applicable ideas interpreting religious experiences entails the individual's disconnection from any finite loyalty, with the increase in the importance of solitariness. This means that Peace, as a religious intuition, functions in distinction from moral or ethical concepts which seek to relate to finite social contexts.

3. THE RELIGIOUS INSIGHT

In our examination of the fundamental religious intuitions, we found that Peace functions in relation to religious experience as a sense of deliverance from the destructive threat of the transience of existence. In the genetic account of religion just rehearsed, we have provided the basis for the conclusion that the context within which Peace is realized transcends moral and social contexts and finds its expression in the realization of permanence radically transcendent of any finite context. We shall find in our consideration of what Whitehead terms the "Religious Insight" a further specification of the importance of the concept of Peace as a religious intuition in promoting the aims of civilization.

We come now to the difficult task of outlining the civilizing function of Peace in relation to Whitehead's metaphysical interpretation of religion. In comparing the sense of Peace with holiness and permanent rightness, we were able to clarify the function of Peace as a religious intuition. And by considering the genetic development of religion from its primitive to its rational form, we specified the relation of Peace as a sense of transcendence to the progressive development from tribal through social to universal religions. Now we must place the sense of Peace in the context of Whitehead's religious insight, the metaphysical elaboration of religious experience.

In *Religion in the Making* Whitehead explicitly considers the metaphysical elaboration of religious experience. In *Process and Reality,* the doctrine of God is discussed both as an interpretation of religious experience and as a metaphysical concept whose functioning is determined by non-religious, metaphysical needs (v. PR 315-316). In *Adventures of Ideas*, the issue is civilized experience and expression, and the sense of Peace is considered in terms of its civilizing efficacy. In spite of these differences we shall find that a consideration of Peace in relation to the religious insight and Whitehead's concept of God will go a long way toward bringing us to an understanding of the importance of Peace and religion to the problem of civilization.

The discussion of religious experience in terms of generic metaphysical concepts is a natural implication of Whitehead's theory of religion. For "religion is the longing of the spirit that the facts of existence should find their justification in the nature of existence" (RM 83). Clearly, therefore, rational religion will require a recourse to metaphysics for general concepts with which to express the emotions and ideas originating in concrete religious experiences.

> The religious insight is the grasp of this truth: That the order of the world, the depth of reality of the world, the value of the world in its whole and in its parts, the beauty of the world, the zest of life, the peace of life, and the mastery of evil, are all bound together—not accidentally, but by reason of this truth: that the universe exhibits a creativity with infinite freedom, and a realm of forms with infinite possibilities; but that this creativity and these forms are together impotent to achieve actuality apart from the completed ideal harmony, which is God [RM 115].

The difference between the phenomenological account of religious experience and this more speculative description is an important one. By recourse to metaphysical description Whitehead hopes to devise religious concepts which will strike deeply into the reality of religious intuitions. The concepts utilized in this metaphysical description are those of the "formative elements" (v. RM 87) which go to form the actual, temporal world. These elements are Creativity, Eternal Objects, and God. The formative elements are so named because the metaphysical description set out in *Religion in the Making*, elucidating Whitehead's phenomenological account of religious experience, is based upon an analysis of the universe into the actual, temporal world and the elements formative of this world. The formative elements are, therefore, fundamental notions in Whitehead's metaphysical description and, as such, are meant to be relevant to all aspects of experience, including religious experience.

The first formative element is "the creativity whereby the actual world has its character of temporal passage to novelty" (RM 88). This notion is surely one of the most problematic in Whitehead's philosophy. Creativity is the "universal of universals characterizing ultimate matter of fact" (PR 31). It is the principle of novelty. The finitude of any given state of nature will always be passing beyond itself to the realization of novel instances of creativity. "The creative process is rhythmic: it swings from the publicity of many things to the individual privacy; and it swings back from the private individual to the publicity of the objectified individual" (PR 229). The creative advance from the disjunctively many elements in the past actual world of a given concrescence to the conjunctive unity of a concrescent occasion is conceived to be a regular process whereby "creation produces natural pulsation, each pulsation forming a natural unit of historic fact" (MT 88).

Creativity is the principle in Whitehead's philosophy accounting for rhythmic, novel process. Creative process may be understood in relation to the fact of transition in the universe. Transition constitutes that character of things whereby an actualized entity enters the constitution of a concrescing occasion via objectification. The element of transition insures the rhythm of becoming and the becoming of continuity in the universe. Creativity provides the pure notion of activity which, along with the epochal character of temporal actual entities, accounts for such becoming.

Two principles basic to Whitehead's philosophy provide a means for grasping the significance of the notion of creativity. These are the principle of relativity and the ontological principle. According to the ontological principle, all reasons are actual occasions. The principle of relativity states that "It belongs to the nature of a 'being' that it is a potential for every 'becoming' " (PR 33). That is, all entities possess the potentiality for contributing to the constitution of a concrescence. "The whole world conspires to produce a new creation" (RM 109). Creativity may only be analyzed in terms of its instantiations as actual entities. This is true for both modes of process in which creativity is expressed: concrescence and transition. Creativity *for* a given occasion—i.e., as relevant to the transition from one occasion to another—is characterizable in terms of the principle of relativity which requires the character of universal potentiality of actual entities for concrescing occasions. In its function as a self-creative act of concrescence, creativity is to be understood in terms of the ontological principle.

In discussing the concept of abstraction in Chapter V, I concluded that Whitehead attempts to maintain a balance between the extreme views illustrated by the Neoplatonists on the one hand and by Bergsonian philosophy on the other. Whereas for the Neoplatonist the most real is the greatest of formal abstractions, for Bergson the reality is concrete, intuitive experience. No doubt Whitehead shares some of the Bergsonian antipathy toward sheer formal abstractions. And if the choice had to be made between the Bergsonian and the Neoplatonic conceptions of the status of abstractions, probably Whitehead would opt in favor of Bergson. But Whitehead does not think that the choice must be made. Whitehead's aim is to cultivate intuitions the generalization of which will allow the philosopher to strike more deeply into the roots of reality. Whitehead's attempt to balance the extremes with regard to the views of the value of abstractions require him to uphold the view of the mutual and dialectical interdependence of percept and concept, of intuition and generalization. For this reason notions such as creativity have a dual role in Whitehead's philosophy. They function both as intuitions of concrete experience and as universals, conceptual constructs which characterize these primary intuitions. In the first role, creativity resembles Bergson's *élan vital*; in the second, Plato's Form of the Good.

In the initial discussion of creativity in Chapter I, we were more concerned with its formal metaphysical character. It may equally well be discussed as a concrete intuition. The intuitive status of creativity can best be seen if it is taken to supply an answer to Heidegger's ontological question "Why is there something rather than nothing at all?" The experience of radical contingency, so much a part of the human situation as characterized by existential philosophers, shares the character of a religious experience since, on Whiteheadian terms, it is an expression of the relation of the finite individual (in his solitariness) to the totality of things. The religious insight which manifests a "creativity with infinite freedom" provides us with a sense of the contingency of things. But, as we shall soon see, when this intuition is combined with an intuition of God, one has a partial answer to the threat of that contingency through an assurance of creative passage.

As I noted in Chapter I, Whitehead, as a metaphysician, was not primarily interested in the question which Heidegger poses. He is much more concerned with the constitution of the world than with its ontological viability. The question asked by Whitehead is "What kinds of things are there?" or "What are the most general characteristics of the things which exist?" This concern means that Whitehead stresses more the formally abstract character of the concept of creativity than its status as a concrete intuition.

The second formative element is the realm of eternal objects "which are in themselves not actual, but are such that they are exemplified in everything that is actual, according to some proportion of relevance" (RM 88). This "realm of forms with infinite possibilities" (RM 115) is part of what Whitehead terms the religious insight. Eternal objects function, via ingression, in the self-creation of each actual entity. An eternal object is an entity "whose conceptual recognition does not involve a necessary reference to any definite actual entities of the temporal world" (PR 70). Eternal objects are potentialities. Actual occasions as formally constituted are wholly determinate. The definiteness of actual occasions is brought about by their determination by eternal objects which are, of themselves, neutral as to their ingression into any actual occasion. "The actualities constituting the process of the world are conceived as exemplifying the ingression (or 'participation') of other things which constitute the potentialities of definiteness for any actual existence" (PR 63). No actual occasion has any character apart from the character given it by its eternal objects. Eternal objects determine the manner in which the world of actual entities enters into the constitution of each one of its members via its feelings. The physical feelings

which initiate concrescence are mediated by eternal objects functioning rela-
tionally—i.e., eternal objects shared by the concrescing subject and the objectified entity.

Eternal objects are pure potentialities. As such they contrast with the
actualities of the temporal world. Novelty is insured only if there are, in
addition to the actualities of any given pulse of temporal process, potentialities which define possible but non-actual states of affairs. An eternal object
is, in contrast to an actual entity, a *potential* entity (v. PR 72).

Eternal objects as potentialities, as forms of definiteness, come in a variety of species.[2] Sense-data, mathematical forms, forms of imperfection
("mud," "dirt"), philosophical concepts (Creativity, Beauty, Peace), are
all examples of what Whitehead means by the term "eternal object." One
particular example, forms of imperfection, raises the question of the relation of Whitehead's doctrine of eternal objects to Plato's theory of forms.
The well-known passage from the *Parmenides* in which Socrates balks at
including forms of imperfection in the realm of Eternal Ideas expresses
Plato's bias toward the concept of perfection as *ideal*. Whitehead does not
limit the term perfection to its ideal expression and, therefore, finds no
difficulty in including forms of imperfection among "pure possibilities."
"Forms are essentially referent beyond themselves. It is mere phantasy to
impute to them any 'absolute reality', which is devoid of implications beyond itself" (MT 69). Plato's view that only forms are perfect is denied by
Whitehead. An eternal object reaches beyond itself for realization in the
temporal world. "Muddiness is referent to mud, and forms of evil require
evil things" (MT 69). As William Christian astutely observes for Whitehead, "a form is not more 'perfect' than a thing." [3]

Although Whitehead compares his concept of eternal objects to the Platonic theory of forms, it is clear that there is a radical difference between
the two concepts. As the Platonist Robert Brumbaugh has informally re-
marked, "Whitehead is Plato turned upside down." The inversion of Platonic doctrine which Brumbaugh notes is clearly seen by comparing the
Whiteheadian concept of "ingression" with the Platonic theory of "participation." Whitehead seems to use the terms interchangeably. But soon the
difference becomes quite clear. For Plato the world of becoming participated
in the forms; for Whitehead eternal objects participate ("ingress") into
temporal actual entities. For Plato the forms were the fundamental realities;
for Whitehead the fundamental realities are the temporal actual entities.
And though Whitehead can still make such Platonic statements as "the
things which are temporal arise by their participation in the things which
are eternal" (PR 63), his meaning is suspiciously un-Platonic. For the ontological principle inverts the relative importance of "temporal" and "eternal"
data in Whiteheadian philosophy. Actual entities are the only reasons. The
forms are in the facts.

As a part of the religious insight, the functions of eternal objects which are of most significance are: (1) their determination of the formal character of actual occasions; and (2) the fact that they are the source of all novelty. The order of the world, the beauty of the world, the zest for life, etc., which provide the primary data the reflection upon which evokes the religious insight, require the intuition of the infinitude of possibilities, as well as a sense of creative process.

But the essence of the religious insight is the intuition of "the completed ideal harmony" apart from which neither the creativity nor the possibilities could achieve actuality. What Whitehead terms the religious insight seems to be a theistic insight. It involves grasping the truth that all order, all value, all beauty, etc., are bound together by virtue of the existence of an ideal harmony which guides creativity and possibility toward the harmonious actualizations of temporal process. This ideal harmony is termed "God."

It is important to recognize, however, that a theistic *insight* is to be distinguished from a religious *intuition*. The status of the concept of "God" in Whitehead's philosophy is highly problematic. For the most part Whitehead speaks of "God" as an interpretation of religious experience (v. PR 518) which lacks the same intuitional status as other fundamental notions. In seeking to found rational religion upon "a direct intuition of a righteousness in the nature of things, functioning as a condition, a critic, and an ideal" (RM 62), Whitehead excludes the concept of divine personality as a fundamental object of direct religious intuition. Noting that Hindu, Confucian, and Buddhist religions have rejected the notion of the intuition of any ultimate personality substrate to the nature of things, and that in the Western world, Christianity and the rational religions of Greece have normally held the belief in a personal God to be based upon an inference, Whitehead points to the necessity of falling back upon the essential agreement of rational religions on "the concept of a rightness in things, partially conformed to and partially disregarded" (RM 65).

Whitehead argues at some length that the notion of a personal God is not an immediate deliverance of intuitive awareness.[4] His arguments in *Religion in the Making* are based mainly on the fact that most of the great religions of the world do not hold to such a view. But, as we have seen, the denial of direct intuition of a personal God is implied, as well, by Whitehead's own description of the intuition of the holy and the sense of Peace. Both Whitehead's historical phenomenology and his phenomenology of individual religious experience lead to the de-emphasis of the element of personality in the construction of a concept of God.

Even though there may be no phenomenological evidence supporting the belief in a direct intuition of the personality of God, Whitehead does not explicitly deny that God is a person or has person-like qualities. This is significant. For, on Whiteheadian principles, such a denial must await the additional evidence provided by a rational interpretation of the phenomenological evidence. For as I have stressed before, rational constructions (i.e., concepts, theories, etc.), though derived from concrete intuitions, are not mere descriptions of these intuitions. The rationalization of experience may provide the means for a more complete analysis of the concrete data of experience. Thus, even though our intuitions do not lead us directly to envision a personal Deity, the metaphysical elaboration of the relevant intuitions may provide evidence for such a view. In any case, the concept of God as a concept interpretative of religious experience has played fundamental roles in Whitehead's metaphysical elaboration of religion. But this concept, it must be remembered, bears only a slight family resemblance to the Judaeo-Christian concept of God. The differences between Whitehead's "God" and the orthodox "God" will be exploited in a later chapter when we discuss the twentieth-century phenomenon of the collapse of the Judaeo-Christian paradigm.

The distinction between "God" as a concept and the religious intuitions which characterize religion is important, for it allows us to understand the relevance of the religious intuition of Peace as a feeling of Eros and of the Unity of Adventure with the religious insight of God as "completed ideal harmony." For in comparing the essence of the religious insight with the sense of Peace, we find that we are dealing with alternate expressions of the same fundamental vision. The completed ideal harmony which expresses the fundamental unity of the religious insight is the content of the sense of Peace. But, paradoxically enough, the sense of Peace is religious in a way in which the doctrine of God is not. The mere provision of initial aims is not, in itself, a religious function. God becomes a religious object when His functioning is set in the context of the totality of experiencing and when the sense of some guarantee of permanence amid the flux is evoked. Peace is just such a sense, but "God" may be encountered as a problem, metaphysically, as well as a religious object. Not so, the sense of Peace. Whitehead treats the concept of Peace as a limiting concept the meaning of which is to be evoked, not completely grasped, in conceptual terms. The language employed to discuss the concept is evocative, metaphorical, and vague. Whereas, at times, Whitehead's discussion of "God" is precise and rigorous, it is never precise in relation to the sense of Peace. Whitehead's metaphorical and poetic language concerning God is saved for Part V of *Process and Reality*. In other portions of that work he describes quite clearly the metaphysical functions of God. It is no doubt for this reason, among others, that Whitehead did not employ as explicitly as he might have the metaphysical language of *Process and Reality* to describe the religious sense of Peace. God's subjective aim at ideal harmony associated with the primordial nature of God is discussed in *Adventures of Ideas* as "Eros," the Platonic concept of "life and mind." God's consequent nature, as discussed in *Process and Reality*, becomes "the Unity of Adventure" in *Adventures of Ideas*. Peace, as we have noted before, is the sense of the Unity of Adventure, including "the Eros which is the living urge towards all possibilities" (AI

381). What Whitehead understands as God's religious function in *Religion in the Making*—i.e., serving as "a completed ideal harmony"—is closely akin to the notion of God in *Adventures of Ideas*. The completed ideal Harmony which gives actuality to the infinite freedom of creativity and the infinite possibilities of Eternal Objects is the Unity of Adventure which is the source of the intuition of Peace. The relationship between the intuition of Peace and Whitehead's concept of God will be clarified by discussing the relation between God and the world of actual occasions in the process of becoming.

Four creative phases constitute a completed event in the Whiteheadian universe. There is, first, the phase of conceptual origination, and, second, the temporal phase of physical origination. The third phase is that of "perfected actuality, in which the many are one everlastingly, without the qualification of any loss either of individual identity or of completeness of unity" (PR 532). From the perspective of an individual actual occasion, the first phase constitutes the provision of the initial aim from God. The second is the origination of the temporal concrescent process via physical prehension. The third phase is the reception into God's consequent nature of the objectively immortal actual occasion. In addition to these phases, there is a fourth in which

> the perfected actuality passes back into the temporal world, and qualifies this world so that each temporal actuality includes it as an immediate fact of relevant experience. . . . The kingdom of heaven is with us today. The action of the fourth phase is the love of God for the world. It is the particular providence for particular occasions [PR 532].

Adequately to conceptualize these successive phases requires that two elements be held in mind in approaching the explication of the creative cycle. The first element is the concept of God in His appropriate primordial and consequent functioning. The second is the world of actual occasions in their subject-superject character. The primordial function of God may be termed "God as lure"; the consequent nature may be designated "judgment." The subjective character of the actual occasion will be termed "appetition"; the superjective character will be termed "satisfaction." God lures and judges; the world "hungers" and is satisfied. The world's appetition is a response to God's lure; God's judgment is a response to the world's satisfaction.

If we concern ourselves with the human mind-body complex, summed up as it is in the temporal string of presiding occasions, the following application of the notion of the four creative phases may be made: The self decides upon a relevant ideal or aim, and seeks, through recourse to the material means at its disposal, to achieve this aim; its successive achievements are registered in God's consequent nature, harmonized whenever possible, and made relevant again to the temporal world. By and large, the relevance will be greatest for the self whose past acts they are. Thus, memory takes on paramount importance here with respect to the providential activity of God.

The judgment of the self's temporal achievements is itself partially accomplished through the very acts of the self in question. Thus, the action of a present self, through the mediation of God, becomes relevant—for good or ill—for a future self, and derivatively, for the entire present and future temporal world. God is both "lure" and "judge," and both functions are aspects of divine providence. The world is both subject and objectively immortal superject, and both aspects contribute to the temporal agency of the world. The cyclical movement of God's providential activity, manifest as lure and judge, combined with the temporal advance of the actual world, implies that what initially began as final cause re-enters the world as efficient cause in order to qualify future final causation.

The fourfold activity, in terms of which the relations of God and the world are considered above, provides a proper matrix for the understanding of the interrelations of the three formative elements we have been discussing as components of the religious insight. In the discussion of the concept of creativity as a component of the category of the ultimate in *Process and Reality,* Whitehead notes that "the ultimate metaphysical principle is the advance from disjunction to conjunction, creating a novel entity other than the entities given in disjunction. . . . The many become one, and are increased by one" (PR 32). The character of temporal process is one of the rhythmic pulsation of plural entities achieving novel togetherness. "The oneness of the universe, and the oneness of each element in the universe, repeat themselves to the crack of doom in the creative advance from creature to creature" (PR 347). The phases of (1) conceptual origination of initial aims for actual occasions, (2) physical origination of actual occasions, (3) their physical reception into consequent unification, and (4) their subsequent reintroduction into the temporal world, are phases of this rhythmic process of the world's becoming many and becoming one.

The vision of God as implicated in the four creative phases constituting the rhythmic process of temporal advance includes the intuition of the creative advance from the infinite possibilities for novelty and the consequent unity of the divine action. The basic metaphysical principle of advance from disjunction to conjunction of the actual occasions constituting the temporal world involves the same fundamental elements as does the religious insight. Thus, Whitehead's basic religious intuition and his basic metaphysical intuition are of the same nature. That is to say, Whitehead's description of religious experience in more phenomenological terms is compatible with fundamental concepts of his metaphysical theory. Reverting again to the metaphysical discussion of the intuition of Peace should make this conclusion obvious. "At the heart of the nature of things, there are always the dream of youth and the harvest of tragedy. The Adventure of the Universe starts with the dream and reaps tragic Beauty" (AI 381).

The "dream of youth" here mentioned is that aim associated with God's subjective aim at ideal harmony. The "harvest of tragedy" is the consequent actualization of the ideal. It is tragic because of the finitude of all perfections and the necessary exclusion which all realization brings. "Decay, Transition, Loss, Displacement belong to the essence of the Creative Advance" (AI 368–369). Youth, which Whitehead defines as "Life as yet untouched by tragedy" (AI 369), is the expression of that Eros, "the agency whereby ideas obtain efficiency in the creative advance" (AI 188). Tragic Beauty is the final unity of Appearance which is woven from a Reality with "the real occasions of the advancing world each claiming its due share of attention" (AI 381). The "Great Fact" is the object of the intuition of Peace because in its union of Youth and Tragedy, of Ideal and Actual, it has provided the sense of each occasion of the world as valued in terms of both its ideal possibilities and its concrete actuality. This Unity of Adventure which is the Realization of Divine Agency in the world is the consequent unity of God including the subjective aim at ideal harmony. The subjective aim, the Eros, is not a mere static envisagement of ideal possibilities. Eros is "the soul in the enjoyment of its creative function" (AI 189). The process of experience is spoken of as "absorption into a new unity with ideals and with anticipation, by the operation of the creative Eros" (AI 356). The Eros is dynamic; it is *creative*. It is "the urge towards the realization of ideal perfection" (AI 354). The element of creativity is bound up with the idea of Eros, or God's subjective aim at Ideal Harmony.

Whitehead employs two concepts to delineate two basic meanings of Peace. The concept of Youth evokes the meaning of Peace as involved in a sense of Ideals; the concept of Tragedy interprets the sense of Peace as related to actualizations. Peace as the crown of Youth is the transcendence of one's individuality by commitment to ideals which transcend personal satisfaction. The sense of the value of high ideals is a peculiar quality of Youth. When there is surrender to ideals based upon a sense of their intrinsic worth, Peace may be obtained. Without such a possibility Adventure would be at a minimum. "Vigorous societies harbour a certain extravagance of objectives, so that men wander beyond the safe provision of personal gratifications" (AI 371).

But between Peace as the crown of youth and Peace as the issue of tragedy there are a number of feelings which approximate that intuition. The other side of the coin from the self-forgetfulness of youth committed to transcendent ideals is the desire for fame, "that last infirmity of noble mind," which leads to an acceptance of the world of others merely as the environment which promotes the realization of self. The desire for fame "involves the feeling that each act of experience is a central reality, claiming all things as its own" (AI 372). In itself an inversion of the social impulse which gives rise to the self-forgetful commitment of transcendent ideals, the desire for fame nonetheless presupposes a social reality beyond the person. Without an audience, or a following, fame would be a meaningless concept. Pure egoism, therefore, is impossible. In the egoistic impulse we see reflected that concern for the worth of a transcendent environment without which there could be no sense of Peace.

Besides the desire for fame, Whitehead finds in the love of particular individual things another perversion of the feeling from which arises the sense of Peace. For in the love of a particular thing there is an indirect form of self-forgetfulness. There has been a transcendence of individuality, but only in a definite and limited way. At its lowest level personal love is nothing more than an attachment to something or someone serving to bring selfish happiness. When such is the case, love renders transcendence impossible. Even the kind of love which leads one to live vicariously through the other (e.g., the love of the father for his son who has realized all the successes which the father never had) is a non-transcendent substitute for the purer emotions leading to self-forgetfulness and to Peace.

There are examples of love which brings transcendence. "Greater love has no man than this, that he lay down his life for a friend." The love which leads to devotion to another often leads away from selfishness and toward a love "where the potentialities of the loved object are felt passionately as a claim that it find itself in a friendly Universe" (AI 373). This kind of love is the sense of Eros which hovers between Peace as the crown of youth and Peace as the issue of tragedy. Eros, which expresses itself in individuals as the "desire for the beautiful result, in this instance" (AI 373), is the closest approximation of the sense of Peace both in its "ideal" and in its "actual" modalities. In Eros there is self-forgetfulness in relation to ideal possibilities, but such possibilities are referred to a single individual. The feeling which expresses the sense of Peace as the issue of tragedy involves a broadening of the sense of Eros to include all individuals, and an intuition of the actualization of the ideal possibilities in relation to these individuals with the consequent transience and decay of perfections.

Between Peace as the crown of youth and Peace as the issue of tragedy lie the complex feelings of desire for fame, love of individual things, the self-forgetful love of another. This is one reason why the concept of Peace is a difficult one to explicate. It is for this reason that I have dwelt upon alternate characterizations of the religious intuition and upon the genetic development of the religious interest. The sense of the holy as a feeling of the value of a finite detail for the totality of things involves precisely the kind of transcendence which gives rise to the sense of Peace. The movement from tribal to universal religions again expresses the need to promote the sense of radical transcendence with which we identify the intuition of Peace. The reason why I have elaborated so upon the meaning of Whitehead's concept of Peace will be evident in the following chapters, for I shall there discuss the relationship between the religious vision of Peace and the cultural interests of art, morality, science, and philosophy in order to demonstrate the civilizing agency of the sense of Peace. In so doing, we shall be able to understand the profound interpretative value of the concepts of cultural aims and interests in promoting the understanding of the meaning of civilized experience.

NOTES

1. "Myths and Rituals: A General Theory," *The Harvard Theological Review,* 35 (1942), 45–79. See also Bronislaw Malinowski, "Myth in Primitive Psychology," *Magic, Science and Religion* (Garden City: Doubleday, 1954), pp. 93–148.

2. See W. A. Christian, *An Interpretation of Whitehead's Metaphysics* (New Haven: Yale University Press, 1959), pp. 202–203, for an inventory of some of the many types of eternal objects.

3. *Ibid.,* p. 203.

4. On this point, one should note Charles Hartshorne's counterclaim that an alternative method of generating a Whiteheadian metaphysics is to consider the theistic intuition rather than the intuition of creativity, or the category of the ultimate, as primary. See "Whitehead's Novel Intuition," *Alfred North Whitehead: Essays on His Philosophy* (Englewood Cliffs: Prentice-Hall, 1963), pp. 21–22. In an article entitled "Whitehead Without God," *The Christian Scholar* 50, No. 3 (Fall 1967), 257–264, and reprinted in *Process Philosophy and Christian Thought,* edd. Delwin Brown et al. (New York: Bobbs-Merrill, 1971), pp. 305–328, Donald Sherburne has contended that the concept of "God" is not essential to Whiteheadian philosophy and has proposed to "naturalize" Whiteheadian metaphysics through omission of the concept of God and its theoretical accouterments. My own position is contained in "The Autonomy of Religion in Whitehead's Philosophy," *Philosophy Today,* 13, No. 4 (Winter 1969), 271–283. There I argue that "God" as an interpretation of religious experience is not a fundamental intuition and, therefore, cannot serve to ground Whitehead's metaphysics. But I also contend that the omission of the concept from Whiteheadian analysis would not fundamentally affect the religious tonality of Whitehead's thought as Sherburne's attempt at a naturalized metaphysics would suggest.

PART THREE

SOME IMPLICATIONS OF THE THEORY

Chapter VII

RELIGION AND THE CULTURAL PROBLEM

THE BURDEN OF THIS CHAPTER will be to uncover that general condition of intellectual culture which Whiteheadian philosophy suggests as the primary threat to the maintenance of a civilized society. Analysis of this "cultural problem" should provide the basis for understanding the necessity for harmonious relations between cultural aims and cultural interests in a civilized society. After an outline of the cultural problem in this chapter, I shall proceed, in the closing chapters, to examine in some detail the effects of this problem upon the exercise of the interests, and the realization of the aims, which define civilized culture.

1. THE RELIGIOUS PROBLEM

In our discussion of the religious insight, we discovered that the formative elements of Whitehead's metaphysical system express his fundamental religious vision. This direct correlation between Whitehead's metaphysics and his theory of religion was also shown in our analysis of the concept of Peace to involve each of those fundamental qualities which make for success in attaining balanced intensity of experiencing. It should not be surprising, therefore, that Whitehead's analysis of the fundamental problem of existence—the cosmological problem—has a religious interpretation.

> The world is . . . faced by the paradox that, at least in its higher actualities, it craves for novelty and yet is haunted by terror at the loss of the past, with its familiarities and its loved ones. It seeks escape from time in its character of "perpetually perishing" [PR 516].

This cosmological problem is encountered by each occasion of experience as it faces the fact that time is a "perpetual perishing." There is an aim on the part of occasions of experience for novelty and intensity of experience. There is, on the other hand, a concern for the maintenance of a grounding in the past experiences of one's world. This is the concern for balance and germaneness in experience. But the temporal and epochal character of the actual world of process insures that the past cannot be preserved in its subjective immediacy. The fading of the past results from the fact that temporality, by definition, is a result of the objectification of past actualities by present experiences. And "objectification involves elimination. The present fact has not the past fact with it in any full immediacy" (PR 517). This problem is "cosmological" in the sense that it is a general problem of existence, affecting each occasion of experience. Whitehead also terms the problem "religious" insofar as it is the principal theme of rational religions. "This is the problem which gradually shapes itself as religion reaches its higher phases in civilized communities" (PR 517). Until the development of rational religions with their visions of radical transcendence, the cosmological problem was not fully recognized. Once recognized, it becomes a religious problem which determines the shape and character of the religious interest. Thus the sense of Peace is the capstone of civilized experience precisely because it is the solution of the religious problem. For just as "the most general formulation of the religious problem is the question whether the process of the temporal world passes into the formation of other actualities, bound together in an order in which novelty does not mean loss" (PR 517), so the most general formulation of the religious solution is the sense of Peace certifying just such a conquest of perpetual perishing.

Here we see a fundamental implication of Whitehead's method of analogical generalization which itself is an implication of the continuity of types of existence expressed in his theory of the actual occasion. The aim of each individual experience at balanced complexity is the basis for the *cultural* aims of Art, Adventure, Truth, Beauty, and Peace. The concern of each occasion of experience for novelty and germaneness is a concern involved in experience at every ontic level. The realization of balanced complexity through the experience of Eros and the Unity of Adventure, unconsciously attained by occasions below the level of personal experiencing, becomes the basis for the resolution of a distinctly *human* problem when interpreted through the religious interest in human culture. The value of such a tightly interwoven skein of analogical relationships is, as we have seen many times before, largely the result of the increased interpretative power of a philosophic scheme in which the primary concerns of individual human cultural existence may be understood in terms of the same principles which explain the basic ontological units of existence. I shall be taking full advantage of the analogical relations between metaphysical and cultural aspects of existence uncovered in previous chapters in my consideration of the relationship of the religious and cultural expressions of the fundamental, cosmological, problem confronting experience.

The cosmological problem has two sides to it. "There is the double problem: actuality with permanence, requiring fluency as its completion; and actuality with fluency, requiring permanence as its completion" (PR 527). In this form the problem can be dealt with successfully only by a recognition of the mutual efficacy and individual incompleteness of the elements of permanence and flux. In religious terms the vision of Peace as the Unity of Adventure, including the Eros which drives toward the perfection of harmony, meets both aspects of the cosmological problem. The detailed discussion of the cosmological problem, however, requires that we supplement our understanding of the concepts of Peace as Eros and as Unity of Adventure by recourse to Whitehead's concept of "God."

The primordial nature of God, expressed at any given moment of the temporal world as God's subjective aim toward the perfection of harmony, expresses the character of permanence as establishing order in the temporal world. The reception of the temporal world into everlastingness, and its transformation in accordance with God's primordial appetition, is the consequent function of God in the world. This consequent function provides to the temporal world objective immortality with the preservation of immediacy. But this is possible only in combination with "the primordial permanence of God, whereby the creative advance ever re-establishes itself endowed with initial subjective aim derived from the relevance of God to the evolving world" (PR 527). God, in His primordial conceptual unity, seeks physical multiplicity. This multiplicity derives from the finite actualities of the temporal world whose *telos* is toward a unity which provides everlastingness of immediacy. Thus are God and the World interdependent. Yet neither can ultimately satisfy the other, for "both are in the grip of the ultimate metaphysical ground, the creative advance into novelty" (PR 529).

> The theme of Cosmology, which is the basis of all religions, is the story of the dynamic effort of the World passing into the everlasting unity, and of the static majesty of God's vision, accomplishing its purpose of completion by absorption of the World's multiplicity of effort [PR 529–530].

Whitehead's characterization of the religious problem emphasizes the fact of perpetual perishing, which evokes the question of whether beyond the flux of temporal passage there is an order in which the value of achieved perfections is preserved. The essence of the religious problem, so defined, is the finitude of existence. We have encountered the problem involved in the fact of the finite character of experience again and again in relation to our discussions of the sense of Peace. We also have had occasion to note a second aspect of the problem of attaining civilized experience. For, in addition to the fact of finitude, there is the threatened dislocation of Appearance and Reality implied in the failure to achieve a balance of novelty and germaneness in an occasion of experience.

The religious problem requires for its interpretation the concepts of creativity and of God in His appropriate primordial and consequent functionings. That is to say, it is the religious insight of creativity, the infinitude of possibilities, and the completed ideal harmony which provides the answer to the cosmological, or religious, problem. It is important to recognize just what this means: the intuition of Peace is possible only when the drive toward ideal harmony, which is the Eros-character of existence, is successful in realizing a Unity of Adventure in which physical realization achieves everlastingness.

The solution to the religious problem, concerned as it is with both conceptual appetition and physical realization, involves two fundamental aspects of existence. First, the solution depends upon the harmonious relationship of Appearance and Reality involved in the achievement of Truthful Beauty. No successful solution to the religious problem is possible if there is a dislocation of Appearance and Reality. Secondly, it involves the overcoming of the inherent finitude of individual experiences by recourse to the completed ideal harmony, the Unity of Adventure, which expresses the result of divine agency in the world. The religious problem results from finitude and uprootedness as they characterize occasions of experience. The fact of finitude has been variously discussed before. I shall now attempt to elaborate upon the quality of *uprootedness*.

In her provocative philosophical analysis of the effects of World War II upon European culture, Simone Weil spoke of the characteristic of *rootedness* in the following way: "A human being has roots by virtue of his real, active, and natural participation in the life of a community, which preserves in living shape certain particular treasures of the past and certain particular expectations for the future." [1] Generalizing this concept of rootedness along Whiteheadian lines, one may say that any action which interferes with the attainment of a balance between novelty and germaneness to Reality in experiencing is contributing to a condition in which Appearance manifests a rootless character, bereft of causally efficacious derivation from the concrete world. It is the function of the Eros to offer persuasion toward the attainment of satisfactions properly rooted in Reality. The loss of such a connection brings on the experience of rootlessness.

At the level of human experiencing, there are two principal causes of the feeling of a dislocation of Reality and Appearance. The first is *ignorance*; the second is *perversity,* or the misuse of freedom. To clarify this contention, which extends the explicit meanings of some of Whitehead's statements, I shall discuss the possible effects of ignorance and of perversity on the realization of the aim of experience.

Whereas finitude is a characteristic of all actual occasions by virtue of the generic structure of Reality as a plurality of passing facts, ignorance, to some extent, is a contingent aspect of experience. Some ignorance does seem to be implied in the fact of the finite character of things, since ignorance is the result of negative prehensions, and negative prehensions are due to the perspective emphasis required by the standpoint in the extensive continuum. Still, a distinction may be made between the ignorance which results from finitude and that which is a contingent fact resulting in a disharmonious realization. Ignorance as a source of religious need is the kind of specific ignorance of individual occasions of experience which interferes with attainment of the aim at subjective intensity. Finitude is a presupposition of experiencing; ignorance of this type is an acquired condition.

Consider an adult human person. The personal order of presiding occasions defining that human person's past and present is such that the subjective aim given to the present presiding occasion is strongly influenced by the decisions and actions of the past presiding occasions of that personal order. The "ignorance" of that person is relative to the knowledge necessary for the optimum achievement of the initial aim. In a personal order of occasions $A, B, C, D \ldots$, where the initial aim given D is partially determined by the character of the satisfaction achieved by A, B, and C, ignorance is a factor which has a cumulative significance in undermining intensity of experiencing.

In addition to ignorance, there is a second factor of experiencing which may cause a dislocation of Appearance and Reality. This factor is perversity. The category of freedom and determination states that "the concrescence of each individual actual entity is internally determined and is externally free" (PR 41). If the ontological principle is combined with this categoreal obligation, one may define the limits of rationality with respect to the freedom of actual occasions. Rationality is guaranteed up to a point by the ontological principle which indicates that actual occasions will manifest internal determination. But there are limits to such rationality in the nature of things since the forms participating in the growth of an occasion, the discovery of which is the purpose of rational analysis, are given for that occasion. "No reason, internal to history, can be assigned why that flux of forms, rather than another flux, should have been illustrated. . . . The actual flux . . . does not disclose any peculiar character of 'perfection.' On the contrary, the imperfection of the world is the theme of every religion which offers a way of escape" (PR 74). The limits of rationalizability are a function of the givenness of experience.

The givenness of experience is a result of all decisions relevant to a certain experience, including the decisions of God and those of the occasions of the past actual world. This element of freedom, categoreally expressed in Whitehead's philosophy, entails a strange consequence. For it would appear from the above discussion that although, according to the ontological principle, actual entities are the only reasons, there are elements of experience which are extant and yet which are not "reasons" in the normal sense. Questions of freedom and self-determination lead one to the limits of rationalizability of the Whiteheadian universe; to ask for specific reasons for free, self-determining activity is to ask a systematically unanswerable question.

> The doctrine of the philosophy of organism is that, however far the sphere of efficient causation be pushed in the determination of components of a concrescence—its data, its emotions, its appreciations, its purposes, its phases of subjective aim—beyond the determination of these components there always remains the final reaction of the self-creative unity of the universe [PR 75].

This analysis of freedom may be interestingly compared to Augustine's discussion of the subject in *The City of God*. Augustine is concerned to show that there is no efficient cause of an evil will. He defines true freedom as obedience to the will of God.[2] Disobedience is a misuse of freedom. Such disobedience cannot be explained by anything except the evil will itself. "For what is it which makes the will bad, when it is the will itself which makes the action bad?"[3] There is no efficient cause, therefore, of an evil will —only a deficient one.

> For defection from that which supremely is, to that which has less of being—this is to begin to have an evil will. Now to seek to discover the causes of these defections—causes, as I have said, not efficient, but deficient —is as if someone sought to see darkness or hear silence. Yet both of these are known by us, and the former by means only of the eye, the latter only by the ear; but not by their positive actuality, but by their want of it.[4]

I think that Whitehead is making essentially the same point as Augustine when he claims that, no matter how far the sphere of efficient causation is pushed in the determinations of the components of a concrescence, there remains the final reaction of the self-creative unity of the universe. Whitehead seems to hold the view that God lures each actual occasion toward the one best possibility among a selection of relevant possibilities. There are three possible meanings of freedom in such circumstances: (*a*) there is freedom both to obey and to disobey God's lure, (*b*) there is freedom only to obey, or (*c*) there is freedom only to disobey. Both Augustine and Whitehead view freedom in the first of these three senses. Augustine allows two kinds of freedom—true freedom, which is obedience to the will of God, and the freedom to disobey, to choose contrary to God's will, which is the freedom of an evil will. And for Whitehead freedom is measured in terms both of conformity and of non-conformity to the lure of God. Obedience to God's lure results in the attainment of maximal subjective intensity amid the particular circumstances in question. Incomplete conformation to that lure will result in a less harmonious actualization. In searching for a reason for the free creative action of an occasion of experience, we shall be able to uncover its cause only insofar as complete conformation to God's lure is evident. In that instance the cause of an action is the final cause of God's persuasive

lure toward the most harmonious actualization. But if there is incomplete
conformation to the best among a set of relevant possibilities, no cause may
be discovered. The cause cannot be in the sphere of final causation since
God lures toward the best possibility. The cause is not discoverable in the
sphere of efficient causation, because of Whitehead's arguments quoted
above. There is neither efficient nor final cause of evil action. The "cause" is
the will of the actor itself.

Whitehead's concept of freedom and determination qualifies any Platonic
stress on the final importance of knowledge in overcoming existential flaws.
For the generalization from Platonic philosophy to the effect that knowledge
of truth entails action in accordance with that truth cannot be applied uni-
versally in a Whiteheadian world in which certain types of action (those
which do not precisely conform to God's lure for a given occasion) defy
rational analysis. The question of the misuse of freedom, and the importance
of ignorance as a causative factor in such misuse, must, therefore, be left
open. Such an openness allows room for the possible perverse use of freedom associated with positive evil actions.

There seems to be a conflict between Whitehead's characterization of the
religious problem mainly in terms of the finite character of experience and
its issue in perpetual perishing; and the implications of his philosophy which
lead to the conclusion that *ignorance* and *perversity* must also be considered
as an aspect of that problem. But the apparent conflict exists only if one
fails to take proper precautions to distinguish the ontological characteristics
grounding Whitehead's theory of religion from the ontic characteristics
relevant principally to human experiencing. For whereas perpetual perishing
is a characteristic of *all* experience, perversity and ignorance, presupposing
freedom and knowledge as they do, are peculiarly related to human experiencing. For knowledge and free will are only trivially expressed at levels
below that of conscious human experience. But at the level of the human
person, characterized by transience, freedom, and novel purpose, all three
religious needs are expressed. For transience entails perpetual perishing; the
possession of freedom entails the possibility of its misuse; and the fact of
novelty in a concrescence means that there is a greater leeway possible in
the choice of which of the possibilities provided by God will be realized. In
such instances ignorance about which of these will provide optimum satisfaction will cause defective realization of subjective intensity. Both ignorance and perversity affect the achievement of the aim of experience by introducing a defective interweaving of Reality and Appearance in the final
satisfaction. The Reality–Appearance disjunction, resulting from a disharmonious realization of subjective aim by high-grade occasions, is conducive
to a state of positive disharmony in experience.

I am not maintaining here that God's provision of the initial aim to occasions of experience is per se a religious function. Whitehead has emphatically stated that "the concept of religious feeling is not an essential element

in the concept of God's function in the universe" (PR 315–316). God has
secular as well as religious functions. And the provision, in the initial aim,
of a graded envisagement of eternal objects is a secular function. But this is
not meant to imply that the provision of the initial aim in human experiencing is completely "secular." For in human beings where knowledge and
free will are important factors in determining the issue of experience, the
lure of God's subjective aim for each occasion, insofar as it seeks to overcome
the disharmonious effects of ignorance and perversity, has a specifically religious character.

The emphasis of Whiteheadian philosophy upon these three aspects of
the religious problem could find some justification in a survey of the various
rational religions. The Christian tradition has emphasized the fact of the
misuse of freedom as the essence of sin, and, therefore, as the principal factor in the religious problem confronted by man. Other religions, like the
Hindu (as expressed in the Upanishads)[5] and the so-called Gnostic heresies
within Christianity, have considered the overcoming of ignorance as a principal means of re-establishing a right relation with the totality of things.
The Buddhist doctrine of the "boundlessness of desire" and of the finite and
limited character of all satisfactions explicitly recognizes human finitude as
a principal generating cause of the religious problem.

We now have a religious problem in a considerably expanded form from
that which emphasizes, mainly, the perpetual perishing of all experiences.
To the problem of perpetual perishing we have found it necessary to add the
fact of potential uprootedness, or the dislocation of Appearance and Reality.
Such uprootedness may be the result either of ignorance or of perversity.
The evils associated with the finitude of existence are twofold: first, experience does not contain in itself the reason for its successor; and second, an
occasion of experience cannot, of itself, prevent the fading of its immediacy.
The experience of the creative synthesis of God's consequent functioning
serves to provide assurance of the continued succession of experiences. Also,
the everlasting character of God's consequent nature provides protection for
achieved value, by providing an order, beyond the temporal order, "in which
novelty does not mean loss" (PR 517). This consequent functioning of
God, as we have seen, is a metaphysical interpretation of the intuition of the
Unity of Adventure, which is one aspect of the sense of Peace. The contingent factor of the religious problem, the threat of uprootedness, is met
by the fact of the divine Eros which lures occasions of experience toward a
novel and creative conformation of Appearance and Reality. This Eros-
function is God's subjective aim at ideal harmony, which expresses the ideal
aspect of the intuition of Peace.

The religious problem can only be overcome by the religious vision of
Peace. That same intuition which is the capstone of civilized values resolves
the fundamental cosmological problem of existence. Here we see the dramatically complex interrelations between the aim of experience at balanced

intensity and the aim at that Unity of Adventure characterized by Truthful Beauty, between the threat of finitude and uprootedness and the promise of Peace as a cultural aim and of religion as a cultural interest. The achievement of Peace involves each of the civilized values. The principles of finitude, process, and individuality insure the necessity that experience as the product of Art must venture beyond present realization if balanced intensity is to be achieved. The principle of individuality is the presupposition of all harmony and, therefore, of all Beauty. True harmony "is the harmony of enduring individualities" (AI 362). Truthful Beauty can be obtained only if "the individual, real facts [which] lie at the base of our immediate experience in the present" (AI 361) are made component factors of Appearance. "The intuition constituting the realization of Peace has as its objective that Harmony whose inter-connections involve Truth" (AI 377). The sense of Peace, therefore, depends upon that Art which achieves Truthful Beauty in some final Unity of Adventure. And if Peace is in evidence such an achievement is assured.

With the discussion of the maintenance of Truthful Beauty we introduce the subject of the relationships between the religious problem and culture per se. In so doing we may realize that the religious problem is, in fact, a general cultural problem insofar as a loss of the sense of Peace and the lack of Truthful Beauty in a society may result from a failure in any or all of the cultural experiences and expressions of the principal civilized interests. It is with this general cultural interpretation of the cosmological or religious problem that we shall be concerned in the remainder of this chapter.

2. THE CULTURAL PROBLEM

The fundamental aim of a civilized society is at Truthful Beauty. Truthful Beauty is realized in an occasion of experience when there is a balance of germaneness and novelty such that Appearance for that occasion provides a novel rendering of the data of the causally efficacious past actual world in conformation with the requisites of the subjective aim of that occasion. Cultural expressions, be they artifacts in the ordinary sense of that term, or concepts, etc., must be importantly related to the Reality from which experience derives. The lack of a fortunate relation between Reality and Appearance means either one of two things: first, that cultural expressions may no longer be relevant to the past actual world, having lost the *fundamentum in re* which gives the expressions their intensity and depth of feeling; or, secondly, that the cultural expressions characterizing a human society may be too closely tied to the world of causal efficacy and, therefore, may lack the elements of novelty, conceptual intensity, and imaginative freedom which are manifestations of balanced complexity in higher grades of experience. In such a case, the society is characterized by an abundance of blunt truth. This condition is not clearly manifest as a part of the religious problem because of its primary emphasis upon *security*. But at the level of general culture it becomes clear that too much grounding in the past, too much love of tradition, too much dependence upon habitual forms of behavior can lead to a loss of the sense of Peace. Adventure is a cultural necessity. Novelty as well as germaneness must be achieved in cultural expressions.

With the achievement of a harmony of novel and germane experiences, the aim of balanced complexity has been achieved. This attainment, in itself, does not insure civilized experience, however. For there is still the possible experience of *finitude* despite the realization of Truthful Beauty.

Whitehead did not explicitly distinguish the two elements of the cultural problem as I have done here. He made the distinction, however, between the sense of ideal Peace (Peace as the Crown of Youth) and the sense of Peace as the issue of tragedy. The first sense is particularly related to the Eros-drive toward maintaining the proper relations between Appearance and Reality; the second refers to that Peace which overcomes the sense of the finitude of all perfections. But no such distinctions between the senses of Peace need be made in most cases. For a culture which has attained the sense of Peace will necessarily have overcome the threat of uprootedness, because the presence of a proper Appearance–Reality relation is one of the prerequisites for a sense of Peace. But the contrary is not the case. There may be creative conformations of Appearance and Reality expressed in the cultural expressions of a society, and yet the sense of Peace may be absent.

We can find some support for the foregoing extensions of Whitehead's theory of civilization in his general approach to the history of civilization found in *Adventures of Ideas*. In discussing the transition from Hellenic to Hellenistic culture, Whitehead contrasts the "speculative" character of the earlier culture with the "scholarly" character of the latter. In the Hellenistic age, "Literature was replaced by Grammar, and Speculation by the Learned Tradition" (AI 133). The primary contributions of the Hellenistic age were the securing of learning by the process of conventionalization and the development of the specialized sciences. But through such developments the Hellenic tendencies toward free imaginative speculation were lost. "The note of Hellenism is delight, speculation, discursive literature: the note of Hellenistic Alexandria is concentration, thoroughness, investigation of the special types of order appertaining to special topics" (AI 134).

Whitehead finds in this contrast between speculation and scholarship a provocative device for characterizing certain broad tendencies in the history of Western culture. After the Hellenic age, the Hellenistic stress upon scholarship was dominant until the Middle Ages. The Renaissance revived the Hellenic spirit. At the close of the Italian Renaissance, the transition from speculation to scholarship was repeated in the specializations of modern science.

In this contrast of speculation and scholarship, Whitehead is illustrating the necessity of novelty and germaneness in cultural expressions. One purpose of free speculation is to formulate more adequate concepts which, when referred to the realities of concrete experience, will be able to evoke novel and more relevant experiences into conscious awareness. Novelty of this sort enriches a society by adding to the reservoir of emotional experiences to which cultural expressions may be germane. Scholarship, on the other hand, is aimed at the precise analysis and classification of matters of fact.

Too much speculation might lead to a dislocation from fundamental emotional experiences. If Appearance outruns Reality—i.e., if cultural expressions are not germane to the intuitions of the majority of a society—uprootedness can result. On the other hand, scholars, concerned only with bare *sensa* and tautologies, concentrate on the analysis of the presentationally immediate world. In such a case, concrete realities may be ignored and only their appearances considered. In either case there is the danger of a dislocation of Appearance and Reality, though it is more likely in the former instance. "Pure speculation, undisciplined by the scholarship of detailed fact or the scholarship of exact logic, is on the whole more useless than pure scholarship, unrelieved by speculation" (AI 138). Speculation of this type is useless because it tends to dissociate itself from its basis in concrete fact. Scholarship, so long as it concerns itself with empirical data, can be hopeful of maintaining some relationship to the realities of experience, however trivial those realities may be. Whitehead's principal objection to scholarship, particularly the scholarship of modern science, is that it tends to "canalize thought and observation within predetermined limits, based upon inadequate metaphysical assumptions dogmatically assumed" (AI 151). Such an approach produces, on the one hand, an overabundance of blunt truth, and, on the other, a dislocation of Appearance from Reality through a concentration upon sense-data and tautologies without a concern for the more concrete realities of existence. In both cases the condition of uprootedness results from a "falling away of the past"—i.e., from a loss of those elements of the realities of the past actual world ignored by the scholarly specialists. This "falling away of the past" coupled with the "outrunning of the past" resulting from an overabundance of speculation threatens human culture with the condition of uprootedness.

In this contrast between the speculative and the scholarly impetus in cultures, it is possible to see an illustration of the kind of tension which results in a society with an unbalanced Appearance–Reality relation. It is equally possible to appeal to a specific historical example to illustrate the manifestation of the threat of finitude to a society. Perhaps the most notable example of this type of society is the Italian Renaissance. Whitehead himself alluded to this period of history in his discussion of the necessity of the quality of Peace to a civilized society. "Apart from [Peace], the pursuit of 'Truth, Beauty, Adventure, Art' can be ruthless, hard, cruel; and thus, as the history of the Italian Renaissance illustrates, lacking in some essential quality of civilization" (AI 366–367). Truthful Beauty and Adventure can be manifest in the cultural expressions of a given society, as was the case in the aesthetic productions of the Italian Renaissance, without evidence of a concomitant moral and religious creativity.[6] Reflecting upon the private life of Benvenuto Cellini, the activities of the Borgias, the political writings of Machiavelli, and the reputations of some of the fifteenth- and early sixteenth-century popes as a contrast to the brilliance of the creative expressions of the Renaissance in Italy, will allow one to grasp the fact that there can, indeed, be a culture which attains an important degree of Truth and Beauty in its expressions without thereby realizing a sense of Peace.

Thus, a dislocation of Appearance and Reality will cause a lack of the sense of Peace, but it is not necessarily the case that a society without a sense of Peace is experiencing such a dislocation. For Peace is meant to overcome the sense of finitude which accompanies any achievement, be it wholly mundane or discordant, or highly novel and creative. The most perfect of achievements is subject to the fact of perpetual perishing. So even societies possessed of the qualities of Truth, Beauty, Art, and Adventure can fail to experience Peace.

Cultures, therefore, generally experience two important challenges to their viability as civilized societies. There is, first, the experience of an imbalance between novelty and germaneness in the Appearance–Reality relation characterizing cultural experience and expression. Such an experience, of course, necessarily involves a lack of the sense of Peace. Secondly, there may be a lack of the sense of Peace in spite of the possession, to an important degree, of the other qualities of a civilized society.

The two aspects of the cultural problem outlined above may be dramatically illustrated if we turn now to an analysis of the condition of our own contemporary cultural milieu. I must emphasize, however, that I am more concerned with clarifying Whiteheadian thought than with articulating with complete adequacy the problem confronting contemporary culture. I shall limit myself to illustrative examples of the cultural problem rather than attempt a more complete analysis of our contemporary cultural milieu, since my main purpose in this work is to provide fruitful interpretative categories for the use of those who can provide a wide-ranging analysis of the conditions of contemporary culture. I shall first be concerned with illustrating the cultural problem as a general condition of contemporary society. In the final chapters I will indicate the manner in which that problem is expressed in each of the specific cultural interests heretofore examined.

Historical examples of the cultural problem are easier to analyze than illustrations from contemporary culture. The past, of course, has a settled character which the present can never duplicate. But there is an added problem in interpreting our present: we are in a neither–nor situation, a period of rather hectic transition. The burden of self-analysis weighs more heavily on some epochs than on others. Creative periods no doubt come easily to an awareness of their temper, the actions and intentions of their great men are "autobiographical" and self-revelatory by their very nature. Ages in decline likewise yield easily to the self-analytic impulse, motivated as they are by the search for the causes of decline. Those epochs in which cultural expressions reach dead center, however, do not find themselves worthy of great interest. The sense of marking time brings on a failure of nerve which does not lead to an honest examination of self. Similarly, those periods in the first stages of creative change, when significant novelties are as yet unrecognizable, do not yield to rational analysis. Apparently we are in such a period of transition. We are able to define the structures of our world insofar as it looks to tradition and the past, but the analysis of the novel elements in our society is an extremely difficult task.

The identifiable structures of our social and cultural systems are to be defined mainly in terms of the frozen insights which gave rise to the "modern" temper in the sixteenth and seventeenth centuries. But the scientific mentality of Galileo and Descartes in which curiosity, rationality, and certainty were the primary values has, in recent generations, grown old and entered its dotage. The modern age which was defined in the beginning by the scientific temper has reached its end in an orgy of technological development. Technology, the bastard offspring of science, stands surrogate for an absent scientific temper. Unlike science which develops from the qualities of curiosity and wonder, technology is fathered by the compulsion of circumstances.

The twin "necessities" which have given birth to the dominance of technique in contemporary society are sloth and the propensity toward violence. Success in war and the active pursuit of leisure have shaped the technological order. Thus we find ourselves in the position of looking, or trying to look, with pride to the progressive advancements of our society which fall predominantly into one of two classes: gadgets or weapons. Neither can serve as a source of inspiration; neither can be the products of a society with any degree of adequate value-orientation. Gadgetry is too trivial, weaponry too inhuman, to inspire a feeling of creativity. In every accomplishment of greatness there must be some element of disinterestedness. Yet, neither our gadgets nor our weapons can lay claim to serving as ends in themselves. Too much blunt truth, too little adventure, prevent the balance between novel and germane experiences and expressions. The trivial and inhuman results of technological ingenuity in so many cases promote the kind of unhealthy Appearance–Reality relations resulting from a loss of Truthful Beauty.

It is for this reason—despair over the puerile developments in a technological society—that many were so hopeful for the scientific success of the space program leading to a landing on the moon. The actual character of that program dashed all hopes that our space adventures would ever have any of the qualities of daring or of risk which had made voyages of discovery so important in our history. The safe and sane manner in which the flights are undertaken weight the program so much on the side of caution and so little toward adventure that the program, after its initial success, appeals very little to the imaginations of either participant or observer. When no decision is made, no action done, which is not perfectly safe and in which every contingency has been considered in advance, little of worth can be accomplished.

The refusal to take risks is the result of a capitulation to the feeling of finitude. The sense of Peace as the Unity of Adventure presupposes the faith and the daring to venture imaginatively into the unknown. To achieve greatness in uncharted areas, risk is a necessity. Our failure to achieve greatness is a function of our overly cautious, timid state of mind which finds no profit in taking chances. Beneath the calculating temperament of the technicians who control our social programs there is the anxiety and fear born of the failure to envision any purpose or goal of existence beyond that of success in one's immediate short-term enterprise.

The static technological order in which safety and efficiency weigh heavily against any attempt at adventure is rapidly being brought to an awareness of the precariousness of its situation by "outsiders"—hippies, intellectuals, the Third World—who in positive work are setting themselves over against the old order. These groups in effect accuse the established order of perpetuating the condition of uprootedness by a refusal to nurture certain positive values of the Western tradition. The "falling away of the past," which is a result of the provincial dogmatisms of established scholarship, has recently been challenged by ethnic minorities who demand that *their* pasts, too, be taken into account, that their names and deeds be recorded in history books. This countermovement is one of the first signs of a shift away from dead center and toward the instantiation of a new set of defining characteristics of society. The thrust of this movement is centered in the "new generation."

The so-called "new generation" is long overdue. The conceptual revolution defining contemporary thought culminated, in principle, with the work of Einstein and Freud just prior to and just after World War I. The effect of that conflict, greater in its social and intellectual implication than any conflict since, was to delay the instantiation of the defining ideas of the new era. Subsequent generations could not afford the time necessary to absorb fully the new ideas. War, depression, war again: this has been our history until recently.

With the misunderstood and much maligned silent generation of the fifties, the cultural revolution began. The new stock of ideas—the continuity of man and nature derived from Darwinian theory which serves as a profound basis for argument against our current ecological policies; the "irrationality of man," a gift of Freudian speculation realized until recently only in literature; the relativity of position and perspective derived from the theories of Einstein and applied at last to social and cultural circumstances—each of these defining characteristics of contemporary times had its first full-scale realization in the silent and beat generations, if only in the brooding and introspective manner characteristic of that generation.

In the new generation, the contemporary scene has become a practical demonstration of the impact of the ideas of irrationality and relativity upon the absolutely rational world fathered by Galileo and Descartes. The generation gap is in its deepest philosophic expression a gap between not merely the under- and over-thirty of our society but between the heirs of the seventeenth-century world-view and those who are the first true children of the twentieth century.

Resistance to the incursion of the new generation has been, as expected, dramatic. To the charge of irrationality directed against economic, political, and social institutions—institutions which breed wars and depressions with regularity—the children of the seventeenth century have answered by demonstrating the ultimate rationality of the technological society in which order and efficiency have effectively established themselves as the primary goals of the social system. To the claim that false absolutes should give way, in religion, art and politics, to a recognition of the relativity of perspectives, the established society has reaffirmed its commitment to the current forms of social and political oppression which deny to the emerging generation any voice in the characterization of cultural significances.

Thus the transformation of values is by no means complete. Our cultural situation is the chaos which it is because no set of values is firmly entrenched in society. We are uprooted from our traditional values and not yet at home with any new ideals. Our cultural expressions cannot achieve Truthful Beauty because we have no coherent realities from which to construct a cultural world.

We might hope to see in our current situation a coming of age expressed in a refusal to depend upon false absolutes and an acceptance of the relativity of all values. But even if it were the case that some concept of value-relativity is the emergent idea which is to define our cultural situation in the future, the identification of the chaos born of a pitched battle between relativists and absolutists as a mature expression of cultural relativism is to be altogether too naïve both about the meaning of relativity and the character of our contemporary situation. The chaos in our value-orientations leads us into a condition in which our own sense of finitude is an overwelming burden. The faith that what is valuable in one's existence will persist beyond the flux of immediate experiences, the faith which can give rise to the sense of Peace, is impossible if one is incapable of discovering a firm place to stand. When every value, each decision, can be brought into serious question, then no value is acceptable, no decision can be firmly made. We are overcome by a sense of the unimportance of our thoughts, actions, or beliefs.

This sense of unimportance is increased by the fact of the quantitative increase in human population which yields the phenomenon of "masses" celebrated in much contemporary literature. Contemporary man is the product, in part, of the impact of the burgeoning population upon social structures. In several crucial respects the fact of "masses" has altered the form of contemporary culture. Masses of people function, first of all, as a threat to the established forms of social organization. The absorption of greatly increased numbers into the social system demands the development of techniques which will enable the reasonably harmonious absorption of the enlarged populations. One clear-cut instance of this fact is the effect of the dramatic increase of college-age individuals in the period of the sixties. The purely quantitative characteristics of the new generation of protest have been too little emphasized. A relatively sensitive individual aware of the birth-rate statistics in post-World War II America could with little difficulty have predicted the generation of revolt by reflecting upon the kinds of radical changes in organizational procedures which would be necessary in order to absorb the masses of students. It is no accident that the generation of protest in American universities is also the generation of undigested masses who may be handled only by highly technical forms of organization.

It is not only as a negative force that the phenomenon of crowding has affected social and cultural organization. Mass culture provides a market for the goods and services of a capitalist economy. The sheer numbers of people insure that almost any product properly advertised, packaged, and marketed will meet with enthusiastic response on the part of at least enough people to provide a profit. The masses of contemporary society present our economy with an almost inexhaustible reservoir of tastes. And the notorious manipulatability of masses means simply that markets may be easily created through advertising. Mass-markets lead to mass-production of a vast array of marketable products which requires an efficiently organized technological order.

The effect of the growth of a technological order in response to the phenomenon of increasing masses of population is to reinforce mass-mentality. If large numbers of individuals are capable of communicating with one another only through the abstract and efficient means of the technological order, there will be little hope of developing the kind of humanistic values which alone can create human relationships in society.

Forty years ago José Ortega y Gasset's *Revolt of the Masses* was acclaimed by a reviewer in the *Atlantic Monthly* in the following words:

> What Rousseau's *Contrat Social* was for the eighteenth century and Karl Marx's *Das Kapital* for the nineteenth Señor Ortega's *Revolt of the Masses* should be for the twentieth century.[7]

Lavish praise from *Time* and *The New York Times Book Review* attested to Ortega's brilliant insights into the coming rebellion of the masses. But, today, when that revolt seems so patently evident, we find his work largely ignored. This would be cause for little concern if we found other prophets voicing the same trenchant ideas which Ortega once proclaimed.

But we do not. Though we are deluged by social prophets, few of them seem to touch the roots of our social chaos.

It is often the fate of a book published "ahead of its time" to be ignored when its time finally arrives. Victor Hugo's dictum "Nothing is so powerful as an idea whose time has come" does not, of course, apply to ideas which have entertained, and have been entertained by, the *cognoscenti* before time has energized them for efficacy. On reflection, however, it appears that the contemporary disregard of the classic Ortegan analysis is rooted in a much deeper and more profound condition than the contempt for the familiar. This analysis, whose modern origins are to be found in such works as Stein's *Der Socialismus und Communismus des heutigen Frankreichs* (1842) and Le Bon's classic examination of *The Crowd* (1895), is increasingly ignored for the simple, if paradoxical, reason that the predicted revolt of the masses has taken place. The mass-man has succeeded in breeching the walls of our intellectual culture. The loudest voices of our time are mass-men disguised as prophets. We are being given advice on strategy by the enemies who would take us over. To outline the temper of our time which has led to this ironic situation is to underline the poignancy of a society burdened almost to collapse by its false prophets.

Any stable human society inhabited by free individuals must possess two qualities: *excellence* and *deference*. Excellence involves the realization of Truthful Beauty. Deference expresses the sense of Peace found in the realization of one's own individual value. The excellences of individuals in a society insure contributions to the creativity and harmony of social interrelations. Deference insures that no one will attempt to extend his influence beyond his area of competence. The revolt of the masses is complete when those individuals who are unaccustomed to the excellence of knowledge are unable to recognize the importance of deference. This is the situation in our society pervaded as it is by the technological state of mind.

We are experiencing what Ortega termed "the vertical invasion of barbarian," [8] the rise to dominance of a class of technicians who possess expert knowledge in an extremely narrow field but know little or nothing of the broader facets of human culture. Our contemporary barbarians are ignorant of the principles upon which rest all significant thought and action. In contradistinction to the geographical barbarians of our Graeco-Roman heritage, we in Western society are "chronological" barbarians. We live outside the civilized world by living beyond it in time. Having outrun the shadow of our past, we are uprooted from the wisdom of our tradition, the only wisdom to which we have any significant access. Disenchantment with established values means that intellectual culture is betrayed both by those within and by those without the mainstream of society.

The polarization of social ideologies means that the condition of chronological barbarism confronts us with *two* distinct threats to civilized order. The unprincipled activity of the technician, the over-specialized man, continually leads away from the sense of harmony and relatedness of the significant cultural interests which have always served as necessary conditions of a civilized society. Besides the technical man there are those minorities which threaten violence to clear away the foundations of established order. The immediate and direct threat comes, of course, from these barbarians-at-the-gates: slogan-shouting, heads filled with practical ideologies, motivated by social grievances—real and contrived—the barbarian-at-the-gates will down the structures just to watch them fall. The passionate sincerity of youth combines with the open hostility of disestablished minorities to make this type of barbarism a real and continuing threat.

Over against the violent minorities, with their true-believer mentality, stand the hippie-style drop-outs who seek in communal experience a revitalization of concreteness and intersubjective commitment. These drop-outs are not being equated in character or in purpose with the proponents of violence. For in the non-violent wing of dissenters there is a program for personal and social existence which eschews resort to direct attack upon established structures. Examining the drop-out mentality we find one type of reaction to the stress and overstimulation of a society whose rate of change makes excessive demands upon the physical and psychological health of its members. This may, indeed, be one of the sanest of all possible responses to advanced technological society. But it is this communal, non-violent life-style which, however much it may be of value in the future, precludes this group from having any immediate impact upon the intellectual culture of a rapidly polarizing society.

The most significant threat to civilized order comes not from violent minorities, the barbarians-at-the-gates, but from the established mass-men, the barbarians-within. Contemporary society has as its sustainers a naïve and dogmatic barbarian horde which threatens to destroy civilization through the insidious fragmentation of intellectual culture. Chronological barbarism, in its two distinct modalities, names the social problem of the age.

Our uprooted and polarized visions of society have the further failing that they are *self-evidently* true to their adherents. The common appeal to self-evidence by contradictory ideologies is a poignant fact of our society. And the intellectual is stymied by such appeals. Like Count Dracula before the crucifix, objective intellectual analysis is neutralized by conflicting claims of self-evidence. Faced by warring and dogmatic truth-claims, the intellectual must either take sides and add whatever authority he possesses to one or the other of the conflicting parties (certainly a very questionable decision), or find a way of dealing coherently with both of the polarized social elements.

This failure of nerve experienced by the intellectual in the face of the polarization of intellectual culture is one of the most significant characteristics of our contemporary situation. The primary characteristic of our contemporary intellectuals is timidity, born of the sense of finitude. Such timidity is a result of the confrontation of the all too many alternatives which serve as possible courses of action. Left to himself the scholar is harmless enough. But the Hamletesque quality of intellectual life becomes dangerous in the extreme when social crises require commitment to *one* among the vast array of possibilities for action. In such a situation, Hamlets too readily accept the leadership of the few Don Quixotes in society who avoid the anxiety of uncertainty through arbitrary decisions. Self-assurance and resolute behavior win the admiration and the support of the timid.

If in no other way ours is a common culture in terms of the problems we confront. Established society, from lower to upper classes, faces problems such as population, pollution, war, minority pressure, which tend to create a community of shared anxieties. In the face of the enormity of social problems, intellectuals in our culture exhibit timidity, insecurity, and fearfulness whenever they are called upon to venture a suggestion about the proper organization and direction of social energies. And it is this condition, born of a radical sense of finitude, which leads many to flock to any leader who seems resolute, self-assured, and certain of the validity of his position.

The search for charismatic leaders, in and out of politics, characterizes an age of indirection and unfocused activity. In a period of indecision and uncertainty it is the man of decision, the man certain of his own beliefs, the man with the *answers,* who will be accepted as savior. Yet it is not just any decisive figure who will command charismatic allegiance, but he who has focused upon the problem and promise of advanced technological society. For the problems which create our contemporary community of anxiety are problems either caused, or to be resolved, by technology.

The palace revolt which has given the technician control of the means of social organization and development is merely one instance of the general enthronement of technique and the technological state of mind throughout society. It is a part of the wholesale stress upon technique over speculation and spontaneity. The conflict between NASA scientists and technicians in which the engineer, heretofore a paid assistant of the pure scientist, has taken over the controls is simply one dramatic instance of the fact that efficient and calculating temperaments have won out over curiosity, speculation, and the search for principles. The technologization of cultural interests is ubiquitous. Even the production and manipulation of religious fervor has succumbed to technology as the well-organized, overly-efficient crusades of the evangelist Billy Graham so well evidence.

All this makes quite understandable the changed conception of social authority characteristic of technological society. In contemporary society technical competence serves as the basis of a new type of charisma, one based upon the skill of the technical man rather than upon mysterious, personal magnetism. An obvious example is that of the American astronauts. Primarily skilled technicians rather than scientists, these men, nonetheless, perform extremely complex operations, the consequences of which are realizations of immensely important goals. Add to this the fact that we seem as a society bent upon destroying the traditional charismatic leaders (King, the Kennedys, Malcolm X), and we see how much evidence there is in favor of the conclusion that our leaders, social and political, are now to be drawn from the barbarians within intellectual culture. When one realizes that the missing ingredient in the exclusively technical man—the knowledge of principles—is the very ingredient without which no civilized society can exist, it becomes extremely important to ask how deeply this orientation penetrates into society.

A sign of just how pervasive the orientation toward technique is is the phenomenon of university education. Many of our universities have capitulated to the idea of the "multiversity" and, consequently, to the idea that the university is not meant to create the well-rounded humanist, but the expert, the specialized man. To the extent that this phenomenon characterizes the university, which is, after all, human culture writ small, the barbarian society is an accomplished fact. For specialization leads to barbarization, to the extent that it promotes a narrowed and dulled vision of the relations between the significant human enterprises forming the cultural context. Specialization is, of course, a natural response to the complexity of human knowledge in advanced technological society. The sense of being of a *knowing* person is a necessary part of the cultural equipment of civilized human beings. But to know something well, to be an expert, one must narrow his focus and specialize. We pay heavily for the feeling of expertise, for intense specialization has inevitably led to the failure of intellectual discrimination which so characterizes our culture.

The irony of this situation is that the chaos brought on by specialization is not prima facie in evidence. For specialization of techniques leads inevitably to the bureaucratization of social structures which lends a certain well-ordered appearance to the institutions serving intellectual culture. But the chaos manifests itself inevitably when a society is confronted by issues which affect all major social groupings or which require the harmonious efforts of all elites. Such problems as over-population and pollution, for example, require the bureaucracy sustaining the specialization of knowledge and technique to perform tasks which no open-ended, loosely structured group of specialized experts could possibly perform. In these instances the call to action is a call to the mobilization of the bureaucracy into a political instrument of the established powers. There is no way of providing the necessary integration of the techniques of social action and analysis except by political fiat. And since the classical charismatic visionary is less and less evident on the political scene, we find that political decisions are made by reliance upon some specific technical proposition. The technical mind dominates at both the popular and the administrative levels of society. In this way specialized elites become expressions of what the people want and what the social machinery requires. The first condition leads to vulgarization of the intellectual culture, the second to its fragmentation.

Specialization rends the social fabric in two dramatic ways. Interdisciplinary communication becomes increasingly less feasible, and the cultural checks and balances which come about through the comparing of activities and concerns among various disciplines are seldom operative. In addition, interdisciplinary communication becomes difficult among intensely specialized experts within the same field, and the more difficult it becomes the more counterproductive it is assumed to be when judged by the criterion of efficiency which technological society imposes upon every discipline.

Thus in a technological society the conflict of alien methodologies, both between and within specialized cultural interests, leads to provincial dogmatisms and the refusal to entertain conflicting semantic contexts. The ambiguity and equivocality of concepts germane to one's discipline is forgotten, and a rigidity of semantic commitments sets in. The specialist who seeks a way out finds that his specialization prevents him from reaching beyond the boundaries of his specialty in any intelligent way.

The condition may appear ameliorated in those instances of the adoption of a single explanatory model by several disciplines, since this could considerably increase interdisciplinary communication. But this is only partially true. The use, for example, of the behavioral model of man by psychologists, sociologists, and political scientists certainly increases the interdisciplinary communication among the behaviorists, but the positive results of such communication are more than offset by the increased tensions and family quarrels which exist among behavioral and non-behavioral theorists within each of the disciplines.

Specialists have become technological minds functioning without an understanding of their relationships to the world of intellectual culture. In reaching for a synoptic vision they can only fail because of the built-in limitations of their vision. Understanding must be grounded in principles. But those of the specialized elites seeking cultural self-understanding are limited to the specialized principles of their discipline. Therefore, the search for cultural self-understanding on the part of the specialized experts leads to the proliferation of reductionist explanations. The specialist, in order to understand cultural experiences, must reduce them to the status of an aspect, instance, or implication of his own specialized knowledge.

This brief sketch of our contemporary cultural milieu will serve to illustrate the cultural problem as we have defined it. We obviously suffer from a dislocation of Appearance and Reality in two dramatic ways. First, since the technological order has come to stress those aspects of our environment which lead to short-term resolutions of our problems, and to the creation of cautious programs aimed at efficiency and economic gain, adventure has been at a minimum. Through an excess of blunt truth we have allowed many of the finer and more subtle components of our tradition to fall away.

This "falling away of the past" has left us adrift without foundations. We have increasingly lost the understanding of *principles,* the beginning-points of thought and action, and have become content with the worst aspects of the pragmatic orientation to our social and cultural problems. Ad hoc solutions are the only solutions available when there is no foundation in principles.

In direct contrast to "the falling away of the past" consequent upon our stress of only selected portions of our past experience, is the phenomenon of the excess of novelty which in many areas of cultural experience and expression is the order of the day. Novelty lays claim to excellence simply for its own sake. The rapid adjustments required by the human organism to the novel changes in the economic and social order must give rise to a sense of rootlessness. Without question, the rate of significant change in advanced technological society is having profound effects upon the sense of meaning and value as it develops among individuals in contemporary culture.

In addition to the sense of uprootedness, the sense of finitude is overwhelming in contemporary culture. The vast array of possibilities open to an individual functions both in a positive and a negative manner to give him an overriding sense of his own finitude. The tenuousness of existence in a society threatened by the economic collapse of its cities, pollution, interracial strife, etc., can only lead to a sense of radical contingency particularly when the rapidity of change is so great that we are simply unable to predict the consequences—good or bad—of decisions which we are pressured to make.

Not only in this negative sense do we experience radical finitude. We have in technological society the problem of "sensible infinity" [9]—i.e., the phenomenon of the myriad ways in which comfort and pleasure may be found. The quantitative possibilities for achieving pleasure and excitement are enormous—considerably greater than any human could ever achieve. The "boundlessness of desire" of which the Buddhist speaks is met in advanced technological society by the boundlessness of the means of satisfying desire. This "sensible infinity" is a cause of great despair in contemporary man. Since so many pleasures must be tasted, no pleasure can be fully experienced. Contemporary man is forced to be a dilettante, a superficial copy of Kierkegaard's "aesthetic man." The ever-not-quite character of existence weighs heavily upon him.

The ignorance of the principles upon which civilized order is based; the perversity of violence which seeks either to defend the old order or to erect a new one on the ashes of the old; the erethic excess of novelty which trivializes the sense of adventure necessary to a viable society—these conditions have brought on the radical sense of uprootedness characteristic of advanced technological society. Coupled with the sense of finitude which confronts contemporary man as the plenitude of possibilities for pleasure and for pain which seem to mock his efforts to gain rational control over his existence, this sense of rootlessness defines the condition of contemporary culture.

The foregoing analysis of the cultural problem in terms of our contemporary milieu is meant to indicate the relevance of Whiteheadian philosophy as an interpretative scheme for clarifying and bringing into focus the fundamental problems which may beset any given culture. We must be reminded, at this point, that "the cultural problem" as we have characterized it is an elaboration of the cosmological problem which confronts each occasion of experience and which in rational societies is interpreted as a *religious* problem. Recalling this fact we can proceed in the following chapters to analyze the possible conflicts between the various modes of cultural interest and the conditions of finitude and uprootedness in terms of the religious resources available for the successful resolution of those conflicts. That is, we can ask after the possible civilizing effects of the intuition of Peace as the sense of Eros and the Unity of Adventure. I shall continue to provide, as illustrative material, comments upon our contemporary situation in the light of the foregoing outline of the cultural problem. In so doing I shall hope to render more coherent and more understandable the Whiteheadian theory of culture through an application of his categories to certain concrete, topical issues crucial to our present situation.

NOTES

1. Weil, *The Need for Roots,* trans. Arthur Wills (Boston: Beacon, 1952), p. 43.
2. Augustine, *The City of God,* trans. Marcus Dodds (New York: Random House, 1950), pp. 384–385.
3. *Ibid.,* p. 385.
4. *Ibid.,* p. 387.
5. See *The Beginnings of Indian Philosophy,* ed. Franklin Edgerton (Cambridge: Harvard University Press, 1965), pp. 182–183.
6. See H. J. Muller, *Religion and Freedom in the Modern World* (Chicago: University of Chicago Press, 1964), p. 41: "There is certainly no correlation between the state of morals and the flowering of culture, as the brilliant, scandalous Italian Renaissance makes sufficiently clear."
7. *Atlantic Monthly* (December 1932), 18–19.
8. See Ortega's discussion of the "barbarian invasion" in *Revolt of the Masses* (New York: Norton, 1955).
9. I owe this fortunate term to Olive Wyon, the translator of Emil Brunner's *Das Gebot und die Ordnungen: Entwurf einer protestantisch-theologischen Ethik* (*The Divine Imperative* [Philadelphia: Westminster, 1947], p. 23).

Chapter VIII

Religion, Art, Morality

Two PRIMARY THEMES underlie our discussion of Whiteheadian philosophy. First, the structure of concrescence presupposes a necessary balance between the requirements of realist and idealist theories of experience. In human experience this leads to the maintenance of a balance between novelty and germaneness in the relations of Appearance and Reality. Secondly, the maximal attainment of the aim of experience at balanced complexity requires the type of social order manifested by human persons and societies. Basing our exposition upon this interpretation of the structure and aim of experience, we have developed concepts of culture and civilization. Our analyzing of cultural aims and cultural interests has provided us with an understanding of the fundamental tools for the discussion of the nature of civilized experience. The discussion of the religious problem and its manifestation as a general cultural problem has set the stage for these final chapters aimed at specifying the relation between religion and the cultural interests of art, morality, science, and philosophy.

In Chapter V we noted how the three principal modes of value-experience—the religious, the aesthetic, and the moral—derive from the basic sense of "worth." All value-experience, according to Whitehead, is fundamentally one, even if through the emphasis of distinct perspectives we can discern differing modalities of such experience. But in our former discussion of concept formation, and in the exposition of Whitehead's genetic account of religion, we noted that the increasing conceptual development of the modes of value-experience means an increased discrimination of the modes, one from the other. This is the process of the civilizing of experience which results in cultural expressions which interact to produce intense and contrasting values, thus promoting the aim at balanced complexity of experience. The fundamental unity of value-experience is an implication of

Whitehead's phenomenology of experience. But the distinctiveness and relative autonomy of the value-interests, and indeed of all cultural interests, is clearly implied by Whitehead's theory of the importance of abstractions and of conceptual constructions. My strategy in this and the following chapter will be to outline the sort of implications of Whiteheadian philosophy for the cultural efficacy of the interests of art, morality, science, and philosophy insofar as they interact with the interest of religion expressed as the sense of Peace.

1. THE CULTURAL FUNCTION OF ART

Art, as a cultural aim, is defined as purposeful adaptation of Appearance to Reality. As such, the term relates to every occasion of experience which possesses sufficient freedom of self-determination to help effect its transition from Reality to Appearance. We have, implicitly, narrowed the range of applicability of the term Art to the human cultural realm in this essay. And we shall further narrow the topic in what follows since we are interested in art in its somewhat less abstract role as a cultural interest. But, even at this level, art is an extremely broad concept. Thus, the fine arts are only special examples of this more generic term. " 'Art' in the general sense . . . is any selection by which the concrete facts are so arranged as to elicit attention to particular values which are realisable by them" (SMW 287).

Aesthetic experience, according to the phenomenological account of Chapter V, is the experience of the immediacy of value. Art objects derive from the various types of expressions of the immediate enjoyment of vivid values. Thus the difference between aesthetic experience and art is no stricter than the difference between experience and expression. And since experience is seldom without its consequent or accompanying expression, the distinction is certainly not a sharp one. "For example, the mere disposing of the human body and the eyesight so as to get a good view of a sunset is a simple form of artistic selection" (SMW 287). Thus, the distinction between the creation and the enjoyment of an aesthetic composition must not be overstressed.

The reason for the close ties between aesthetic creation and enjoyment, on Whiteheadian grounds, is obvious. The creation of a work of art requires symbolic reference from the reality of one's emotional experience to the appearance of the painting, poem, etc. Similarly, the enjoyment of that work of art requires symbolic reference, moving in the opposite direction, between the symbols of the art objects and the emotions of the aesthete. The elicited emotions will be somewhat distinct for each individual percipient, but the work of art should serve to elicit the enjoyment of vivid values. The art object may serve to elicit emotions which were heretofore locked below the level of conscious experience. The percipient, enjoying a work of art, is approximating, therefore, the process of artistic creation by virtue of the fact that he is altering, however slightly, the status of the relations between Appearance and Reality for the occasions of his personal order of experience.

Human art supports the aims of Truth, Beauty, and Adventure. The type of truth-relation promoted by art is that which expresses a community of subjective form between Reality and Appearance. This type of truth-relation, which was discussed in Chapter IV in some detail, is of great importance for the higher phases of civilized experience. For example, the conformation of subjective forms is "the whole basis of the art of litera-ture" (S 83). The emotions elicited in response to verbal symbols intensify the emotions elicited by the contemplation of their meanings. The same principle holds true for music. Listening to an orchestra encourages one to refer symbolically from the music to the variety of emotional response. In the most fortunate of artistic circumstances, we have little if any concern for more direct kinds of truth. A missed or a sour note occurring in a musi-cal performance is likely, however, to cause one to seek the person responsi-ble for the aesthetic blunder. A conductor's discovery of the culprit is an example of the usefulness of the less subtle type of truth-relation in art. For the conductor, both types of symbolic reference are important. If he cannot locate the source of disharmony in the orchestra, he will not be likely to evoke the aesthetic attention to elicit the more subtle type of truth-relation.

The enhancement of Beauty is, of course, one of the ideal aims of art. And it is closely tied with the aim at Truth. For the symbolic transfer of emotion, which is the basis of truth in art, is also the criterion for Beauty. For emotional responses to the elements of a work of art must be harmo-nious. Therefore, the details of aesthetic experience or expression must not evoke conflicting emotions. The presence of conflicting or irrelevant details can only produce emotions which inhibit the overall effect upon the per-cipient. "Each little emotion directly arising out of some subordinate detail refuses to accept its status as a detached fact in our consciousness. It insists on its symbolic transfer to the unity of the main effect" (S 86). A sour note during an orchestral performance is a subordinate detail whose symbolic reference to the unity of the main effect is not aesthetically pleasing.

Although Adventure is not one of the explicit aims of human art, it is often an essential by-product. This is best seen by noting the significance of the transitions within and between successive styles of art. Two problems must be overcome in these transitions. There must be change in the form and style of artistic expression, or art becomes mere tedious repetition, but the change must not come before the creative possibilities of that particular style have been adequately elaborated. "Mere change before the attainment of adequacy of achievement, either in quality or output, is destructive of greatness" (SMW 291). If these two principles are adequately followed, the adventurousness of art is of profound service to human culture by pro-viding, when necessary, novel stimulation toward the enjoyment of the aesthetic content of the emotional lives of its members. Art provides the sense of Adventure because it allows for an unparalleled use of human freedom. Autonomous artists, relatively free from the claims of morality or religion, are able to proclaim insights grounded in their deepest intuitions. Art so produced may be evil or very good, but at its best it is likely to be adventurous.

Art is unquestionably a civilizing agency. But it can also serve, in its lesser forms, to inhibit the growth of a civilized society. That is to say, art may well be a causative factor in the production of "the cultural problem." The reason for this possibility is that art, like all other cultural interests, is conditioned by the inevitable fact of finitude and the possible negative consequences of ignorance and the misuse of freedom.

I have already noted that, in Whitehead's view, human art is characterized by artificiality and finiteness. The quest for finite perfections which is the aim of human art, both as creation and as enjoyment, may also be its downfall. Without a sense of the permanent worth of artistic creations and of aesthetic enjoyment, artists may suffer a failure of nerve which could take all but the most immediate significance from their art. Commitment to aesthetic enjoyment is a tragic commitment. For all realization means loss. Artistic creations and aesthetic enjoyment suffer the passage of time as do all experiences and expressions. Because of the delicacy and transience of such perfections, many consider aesthetic pursuits frivolous and conceive the business of men to be merely the control of environments for practical ends rather than for aesthetic enjoyment. But, from the aesthetic point of view, the level-headed engineer who plans and builds for the needs of present utility, expecting obsolescence, is no substitute for the arrogant, yet tragic, figure of Ozymandias. One problem for the artist is to maintain his sense of purpose while creating and enjoying vivid, yet transient, values.

It is the religious intuition of Peace which can provide a sense of purpose for art. The religious insight, discussed in Chapter VI, contains a sense of the completed ideal harmony, integrating free creative passage with definite possibilities. This is the intuition of Peace which is "a trust in the efficacy of Beauty" (AI 367). The intuition of permanence is a primary offering of religion to art.

The religious intuition of permanence can benefit art in two ways. First, it can provide a means whereby the transience and finitude of aesthetic perfections may be accepted. If, besides the temporal order, there is an order "in which novelty does not mean loss" (PR 517), then the creation and enjoyment of finite, transient values in art need not be frustrated by despair and a loss of the sense of ultimate purpose. But, beyond this, religion may provide subject matters for art which have ultimate significance. Much art is comprised by creative expressions of such themes as love, death, etc., themes which are central to religious experience and expression. Specifically religious content, though not essential to art per se, is one means whereby the artist may be assured of dwelling on the central themes of human existence.

Finitude is not the only threat to art. The threat of the loss of novelty or germaneness must likewise be met. This threat will express itself in the form of *aesthetic ignorance*. There are two broad types of aesthetic ignorance. One is igorance of technique. Without a mastery of the aesthetic canons of one's particular art, and a knowledge of the proper emphasis of technique in art, there is little possibility of creative aesthetic expression. The second type of ignorance is most often termed *insensitivity*. Without a reservoir of profound emotional feelings from which to draw, the artist produces a work which, no matter how technically correct, is dull and insipid.

There are two significant ways in which an ignorance of technique may adversely affect aesthetic achievements: by an emphasis upon novelty at the expense of the more traditional canons of art, or by too great a stress upon technique and an insufficient stress of the novel factors of aesthetic expression. Avant-garde artists tend to stress the element of novelty in art. Artistic creations which are born of a quest for novelty for its own sake often lack the necessary quality of truth. The momentary interest generated by such art is not sustained by a foundation in relevant emotions in the artist or in his public. In such a case art becomes idiosyncratic to the individual artist. The subjectivity of aesthetic experience and creation implied in such art militates against any widespread social efficacy. Relevant aesthetic expression is at a minimum. This is not to say that novelty in art necessarily leads to negative results. There are circumstances, as we shall see, when the press toward novelty is the only alternative in achieving aesthetic value. Novelty cannot be an end in itself; it must remain a means for the expression of aesthetic intensity.

A more general defect in art results from a stress upon tradition. A certain amount of tradition, of course, is essential to art, and its necessary elements are embodied in those general aesthetic techniques to which almost every artist appeals in the production of art objects. Such canons are rules for the promotion of appropriate symbolic interconnections between Appearance and Reality. But Reality is in process. Therefore, only the most general canons will be appropriate in the face of human social changes.

Art suffers most when it clings to expressions which have been outmoded by changes in the emotional underpinnings of a social grouping. Changes in sentiment, taste, and general emotional tone produce novel aesthetic needs which should stimulate novel aesthetic productions. If the artists, for whatever reason, are unable to meet these new needs, they lose their ability to express truth and ignore the need for adventure. An important implication of Whitehead's theory of the Appearance–Reality relation is that Reality and Appearance may possess different tempos. Both the quest for novelty in Appearance and the quest for stability in Appearance may, therefore, lead to a loss of concrete realities.

The cultural efficacy of human art is challenged so by this problem of the balancing of novelty and germaneness because of the true importance of technique. Consider the relation which exists between the performer of a particular musical work and its composer. The techniques involved in learning to play a particular composition and in its actual performance are highly intellectualized pursuits which require little symbolic reference to or from the emotional feelings of derivation of the musician. For a performer does not have to create the complex proposition illustrated by a musical composition, he must only use his technical skill to objectify that proposition in a musical performance.[1] Critics and audiences distinguish a first-rate musician from a mere technician by his possession of, in addition to technical excellence, a certain idiosyncratic creative talent which enhances the aesthetic potential of a musical composition. The "flair" of a Rubinstein or the "intensity" of a Horowitz is an example of such a distinguishing trait. The presence of creative artists in the performing arts is of great importance to the cultural efficacy of art.

The debilitating effects of technique in art are felt beyond the performing arts. The urge toward imitation is a case in point. To the untalented or unpracticed poet, the writing of poetry is often a mere exercise in the imitation of another's art. This may mean that one's potential for aesthetic creation, however slight, will be reduced to the vanishing point because of a lack of concern for the need of symbolic reference from one's own emotional experiences. True poetry expresses such primitive emotional experiences in the sophisticated techniques of language. The overemphasis upon technique or style can mean only that the poetic expressions have little or no foundation in the experiences of a poet. And, if such be the case, they are not likely to elicit emotional response from the public exposed to such poetry.

The same source from which the intuition of the Unity of Adventure comes, offering to art the sense of ultimate purpose, can supply the answer to the threat of uprootedness. Eros, the subjective aim at ideal harmony, acts as a lure toward maximal achievement of harmony both internal to an experience and beyond it. In human experience, where freedom is of great significance, the subjective aim is wide enough to include alternate possibilities for attainment. One function of Eros is to maintain the ground for free creative action within the possibilities allowed by the givenness of the past.

The techniques of art are related to the religious insight in a simple and relatively direct fashion. The symbolic interconnections required for successful aesthetic experience and expression require that the aesthetic canons which guide the artists' creativity be compatible with the purposes of the social complex generally considered.

No elaborate community of elaborate organisms could exist unless its systems of symbolism were in general successful. Codes, rules of behaviour,

> *canons of art,* are attempts to impose systematic action which on the whole
> will promote favourable symbolic interconnections. . . . Such rules will be
> found in general to impose upon society behaviour in reference to a sym-
> bolism which is taken to refer to the ultimate purposes for which society
> exists [S 87–88; italics mine].

The imposition of canons of art which are compatible with the other principal types of symbolic interconnections within a society is necessary to the
health of that society. Such canons usually arise naturally in the process of
the maturity of a society. But, as the movement of Socialist Realism in post-
revolutionary Russia has illustrated, when circumstances preclude the natural development of aesthetic norms, they are likely to be imposed by
political fiat. Whitehead's point in the quotation above is that socially
responsible art must derive its canons from the ultimate purposes for which
the society exists. If these purposes are reflections of those implied by the
religious insight, a society will likely have aesthetic expressions compatible
with those ultimate purposes.

The second type of aesthetic ignorance is insensitivity. The artist must
have richness of experience from which to draw his aesthetic intuitions. But
more than that he must have sensitivity to the proper way in which the
creation of Appearance is to be performed. The proper balance of novelty
and germaneness can only come from an insight into that element in the
universe which seeks to foster such a balance—i.e., the Eros luring each
occasion of experience toward maximal harmony. As we have noted before,
there are three primary elements relevant to the determination of a concrescence. There is the potentiality expressed in God's provision of the initial aim with a breadth of possibilities for realization. There is the givenness
of the past, one element of which is the superjective character of God.
Finally, there is the freedom of the experiencing subject. Each of these
elements partially determines the limits of the others.

From the point of view of human experience, the givenness of the past
designates the reservoir of primitive experience from which aesthetic creations are drawn via symbolic reference. The experience of purpose in the
creation of a work of art is an experience of a subjective aim drawn, via
the interpretation and selection implied in conscious experience, from the
initial aim. The freedom of the artist is expressed both in terms of the
selection of a given aim from the width of possibilities provided in the initial aim and in his choice of maximal or minimal fulfillment of the aim.

The religious man experiences providence in the following ways: (1) in
the persuasive lure of the subjective aim, (2) as conditioning the givenness
of the past via his own immanent presence, (3) in the anticipation of the
final acceptance of his achievements into the consequent Unity of Adventure. In such experiences the religious man attempts to remain open to the
lure of God, adjusting the initial aim in accordance with those aspects of
givenness in the past which express God's will for that particular occasion.

Such religious response is made with the subjective form expressing the intuition of Peace.

I have indicated that the artist's sense of trust in the efficacy of Beauty, his sense of ultimate aesthetic purpose, may be enhanced by the religious insight of the Unity of Adventure. Whitehead would, of course, make no claim that all good artists must be self-consciously religious. The intuition of Peace, providing the sense of final purpose for cultural expression, need not be interpreted in terms of the relation of God and the world. But Whiteheadian philosophy does indicate that religion can serve art by making it more responsive to that final sense of purpose, if only through the inspiration of religious lives or through education via religious dogmas.

Artists, in order to produce art objects which have the qualities of Truth and Beauty, must in some fashion attune themselves with that element in the universe which aims at the conformation of Appearance and Reality. The determination of the proper actions of a given occasion in its attainment of intensity of experience is a result of mixing the efficient determination of the givenness of a particular occasion with the final causation manifest in the initial aim. If one recognizes the elements of deity in the givenness of experience and in one's finite purposes, goals, or desires, one is free to choose to act in accordance with those elements.

The truly religious man has achieved one prerequisite for becoming a true artist. But there are a number of reasons why the possession of a profound religious consciousness does not necessarily produce a great artist. The emotional experience of the religious man may not be broad or subtle enough to provide important raw material for symbolic reference, and his knowledge of techniques of artistic expression may be, and often are, at a minimum. Religious men, such as prophets and mystics, may have no desire to attempt to depict in narrative or plastic form the content of their religious experiences. Contemplation, preaching, and actions may be the substitutes for more specifically aesthetic creations.

The relation of religion and art, on Whiteheadian grounds, may be much more indirect than one might suppose from the views expressed above. For "God and the World," as one of the ideal opposites in terms of which Whitehead's cosmology is summarized in *Process and Reality*, "embody the interpretation of the cosmological problem in terms of a fundamental metaphysical doctrine as to the quality of creative origination" (PR 518). Such an interpretation need not be made. The experience of creative origination, conceptual appetition, and physical realization, need not, as we have repeatedly said, explicitly involve a concept of God or of His relation to the temporal world. The existence of high-grade, explicitly religious art indicates that the explicit and conscious recognition of the element of deity in the world can stimulate the production of creative aesthetic expressions. But a wide range of types of art are, of course, of a wholly other emphasis. Much so-called secular art has been held to be truly religious, if implicitly so. Thus Paul Tillich's critique of the school of Expressionism in art as having a special affinity for religious subject matter,[2] and Whitehead's analysis of Wordsworth's nature poetry,[3] illustrate the point that the implicit relation between art and religion may be fully as important as its explicit relation.

Implicitly religious art is that art which discloses or elicits those factors in the givenness of the experience of the artist and his public relevant to the promotion of present action in accordance with the element of Eros in things which drives toward a conformation of Appearance and Reality. The aim of specifically religious expressions should be toward the enhancement of this achievement, in both explicit and implicit fashions, on the part of the creative artists of a given culture.

The sense of Peace undergirds the enterprise of art in its task of proclaiming, in creative expressions, the quality of Truthful Beauty. But at those times when the sense of Peace is absent from a culture, the artist functions as prophet, proclaiming the loss of religious vision. But even, and especially, such a proclamation depends upon a sense of the importance of Peace and the hope for a renewal of the sense of Peace as Eros and the Unity of Adventure. In such instances the sense of the tragic quality of art becomes quite strong: the sense that in order to express Truthful Beauty one must advertise the tragedy involved in the loss of the religious vision.

2. ART AND TRAGIC BEAUTY

The principal truth proclaimed by artists in this century concerns the sense of uprootedness and finitude resulting from the loss of the experience of Eros and the Unity of Adventure. This message of the failure of Peace has been expressed most directly under the guise of the proclamation of "the death of God" which forms the theme of so much contemporary literature.

In *The Brothers Karamazov*, Dostoevski had Ivan, one of his principal characters, declare: "If God is dead, then all things are lawful for men." About the same time (1882), in his *Joyful Wisdom*, Nietzsche proclaimed, "God is dead." The philosophy of *Existenz*, one phase of which reached its high point with the publication of Jean-Paul Sartre's *Being and Nothingness* in the 1940s, drew the logical conclusion: "All things are lawful for men"; human beings are radically free and completely responsible for each of their actions. This existentialist syllogism contains a truth which art has tried to proclaim in so many different ways in this century.

The significance of the claim that God is dead depends, of course, upon the nature of the now-defunct deity. The God which is proclaimed dead was the Judaeo-Christian God—the Supreme Being, perfection itself, the Creator and Sustainer of all things. This God was omnipotent, omniscient, omnipresent. He was the source of all positive value, and He it was who sought to save the world from evil. The loss of the experience of God involves the loss of an absolute point of reference in accordance with which to judge the significance and meaning of nature and human life. Uprooted from the traditional source of meaning and value, twentieth-century man has expressed in his art a radical sense of finitude which threatens to overwhelm him.

> Alone in the time-space continuum [man] knows now of a certainty that none of his subjective wishes can ever influence the course of events. He is a victim of time, sensible to the passage of years and cut off forever from the divine source, aware of the nothingness of the grave. And the writers of today are afflicted with this metaphysical nausea. God is, as in *Waiting for Godot,* a shadow of desire, an empty word, a promise of hope that will never be kept.[4]

In works such as Franz Kafka's *The Castle,* the silence and indifference of the divine, and the anxiety, frustration, and antagonism of man in the face of this indifference is portrayed with chilling effect. Written with a listless humor which evokes a sense of futility, Kafka's novels are paradigmatic expressions of the truth which the art of the twentieth century proclaims with so many variations—the truth that the Judaeo-Christian God is dead.

The poetry of William Butler Yeats celebrates the end of a religious era and prophesies the coming of a new religion.

> Turning and turning in the widening gyre
> the falcon cannot hear the falconer
> Things fall apart, the center cannot hold
> Mere anarchy is loosed upon the world
> The blood-dimmed tide is loosed
> And everywhere the ceremony of innocence is drowned.

The voice of the "falconer" cannot be heard; we are too far distant from the center of things. Violence and anarchy result when religion loses its hold upon a culture. Our destiny, according to Yeats, is to live in a period of the collapse of religion. Our only choice is to await a "Second Coming."

> And what rough beast,
> its hour come round at last,
> Slouches towards Bethlehem to be born? [5]

James Joyce, as sensitive as any man to the collapse of religion in twentieth-century culture, expressed his feelings concerning the collapse of Western religion through the principal character of *A Portrait of the Artist as a Young Man.* Stephen Dedalus expresses Joyce's twin "vocations"—as artist and as saint. St. Stephanus, the first Christian martyr, and Daedalus, the legendary artificer of Greek mythology, provide the inspiration for Joyce's poetizing of his own formative years. When, in the end, Stephen decides upon the vocation of the artist, it is with a specific goal in mind.

I go to encounter for the millionth time the reality of experience and to forge in the smithy of my soul the uncreated conscience of my race.[6]

Joyce, under the inspiration of Daedalus, wishing to forge the "uncreated conscience" of his race, is expressing the desire to produce a new conscience, a new religio-ethical standard, a way out of decaying Western culture. It was Daedalus, after all, who "forged" the wings which allowed Icarus, his son, and himself to escape from the labyrinth. Joyce likewise wished to create a means of transcending the cultural situation into which he was born. Few, of course, have found in his masterpiece, *Finnegans Wake*, the tool of that transcendence, though none would doubt that such was his aim: to escape the strictures of a culture decaying because it had lost its conscience resident heretofore in the now-defunct Judaeo-Christian paradigm.

Hermann Hesse's novels, from the early *Peter Camenzind* to *The Glass-Bead Game*, examine in anxious tones the relation of religion and art in terms of the artist's futile search for religious absolutes. The novel *The Glass-Bead Game* has as its theme the unsuccessful attempt to synthesize art, science, and religion through the use of an elaborate formal symbol-system reminiscent of the Platonic strategy of achieving "The Good." But for Hesse the rift between the intellectual and the emotional qualities of existence remained, in the absence of belief in God, too great to overcome.

The persistence of the theme of religion as a central problem of the artist is unmistakable in twentieth-century literature. The absence of God leaves the artist, who must depend, implicitly or explicitly, upon that sense of Eros which secures Truthful Beauty, with only one last truth to tell—the truth that the substratum of truth, God as the sense of Eros, is dead. It is not the actual existence of God which is at issue so much as the *belief* in His existence. As the poet Wallace Stevens has said:

> God may or may not exist as an independent absolute *thing,* an object, so to speak, for scientific exploration. He assuredly exists as a necessary postulate of the poetic imagination, embodying in concrete form the perfected projection of life, which alone can satisfy the will.[7]

Stevens, who often described himself as "absolutely without religion," nonetheless recognized the importance of the religious vision to art. And when religious belief is no longer possible, art stands, uncomfortably, as religion's surrogate. "The relation of art to life is of the first importance in a skeptical age since, in the absence of a belief in God, the mind turns to its own creations."[8]

We cannot find even in the most contemporary expressions of the literary artist any proclamation of a new religious vision. A new religion may be rising, an uncertain phoenix, out of the ashes of the old, but it is yet to be recognized. Instead of proclamations of the new, we have poignant satire of the old. In the discussion of Adventure as a cultural aim, I quoted Whitehead's words "Satire is the last flicker of originality in a passing epoch as it faces the onroad of staleness and boredom" (AI 358). The abundance of religious satire in contemporary art signals, perhaps, at least the beginnings of a transition to a new sensibility.

In the works of Kurt Vonnegut, Jr., we find some extremely sensitive religious satire. In *The Sirens of Titan* Vonnegut creates a new religion served by "The Church of God the Utterly Indifferent." In this parody of Christian Calvinism, Vonnegut creates a *reductio ad absurdum* of any orthodox Christian attempt at justifying the ways of God to man. In *Cat's Cradle*, Vonnegut invents *Bokononism*, a religion whose theology is self-consciously grounded upon *foma*, "harmless untruths," and whose moral principles are expressed in such propositions as "Pay no attention to Caesar; Caesar has absolutely no idea what's going on."

Robert Heinlein, a science-fiction writer, has provided an interesting satirical treatment of Christianity in his underground classic, *Stranger in a Strange Land*. The hero of this novel, Michael Valentine, is half-human, half-Martian. He suffers martyrdom on earth in an attempt to establish his religion of mutual love. This martyrdom comes mainly because Michael has stressed the sensuous as well as the spiritual implications of the love-relation in his construction of a religion. This work serves to reduce to absurdity both the original Christian vision and our modern misconstrued version of it.

The British rock opera *Jesus Christ Superstar* is perhaps one of the most significant examples of contemporary religious satire. Its lyrics and musical themes provide an exciting adventure in satire, largely because the Superstar superman which Jesus Christ has become in the eyes of the Church is tried, in words and music, and found wanting, while the believable Jesus behind the image strains the credulity of the orthodox faithful. In the opera, the Judaeo-Christian God is parodied as a ruthless puppet-master who uses both Jesus and the naïve and sincere Judas Iscariot for the working out of His inscrutable purposes.

Religious satire of the type we have mentioned is a final expression of Adventure in a declining epoch before the advent of a new religious vision. Art, in order to express Truthful Beauty, has had either to express directly the tragic truth of the loss of Peace, or to resort to the parody which softens the impact of the collapse of the religious vision, through a demonstration of the inadequacy of the forms through which that vision had been expressed.

The phenomenon of the death of God means that the traditional source of the sense of Peace is no longer available. One might well expect that, confronted by this fact, cultural expressions would increasingly evidence a search for new guidelines, channels through which to experience anew the Eros which promises some fundamental harmony of Reality and Appearance. This in part explains the highly tentative and transitory character of so much of the aesthetic expressions of contemporary culture.

It has become a truism of the art critic that, beginning with the twentieth century, there has been a general decline in the life expectancy of schools of art. Since the end of the nineteenth century only two styles of painting have had any lasting influence, the Impressionist movement which endured from the last quarter of the nineteenth century to the early years of the twentieth, and Abstract Expressionism, which lasted through the forties and fifties of this century. The list of the remaining significant movements in painting constitutes a catalogue of ephemera: the Futurists, the Fauvists, Cubism, Surrealism, "Pop" and "Op" art—each hurrying off the scene to make room for the next. One lesson learned by the art of the twentieth century is that the experience of Beauty, like all experience, is ephemeral. Existence is ever-not-quite. Beauty, as the achievement of harmonious intensity, always involves tragedy. The actualization, through the attainment of satisfaction, of the subjective aim of experience spells the end of an occasion of experience. Tragedy, which for Whitehead means the loss of beauty, is involved in every time-bound occasion of experience. The threat of finitude under such ontological conditions would be overwhelming were it not for the possibility of the sense of the Unity of Adventure—the intuition that one's experiencing passes into the formation of other actualities beyond the present. Permanence is not essential to art. The ephemerality of art is of the essence of experiencing. The sense of a permanence transcending temporal occasions of experience is the gift not of aesthetic but of *religious* insight. From the perspective of Whiteheadian philosophy, the contemporary developments which lead toward "the happenings" of such expressions as "action painting" or of kinetic art, in spite of the threat of too much novelty, evidence a significant insight into the nature of art and of beauty itself—that beauty is ephemeral by its very nature.

Artists have always recognized, at one level, the ephemerality of the aesthetic experience. The reply of most artists to the question "Which of your works is your favorite?" would no doubt be "The work now in progress." The enjoyment of the aesthetic *process* is sought in the experience of enjoyment of the finished product. In fact the poignant emotion which overcomes an artist at the moment of the completion of a work of art testifies to the Whiteheadian insight that the final "satisfaction" of an ideal aim is fraught with the sense of tragedy—the fading of intensity. It is said of the poet Carl Sandburg that he always cried over beautiful things, knowing that nothing beautiful lasts. Realizing that beauty is ephemeral, the artist is driven by the sense of finitude to seek an intuition of permanence. That intuition is the sense of Peace as the harmony of finite perfections, the Unity of Adventure.

The cultural task of art in contemporary technological society is the acceptance of the fact that permanence is no longer possible in art.[9] Dynamic, kinetic art is the art of a functionally oriented society. Process philosophies of the type of Whitehead are designed to interpret the cultural significances of such societies much more successfully than are substance-oriented philosophies. The recognition of finitude as inherent in the ever-not-quite character of existence allows for the confrontation with a fundamental fact of cultural existence in contemporary society. But beyond the acceptance of finitude consequent upon the ephemerality of beauty, art has a substantive function as well: to proclaim, if possible, a new religious vision emerging beyond the collapse of the Judaeo-Christian paradigm. The Whiteheadian religious insight, equipped as it is with a distinctly different conception of God's functioning, can provide the initial stimulus to seek that Eros in existence which drives toward a harmony of Appearance and Reality. Beyond the death of the Judaeo-Christian paradigm, and the sense of uprootedness involved in that loss, lies a new religious sensibility in which the senses of Eros and the Unity of Adventure function to secure the finite and uprooted experiences of contemporary culture. It is the function of art to proclaim the truth of this new sensibility.

The new religious vision will emerge by virtue of a reflection on the ephemerality of Beauty, an acceptance of finitude. The novelty and erethic fervor of contemporary society expresses the fact that process, and not substance, rules in art. Aesthetic experience is poignant in the extreme. The proclamations of art already contain the embryonic expressions of a new religious vision—a vision grounded in tragic beauty. It is the sense of Peace which brings us to a realization that existence is ever-not-quite and that, beyond our own finite actualizations, there is a tendency toward congruence of Appearance and Reality and a consequent realization of permanence. Art proclaims what Whiteheadian philosophy proclaims: Existence is transitory; individual attainments are beyond complete enjoyment; beauty is tragic —but beyond the ephemerality of the aesthetic experience, beyond tragic beauty, there is the sense of Peace which prevents cynicism and overcomes despair.

3. MORALITY AND THE CONTROL OF PROCESS

We have had occasion before to stress the importance of the category of subjective intensity in the interpretation of the aim of experience, both in its individual and in its cultural modalities. This category defines the aim of experience as an aim at intensity in the immediate present and in the relevant future. I have suggested that these two aspects of the aim of experience give a systematic foundation for Whitehead's view of the relations between aesthetic and moral experience. Aesthetic experience is concerned primarily with the immediate realization of value, while moral experience aims at the achievement of importance for a finite selection of others in the relevant future. The relation of art and morality, expressed in this manner, must be recalled in the following consideration of the relations of religion and morality. For the discussion of religion's contribution to moral experience and expression will be similar, in form, to that of the discussion of the last section. The difference is that, while art expresses its relevance from the perspective of the immediacy of the present, "the greater part of morality hinges on the determination of relevance in the future" (PR 41).

Morality is "the control of process so as to maximize importance" (MT 13–14). It is possible, as in the case of art, to distinguish between experience and expression. Moral experience is a "control of process" consisting in the attention to the "detailed occasion" (v. MT 28) and its relation to the anticipated future beyond itself. Moral expression is the actual maximization of importance through the expression of one's moral intuitions, using the vehicle of moral codes, rules of behavior, etc. The distinction between moral experience and expression can be seen by noting the *moral* character of the adjustment of Appearance to Reality.

> An actual individual . . . has truck with the totality of things by reason of its sheer actuality; but it has attained its individual depth of being by a selective emphasis limited to its own purposes. . . . The selectiveness of individual experience is moral so far as it conforms to the balance of importance disclosed in the rational vision; and conversely the conversion of the intellectual insight into an emotional force corrects the sensitive experience in the direction of morality. The correction is in proportion to the rationality of the insight [PR 22–23].

It will be helpful to interpret this statement of Whitehead in terms of the Appearance–Reality relation. In the self-formation of an occasion of experience, two relevant senses of morality are present. The first is that which characterizes the transition from Reality to Appearance. The selective emphasis of an occasion is moral insofar as it maximizes importance. Such importance is achieved when the rational concepts emerging from high-grade occasions of experience expressing those factors of primitive experience are capable of promoting intensity beyond that given occasion. The second sense of morality refers to the symbolic reference from Appearance to Reality. If the Appearance (concept, image, etc.) has emphasized the relevant factors of experience, then the referring of that Appearance to its origin in emotional experience will correct the rationalized concept by providing an emotional force conducive to the maximization of importance. Consider human moral experience: in the first instance there is a generalization of a concept from particular experiences; in the second, the application of that concept to a particular instance in the experience of a personal order of occasions.

The commandment "Thou shalt not bear false witness" expresses the moral intuition that telling the truth is one way of insuring harmony of experience. We may say that telling the truth is morally good, in Whitehead's view, if that action results in harmonious consequences to the extent that it is asserted, and in the manner implied, in the conceptual formulation of the maxim. Similarly, the maxim is morally sound if it evokes actions which promote such harmony. In brief, an action is morally good if it pro-

motes harmony and intensity of experience within a selected context; a so-
called "moral maxim" promotes moral good if it elicits such action. "Moral
codes are relevant to presuppositions respecting the systematic character of
the relevant universe. When the presuppositions do not apply, that special
code is a vacuous statement of abstract irrelevancies" (MT 13).

Moral maxims—"Do not kill," "Always tell the truth," etc.—seek to
promote certain broad types of systematic action which, on the whole, promote intensity and harmony of experience within the social context presupposed by the maxim. These maxims should be such as to allow for alteration
and re-interpretation when necessary. For reality is in process; conditions
change. Particular moral actions must be performed on contextual criteria
which allow adequate analysis of the character of the reality from out of
which the relevant future will be constructed. The continual reassessment
of actions relevant for the future requires a constant check upon the relation between Reality and Appearance in any given situation.

Every moral code is derived from a special set of social circumstances
beyond which its relevance is questionable. But Whitehead recognizes the
need to search for the "highly general principles underlying all such codes"
(AI 376). These principles are: the generality of harmony and the importance of the individual. These two principles, the first indicating the general
concept of "order," the second, the particular concept of "love," express the
two extremes in terms of which the validity of moral experiences and expression is to be judged. Too often morality is discussed only from the
point of view of the maintenance of a type of social order to which individuals are subordinate. It is to morality in this sense that Whitehead's statement "Love . . . is a little oblivious as to morals" (PR 520–521) refers.
A valid moral code must always seek to resolve the seeming antithesis between the impersonality of order and the personal character of love.

The means of harmonizing these two contrasting aims is to combine the
factors of personal transcendence and personal affirmation in moral expression. All types of order should be judged according to their ability to support intensity of experience in individual occasions of experience. Individual
actual occasions should be judged by a twofold criterion: intrinsic strength
of experience and optimum influence in promoting a high-grade variety of
order. The moral code which best meets this criterion preserves the health
of a society.

In addition to these two general objective criteria by which a moral code
is to be judged, it is possible to find in Whitehead's philosophy the basis for
the elaboration of certain subjective criteria which are prerequisites for the
making of valid moral decisions. These criteria may be derived from the
categoreally based requirement that moral experience should consist in the
maximization of importance in the *relevant future*.

"The relevant future consists of those elements in the anticipated future
which are felt with effective intensity by the present subject by reason of the

SOME IMPLICATIONS

real potentiality for them to be derived from itself" (PR 41). One obvious
implication of this statement is that different subjects will determine different futures. And the scope of the relevant future determined will be a function of the content of one's experience, one's ability to reflect upon it and ac-
curately to discriminate its significant elements, and the motivation for the
utilization of these discriminations. Now, according to the objective moral
criteria discussed above, a moral code is adequate if it promotes the generality of harmony and the importance of the individual. In order for such
a code to be followed, an individual must be able to derive from his experience a feeling of anticipated importance for a broadly determined future.
Two subjective qualities are necessary if this is to be accomplished. The first
is rationality; the second is disinterestedness.

Rationality is necessary in making a moral decision: in determining a
relevant future, the present subject must feel elements in the anticipated
future with effective intensity, by reason of the real potentiality for them
to be derived from itself. Such feeling, if it is to be relevant to a broadly
determined future promoting a generality of harmony, requires subtle rational analysis of one's anticipated future.

Disinterestedness, the second subjective criterion, is necessary since it is
the *future* which is being decided upon. The two dimensions of that future,
from the perspective of a moral decision, are the future occasions of the
personal order of occasions comprising the moral agent, and the futures of
the other nexūs of entities defining the relevant future of the subject. Self-
interest, in its most basic sense, cannot be served since there is no radical
persistence of the moral agent beyond its act of decision. Thus the aim of
an occasion of experience at subjective intensity in the relevant future must
be a rational and disinterested one. As Charles Hartshorne has said of his
own similar philosophical stance:

> Reason surveys ultimate consequences, and when our personal sequences
> are all in the past, then it will not be we who still profit from the pleasant-
> ness of the experiences making up the sequences. It will rather be the sur-
> viving individuals, and God. Thus the rational aim of an actual entity must
> be disinterested.[10]

The general value of morality in promoting civilized order is obvious.
For components of the social order, such as legal structures, political institutions, and cultural mores, are all expressions of the moral order of a culture.
But if we ask what specific cultural aims are promoted by the moral interest, we shall find that the subject of morality may be most relevantly discussed in terms of the promotion of the qualities of Truth, Adventure, and
Peace.

Both art and morality require a measure of blunt truth. But art does not
require large-scale and direct conformation of Appearance and Reality since
it attains its goal via symbolic truth-relations of a more indirect and subtle
sort. Morality, which is concerned with effectiveness for the future, must

have a high degree of correspondence of Appearance to Reality. The maximization of importance requires a correct judgment concerning the character of the relevant future. Such a judgment can be made only if one is able to analyze correctly those elements in the givenness of the initial physical prehensions which will be likely to persist into the future. This implies the presence of a strong and direct truth-relation between Appearance and Reality in valid moral experience and expression. Thus morality promotes and sustains truth-relations of the direct sort.

The moral interest safeguards truth in two ways: in promoting the elaboration of certain general moral principles based on commonly held moral intuitions, thereby maintaining the large-scale truth-relations which serve as the general defining characteristics of the type of social order in question; and in stressing the constant attention to context. Such a stress enables one to seek a continual reassessment of the possible alternatives for moral actions and of the concrete requirements of present experience. This increases the possibility of the maintenance of specific truth-relations in these circumstances. Whitehead explicitly recognizes the function of morality in promoting broad-based truth-relations when discussing the foundation of the motivation for scientific activity in moral experience.

> That we fail to find in experience any elements intrinsically incapable of exhibition as examples of general theory, is the hope of rationalism. This hope is not a metaphysical premise. It is the faith which forms the motive for the pursuit of all sciences alike, including metaphysics. . . .
>   The preservation of such faith must depend on an ultimate moral intuition into the nature of intellectual action—that it should embody the adventure of hope [PR 67].

The concern for the maximizing of importance for the relevant future entails a concern, not only for Truth, but for Adventure as well. The adventure of hope is possible because morality recognizes an aim at the ideal. The concern for the relevant future entails an anticipation for the future beyond the present occasion, as well as a concern for the character of givenness potentially determinant of that future. The factor of anticipation in moral experience leads, under ideal conditions, to a promotion of Adventure. "Morals consists in the aim at the ideal, and at its lowest it concerns the prevention of the relapse to lower levels" (AI 346).

It may seem somewhat paradoxical to argue that morality promotes adventure in a society when "the champions of morality are on the whole the fierce opponents of new ideals" (AI 346). Nevertheless, since Adventure is concerned with transcendence beyond achieved perfections, and since morality contains an element of anticipation in its very structure, morality and Adventure have coincident purposes. The contextualist implications of Whiteheadian moral theory leave open the possibilities of dynamic moral decisions which, by taking into account the wide variations of the circumstances within which moral decisions must be made, could promote adventurous actions. An unyielding conservatism characterizes moral experience and expression only when this necessity of contextual reference is denied.

To promote the qualities of Truth and Adventure, it is essential that morality be sustained by the intuition of Peace. Morality is concerned with the relevant future. This implies a specific context. "The [best] moral code is the behaviour-patterns which in the environment for which it is designed will promote the evolution of that environment towards its proper perfection" (AI 377). But the limitations set upon the context, in extent or duration, are arbitrary. The most limited moral context for human beings is that of a single presiding occasion in its anticipation of its relevance to the next occasion in that series. This is the experience of self-determination which is the foundation of all morality. "The actual entity, in a state of process during which it is not fully definite, determines its own ultimate definiteness. This is the whole point of moral responsibility" (PR 390). But for morality to have any meaning in a human social context, there must be transcendence relevant to other human beings and societies, not just to the successive occasions of one's own personal order.

> Beyond the soul, there are other societies, and societies of societies. There is the animal body ministering to the soul: there are families, groups of families, nations, species, groups involving different species associated in the joint enterprise of keeping alive. These various societies, each in its measure, claim loyalties and loves. In human history the various responses to these claims disclose the essential transcendence of each individual actuality beyond itself [AI 376].

The sense of Peace extends and purifies moral experience and expression by providing that ultimate sense of transcendence between individual attainments. The first, and most important, contribution of religion to morality is just this. The feeling of objective immortality, "the anticipatory feelings of the transcendent future in its relation to immediate fact" (PR 425), provides the pivotal point at which morality passes over into religion. For whereas "morality emphasizes the detailed occasion . . . religion emphasizes the unity of ideal inherent in the universe" (MT 28). The primary distinction between morality and religion is found in the dimensions of the order to which each is meant to be relevant. Morality considers the relevant future to be a finite selection of future occasions, while for religion the context is unlimited. Religion concerns the objective immortality of individual experience in the everlasting nature of God. A faith or trust beyond what is specifically experienced is involved in the intuition of Peace. Morality is concerned with those elements in the future of an occasion which are felt, via anticipation, as potentiality derivable from that occasion. The sense of Peace in religion extends the feeling of anticipated relevance to the whole of future experiencing.

For this reason the sense of Peace delivers morality from the aberrations threatened by the experience of *finitude*. One of the first lessons of experience is that all realization involves exclusion. The choice of finite means for the realization of finite ends will invariably result in the exclusion of some "goods" and the realization of others. The sensitive moralist is perhaps more acutely aware than most men that striving after the best necessarily entails the tragic loss of potentially realizable value. The intuition of Peace provides the moral agent with the sense of a transcendent context within which the necessary loss involved in chosen realizations is not a source of final disharmony.

The most vitiating aspect of the finitude of morality stems from the fact that moral judgments, as judgments of the relevance of present to future experiencing, must be made from the perspective of individual occasions with their own finite interests. This tends to prevent the attainment of disinterestedness, one of the prerequisites for sound moral decisions and actions.

> The antithesis between the general good and the individual interest can be abolished only when the individual is such that its interest is the general good, thus exemplifying the loss of the minor intensities in order to find them again with finer composition in a wider sweep of interest [PR 23].

Such a merging of individual and general interests can only come about through the attainment of the quality of Peace. For the general good must, on Whitehead's terms, be really general. As long as one's definition of the general good is in terms of "my family," "my country," or "in the short run," the ego-centric element is still much too emphatically present. For "the essence of Peace is that the individual whose strength of experience is founded upon this ultimate intuition, thereby is extending the influence of the source of all order" (AI 377). Religion, with its expression of the vision of objective immortality as a gift of the consequent nature of God, provides a means whereby the fullest transcendence of individual interest is possible. This is one way in which religion may be said to "complete" morality.

This completion of morality by transcendence is an implication of Whitehead's characterization of the religious and the moral interests. For since morality is defined in terms of relation within a finite context (the relevant future), the questions of the transcendence of morality arise each time that finite context is transcended. The conception of religion as based upon the intuition of the relation of an individual to the totality of experience implies that the transcendence of a finite context will involve a movement from a moral toward a religious reference.

Whitehead is by no means alone in his conception of the relation between morality and religion. A view quite like Whitehead's is held by Paul Tillich, who considers the relation between morality and religion to be that of the "conditioned" to the "unconditioned." [11] And Stephen Toulmin has provided a similar analysis of the relations between morality and religion, which he bases merely upon a philosophical analysis of certain ethical situations.[12] Toulmin claims that in some ethical situations one may encounter

questions for which no satisfactory *ethical* answers are possible. Only insofar as such questions refer to the relevant ethical context may they be answered in ethical terms. For example,

> The question, "Why ought I not have two wives?", calls to begin with for
> reasons referring to the existing institutions; secondly, may raise the more
> general question whether our institution of "marriage" could be improved
> by altering it in the direction of polygamy; thirdly, transforms itself into
> a question about the kind of community in which one would personally
> prefer to live; and beyond that cannot be reasoned about at all.[13]

Questions precluding answers which appeal to an accepted mode of social
practice are "limiting questions" for Toulmin, since they transcend the
limits of merely ethical reasoning.[14] But even though ethical answers are
not appropriate for such limiting questions, religious answers may well be.
Thus the question "Why ought I not have two wives?" when pressed beyond the limits of strictly ethical reasoning, may still appropriately receive
such an answer as "Because it is against God's law to do so."

Toulmin, in his analysis of ethical situations, is pointing to the same general fact which we have found to be an implication of Whitehead's metaphysics: moral concerns lead to religious concerns when the relevant moral
context is brought into question and is transcended. But I should be quick to
add that Toulmin is not seeking to express any *metaphysical* views concerning morality or religion, but wishes merely to consider the *logic* of ethical
situations.[15]

I have said that morality, on Whiteheadian grounds, is "completed" by
religion through transcendence. Such a completion consists in overcoming
the finitude inherent in the moral perspective. But there is another sense in
which religion may be said to complete morality. The extremes of the over-
emphasis of either traditional or novel factors in experience, which were
found to militate against the value of art to culture, affect morality as well.
The dislocation of Appearance and Reality, which we have termed the state
of uprootedness, from the moral perspective, is the result of a failure to
meet one or both of the subjective criteria for moral action discussed above.
A failure of rationality or of disinterestedness in moral deliberation and
actions can disrupt the Appearance–Reality relation in the experience of the
moral agent and the experiences of those who constitute his relevant future.
These failures, of course, relate to the two factors of the religious problem
which were cited as potential causes of uprootedness: ignorance and perversity.

Moral ignorance is ignorance of the relevant context in terms of which a
specific moral decision is to be made. This ignorance results in a disharmonious realization of experiences in the relevant future. The most obvious
example of moral ignorance in a human social context is the rejection of
contextual morality in favor of dogmatic implementation of moral maxims.
Such a dogmatic affirmation may be the result of an ignorance of the proper

range of creative relevance of the maxims. If such is the case, the set of symbols expressing the required patterns of behavior cease to be valid expressions of present experiencing, and the prescribed actions are no longer those which will maximize importance in the relevant future. A moral code which applies beyond its context in space or in time influences attempts at symbolic reference which will undermine the potential truth-relations characterizable in terms of present experiencing, and will, likewise, stultify any possible adventure beyond traditional modes of effective action.

Whitehead cites the Biblical proscription of work on the Sabbath as an example of a moral maxim which has been applied far beyond its relevant context. If such maxims are held to be germane to the ordering of general social behavior, then the aims of Adventure and Truth which are supported by moral experience and expression will not be given sufficient support within a culture. The very existence of moral codes allows for too great a reliance upon their specific verbal requirements. For this reason, moral codes, political constitutions, etc., should be left somewhat vague in order to facilitate the adjustment to changing circumstances.

The answer to the threat of the promulgation of dogmatic moral codes is obviously not radical contextualism which denies any guidelines. Whitehead is concerned only that there be a sensitivity to the cultural relativity of moral injunctions. This sensitivity is a function of the rationality of the moral agent. Every experience has an initial aim whose content is based upon a "graded envisagement" of all possibilities relevant to that particular occasion. This aim is conditioned by the givenness of the past and, in its final character as fully formed subjective aim, by the freedom of the actual occasion. *Given that context*: the initial aim is the relevant aim. No other context will require just that aim for the realization of maximum intensity. To be able to make correct moral judgments, one must be sensitive to the lure of Eros toward subjective intensity of experience. For insofar as a moral decision is a *reasoned* one, the reasons must be determined in large part by a rational analysis of that lure. Just as in the case of artistic creation, the knowledge of the Eros may or may not be conscious, and may or may not have explicit religious significance. But it is nonetheless true that the religious emphasis upon the importance of discerning God's will in each situation does, on the Whiteheadian view, have important moral implications.

Besides moral ignorance, the condition of uprootedness may also be caused by moral perversity. In discussing the religious problem in Chapter VII, I defended the view that Whitehead's concept of freedom allowed for the possibility of perversity—i.e., free actions which seek to thwart the fulfillment of the lure toward subjective intensity of experience. The chief motivation of perverse actions derives from the same principle from which derives the possibility of moral disinterestedness. An important implication of Whitehead's doctrine of the self as constituted by a nexus of actual occasions sustaining personal order is that the fruits of an action will not, in the strictest sense, be gathered by the actor himself. Such an implication can lead either to disinterestedness, or to a *carpe diem* viewpoint whose moral guideline is the knowledge that "As I sow, so shall another reap."

Perverse actions directly interfere with the promotion of truth in a social context. This can easily be seen by considering a simple example. Truth is the conformation of Appearance and Reality. A lie is a misrepresentation of the true Appearance–Reality relation. A lie told by Smith to Brown contributes data to the experience of Brown which weaken the efficacy of symbolic reference from those data. Constructions of Appearance utilizing those data will manifest a minor dislocation from Reality.

The implications of moral perversity on Whiteheadian grounds are much more profound than on many other views because of Whitehead's metaphysical realism. Perverse actions have consequences beyond those which directly inhere in the relations of human beings in a social context. They affect, however slightly, the aim at ideal harmony. Since the future experiences derived from a given moral subject must be harmonized in accordance with the aim at subjective intensity, the freedom of man, when used perversely, can fundamentally affect the attainment of harmony in the world. "The initial aim is the best for that *impasse*. But if the best be bad, then . . . the chaff is burnt" (PR 373). Initial aims are provided in accordance with the existing possibilities for realization. This is the metaphysical basis for Whitehead's contextual morality.

In the foregoing discussion of the moral interest, I have tried to show how the Whiteheadian conception of the relations of religion and morality allow religion to make the following important contributions to morality. First, through that element of the religious insight grounded upon the anticipation of objective immortality (i.e., the sense of Peace), religion "completes" morality by providing a vision of the source of all order to serve as the context for moral deliberations and actions. Second, the Eros conditions moral actions by the provision of a rational aim in terms of which moral decisions may be made. Finally, an intuition of Peace as the realization of the actual harmony attained in the Unity of Adventure provides the sense of new possibilities for future actualizations. Before concluding our discussion of the moral interest, I intend to indicate the relevance of Whitehead's philosophy for the resolution of the contemporary crisis in the relation of religion and morality.

4. THE SECULARIZATION OF MORALITY

Contemporary theorists of religion often yield to the temptation to believe that the secularization of religion and theology is the direct result of the rationalization of human experience. Echoing the Hegelian argument that the transition from the *Vorstellungen* of religion to the rational concepts of philosophy has brought an end to the need for transcendent reference in religious language, contemporary theorists have found the "sacred" character of religion intrinsically tied to mythological forms of thought and expression which can have no significant role in a semantic context in which "scientific" and "secular" concepts constitute the criteria of meaning. Philosophic and theological programs based on this belief seek to translate traditional religious language into some alternate semantic context—that of linguistic empiricism in the case of Paul Van Buren,[16] or of urban sociology as in the program of Harvey Cox,[17] to give but two examples. The effect of such a translation is, of course, the reduction of religious language to the language of ethics, that is, to language about the evaluation of norms for human conduct. If religion is to survive as an autonomous cultural interest, it must be able to defend itself against the various ethical reductionists who would reduce it in meaning and value to an expression of the moral interest.

One of the implications of our remarks on the religious interest in relation to its cultural context has been that any philosophic program which refuses to recognize the religious interest as a fundamental mode of cultural self-realization greatly impoverishes the sources of thought, action, and feeling to which civilized men refer for self-understanding. Whitehead's explicit recognition that the aim of an adequate cosmology must be to "bring the aesthetic, moral, and religious interests into relation with those concepts of the world which have their origin in natural science" (PR vi), together with the explicit cultural value he gives to the religious vision as Eros and the Unity of Adventure, places him squarely against any devaluation of the importance of the religious interest. Nevertheless, one consequence of the collapse of the Judaeo-Christian religious paradigm, proclaimed in art and experienced throughout contemporary culture, is the widespread reduction of religion to the moral interest.

Even Whiteheadian philosophy is being "revised" by those embarrassed by its avowedly religious tonality. Donald Sherburne, one of the most acute interpreters of Whitehead, has announced his intention to rid Whiteheadian philosophy of the concept of God and, consequently, to establish the relevance of Whitehead to classical religion solely in ethical terms. Sherburne writes that

> Exorcising the concept "God" from the [Whiteheadian] system leaves me in a stance very similar to that of Paul Van Buren, who holds that the essence of Christianity is an ethical message about how to live a life and that "God" talk is a dated, misleading . . . obscure way of saying what Christianity wants to say about what it is to be a man and to live a moral life.[18]

Sherburne's claim that the "naturalization" of Whitehead's metaphysics leads to the reduction of Whitehead's theory of religion to an "ethical message about how to live a life" is one more expression of the contemporary embarrassment with the religious interest in an increasingly secularized world. However much one might wish to free Whitehead from some currently unpopular theological ballast, the distinctly religious tonality of

Whiteheadian thought is an unquestionable datum which cannot be avoided without doing great damage to his philosophy.

Any attempt to interpret religious experience solely in ethical terms must fly in the face of the Whiteheadian theory of religion developed in Chapters VI and VII. There we indicated that morality and religion have distinctive origins in human experience, and must function as autonomous interests. We also pointed out the way in which Whitehead's affirmation of a distinctively religious modality of experience in terms of the historical progress of positive religion suggests the need for an increasing independence of the cultural interests of morality and religion.

The single most important change in contemporary culture, insofar as the relation of the religious and moral interests is concerned, is that of the secularization of morality. The phenomenon of the collapse of the Judaeo-Christian paradigm has left the moral interest uprooted, without the theological *fundamentum in re* which has served as its foundation since the beginnings of Western culture. A radical contextualism has supervened upon absolutist ethics as the cultural expression of moral feeling and action. The moral man, of the twentieth century, like his artist counterpart, is faced with the radical sense of finitude born of the experience of moral relativity. Through the acceptance of finitude the moral interest, like the artistic, will find renewed cultural efficacy. The sense of Peace cannot come from the traditional source, viz., the Judaeo-Christian God. Hope for a revitalization of the civilizing function of the moral interest lies beyond the contemporary "crisis" in the relations between morality and religion.

This crisis results from the civilizing of experience which demands the increased autonomy of each of the cultural interests. Such a demand militates against the practical dominance of the moral over the religious interest which has been characteristic of Western culture since the "establishment" of Christianity in the fourth century.

The predominantly moral interpretation of religious experience and expression in our Western tradition is supported by at least three important historical considerations. First, the Judaeo-Christian God has been conceptualized primarily in terms of the function of lawgiver. This Old Testament concept has established a type of theistic interpretation in which the divine is envisioned as moral guarantor and judge. Such a concept understandably determines the intrinsic relations of religious and moral interests in our tradition.

But the concept of God as moral guarantor turns out to be an arrant provincialism. Judaic monotheism, which sought, in the beginning, to express religious ideas in the broadest possible terms, nonetheless maintained, for the greater part of its development, the direct relevance of these ideas to the Jewish nation alone. This means of producing increased rationality through extended generality was only slightly superior to the Roman attempt to maintain the widest possible vision of geographical and social inclusiveness.

Both conceptions of religion were vitiated by the same kind of finitude. Such interpretations of religious experience invariably lead to a this-worldly, moralistic religion, ruled by space and time. But even if the interpretation of God as moral guarantor and judge were feasible and desirable, the autonomy of the religious interest need not be affected. There is no reason why the moral functioning of God need be understood as religious. God can certainly have secular functions. Kierkegaard demonstrated this point in his examination of the teleological suspension of the ethical. Whitehead's concept of God entails the exercise of important non-religious activities, as we have stated previously.[19]

A second reason for the reduction of religion to morality lies in the problem of legitimation. The employment of religion and of primary religious objects to legitimate ethical ideals and practices has been an almost universal phenomenon in social evolution. If Moses had come down from the mountain to face a disorganized and demoralized people with tablets of clay bearing Ten Commandments for which he claimed sole authorship, he would have no doubt been lynched. The cry "God has spoken" is an incantation which has magically transformed a great deal of magnificent poetry into an equal amount of rigid dogma. As long as it is suspected that the appeal to God is necessary in order to validate ethical propositions, the confusion between morality and religion will continue.

Read in terms of the principle of legitimation, the development of Western Christianity may be told as the story of the increasing moralization of the religious element. The short step from Jesus to Saint Paul was a move from the priority of unreflective love to subordination of the claims of love to those of "justice" and the "powers that be." The direct influence of Jesus and His message of uncompromising love increasingly took a back seat to the theological rationalizations of Saint Paul. It was an even shorter step from Pauline Christianity to the "establishment" of the Christian faith by Constantine and Bishop Hosius in the fourth century. The claims of Christ were molded to suit the established political structure. The perfectionist, spirit-filled sectarians maintaining the tradition of love were destroyed or persecuted until their influence was broken.

The third phase in the moralizing of religion came with the barbarian invasions of the Roman empire in the fifth century. The religious establishment accepted a *détente* with the barbarian inheritors of the Roman political institutions which set the pattern for the development of our modern Church-State relationships—the cloistered elements maintaining the distinctly religious tonality of Christianity over against the papal establishment which was largely concerned with political matters. The Reformation altered these conditions of religion very little. Lutheranism and Calvinism developed primarily into institutions for the legitimating of social value systems, as the work of the sociologist Max Weber so profoundly indicates.

The conditions of religious experience and expression in the contemporary period are such that we are freed from the necessity of employing the authority of the religious interest to support the *status quo*. The secularization of social existence, the pace of which has accelerated since 1789, has produced increasingly disestablished and sectarian expressions of religious feeling which do not function at all to maintain bonds of social unity. The contemporary technological society sustains order without the need of external stimuli to promote moral commitment. Thus we no longer require religious sanctions to maintain social order. This phenomenon no doubt entails the loss of some of the traditional modes of exercising power which have belonged to all established religions. But read from the perspective of the theory of culture which we are presupposing in this work, some form of disestablishment is an essential precondition for the discovery by a religion of its own autonomous essence.

A third basis for the tendency to reduce religion to the moral interest can be traced to the philosophical sources in modern philosophy for the examination of religion. If modern philosophy has a story to tell, it is of the futility of employing doubt as the primary tool in the quest for certainty. Viewed methodologically, philosophic activity from Descartes through Hume and Kant to Hegel was one grand *reductio ad absurdum* of the skeptical method. One of the principal victims of that doubtful certainty which vitiated modern thought was the cultural interest of religion. Cartesian doubt made of the primary religious object a bare metaphysical principle whose only purpose was to save Descartes' philosophic system from incoherence. Hume managed to reduce the religious interest either to the status of "sophistry and illusion," or to a form of practice, or "custom," to which he denied rational status. Kant, in placing limits upon reason to make room for faith, reduced rational religion to certain experiences and expressions which direct the will toward obedience to the moral law. Hegel's speculative attempt to revitalize reason in its theoretical mode resulted in reducing religion to a congeries of *Vorstellungen,* mere pictorial representations of the truth which only philosophy may adequately attain.

It was not until the late nineteenth and early twentieth century that the philosophic investigation of religion as an autonomous enterprise began to come into its own. Inspired by anthropological studies into the religions of non-Western societies, phenomenologists such as Otto and Van Der Leuuw,[20] as well as radical empiricists such as William James,[21] began to provide strong evidence that religion, as experienced and as expressed, must be understood in some other way than as "morality tinged with emotion." In addition, contemporary philosophies of language analysis have done much toward supporting the autonomy of religion by directing attention to the distinctiveness of its linguistic expressions vis-à-vis the languages of alternative cultural interests.[22]

We have considered in some detail the Whiteheadian basis for maintaining the autonomy of religion as a cultural interest. In Chapter V the rationale for such autonomy was provided in terms of an analysis of the origin in experience of the intuition of holiness. For Whitehead, the experience of moral obligation, the search for "rightness," is radically distinct from the experience of the value-contrast of a finite individual to the infinite totality of things, which evokes the sense of holiness. Concepts of "the right" and "the holy" are predicates possessing distinctly different experiential values. In teleological terms, the difference between morality and religion is the difference between the short or long run and the *interminably* long run. The first two considerations make moral sense—i.e., it is perfectly reasonable to ask after the consequence of one's decision or action in short- or long-run terms. But to ask about the consequences for an everlasting future precludes any kind of ethical analysis. The question of the value of experience for the interminably long run does make some sense, however. At least this seems to be true because so many saints, martyrs, and other religious virtuosi have asked just this question. There must be a sense in which to say "He is a good man" and "He is a holy man" mean significantly different things. The basis of that difference is to be found in the supposition that one is "good" or "right" when one is concerned with the consequences of one's intentions or actions for some finite selection of individuals considered through some finite temporal order. On the other hand, one is "holy" when one envisions one's experience *sub specie aeternitatis*.

If it is true that one may be moral or immoral when finite consequences of experience are relevant to the analysis, and holy or unholy when the *sub specie aeternitatis* quality of a thought, action, or feeling is considered, then it is clear that the same experience may be both "good" and "unholy" or "bad" and "holy." Thus Jesus' anointing at Bethany involved the use of precious ointment which could have been easily sold to the benefit of the poor. The moral indignation of the disciples at the misuse of the ointment seems to have been quite in order. The disciples were "morally" right and Jesus "morally" wrong. On the other hand, Jesus was a participant in a holy event of which the disciples could only be dimly aware. Or to cite an even more obvious example: in betraying Jesus, Judas Iscariot was certainly guilty of a moral failing. But he was unquestionably participating in a holy event. The *felix culpa* must be seen, religiously, as the result of an action which played a significant function in the enactment of God's plan of salvation (cf. Jn 11:49–52, where Caiaphas, "as high priest, made the prophecy that Jesus was to die . . ."). Examples such as these point up the inevitable confusion which would result from always insisting upon a congruence in a single action of religious and ethical consequences.

The contemporary conditions of both the aesthetic and the moral interest involve the necessity of the acceptance of finitude. Absolute standards of Beauty and Goodness are equally unavailable. Whitehead's philosophy provides both artists and moral agents with a means of accepting the inevitable finitude of cultural experience. The ephemerality of Beauty is a positive,

210 SOME IMPLICATIONS

though essentially tragic, fact in a Whiteheadian world. Similarly, the acceptance of the radically contextual character of morality not only does not vitiate the moral interest, but actually paves the way toward the realization of the complete autonomy of religion.

NOTES

1. For a more detailed discussion of the relation between the artist as composer and as performer, see Donald Sherburne, *A Whiteheadian Aesthetic* (New Haven: Yale University Press, 1961), pp. 173–177.
2. See Tillich's "Protestantism and Artistic Style," *Theology of Culture* (New York: Oxford University Press, 1954), pp. 68–75.
3. See Chapter V of SMW, "The Romantic Reaction."
4. Charles I. Glicksburg, *Modern Literature and the Death of God* (The Hague: Nijhoff, 1966), p. 15.
5. Yeats, "The Second Coming," *Modern Verse in English 1900–1950* edd. David Cecil and Allen Tate (New York: Macmillan, 1958), p. 117.
6. Joyce, *A Portrait of the Artist as a Young Man* (New York: Viking, 1959), p. 253.
7. Quoted in Samuel French Morse, *Wallace Stevens: Life as Poetry* (New York: Pegasus, 1970), p. 55.
8. *Ibid.*, p. 23.
9. For a discussion of this conception of the role of art in an advanced technological society, see Alvin Toffler, "Information: The Kinetic Image," *Future Shock* (New York: Random House, 1970), Chapter 8, section 2.
10. See Hartshorne interview in *Philosophical Interrogations,* edd. Sydney and Beatrice Rome (New York: Holt, Rinehart, 1964), pp. 339–340. John Cobb, following Hartshorne's lead, has given an account of Whitehead's concept of morality in his *A Christian Natural Theology* (Philadelphia: Westminster, 1965), pp. 113–130.
11. See Tillich's *Morality and Beyond* (New York: Harper & Row, 1963), pp. 22–30.
12. See Toulmin's *An Examination of the Place of Reason in Ethics* (Cambridge: Cambridge University Press, 1953), pp. 202–221.
13. *Ibid.*, p. 202.
14. See *Ibid.*, pp. 152–153, 217–218.
15. Schubert Ogden (*In the Reality of God* [New York: Harper & Row, 1966], pp. 27–39) has attempted to use Toulmin's concept of limiting questions to support his argument that all moral or ethical situations presuppose a religious faith in "the abiding worth of life." Delwin Brown's "Process Philosophy and the Question of Life's Meaning" (*Religious Studies* 7 [1971], 13–29) employs much the same kind of argument to show the way in which Whiteheadian philosophy provides a fruitful basis for asking the "question of life's meaning."
16. Van Buren, *The Secular Meaning of the Gospel* (New York: Macmillan, 1963).
17. Cox, *The Secular City* (New York: Macmillan, 1965).
18. Sherburne, "Whitehead Without God," *Process Philosophy and Christian Theology,* edd. Delwin Brown et al. (New York: Bobbs-Merrill, 1971), pp. 305–306.
19. See the discussion of the concept of God in Chapters II and VI.
20. See Otto's *The Idea of the Holy,* trans. John W. Harvey (New York: Oxford University Press, 1953) and Van Der Leuuw's *Religion in Eessence and Manifestation,* trans. J. E. Turner (New York: Harper & Row, 1963).
21. See James's *Varieties of Religious Experience* (New York: Longman Green, 1902).
22. See, for example, Ninian Smart, *Reasons and Faiths* (London: Routledge & Kegan Paul, 1958).

Chapter IX

Religion, Science, Philosophy

THE RELATIONS OF RELIGION to science and philosophy are determined by their respective roles as cultural interests. In Chapter V we noted that cultural interests were based upon various types of abstraction from the unity of an occasion of experience. Religion, as a value-interest, is based upon a selective abstraction from concrete experience; science, upon formal abstractions from a selected subject matter; and philosophy, upon formal and, in principle, nonselective abstractions. In the last Chapter we were concerned with religion, art, and morality—three interests which share a common origin in value-experience. But in this Chapter the differing origins of the three interests under consideration will mean that the *distinctiveness* of these interests will be of somewhat greater significance.

1. THE ADVENTURE OF SCIENCE

Before discussing Whitehead's view of the civilizing function of science, its negative potentialities, and the aid which religion can provide it, I shall consider, briefly, Whitehead's concept of the type of relation which exists between religion and science. We shall see that Whitehead stresses the intrinsic interdependence of religion and science, as well as the autonomy of each. It is the radical distinctness of the two enterprises which has more often received attention by contemporary philosophy. For example, existentialist thinkers, utilizing the model of the subject–object relationship, have stressed the objective impersonality of the world of science as over against the subjectivity and "authenticity" of the personal world of human beings.[1] Analytic philosophers too have emphasized the distinctness and autonomy in structure, aim, and logic of scientific and religious languages.[2]

Whitehead's metaphysics allows him to stress the distinctive functions of religion and science. But his theory of experience requires him to be concerned, as well, about the foundation in experience of both of these interests. Thus he says, "Religion deals with the formation of the experiencing subject; whereas science deals with the objects, which are the data forming the primary phase in this experience" (PR 24). Since Whitehead places the subject–object distinction within the context of an occasion of experience, the type of existentialist approach to the relations of religion and science characterized above is undercut. Also, the distinctions between the structures and aims of differing languages and concepts are to be understood only if they are seen, ultimately, as differential abstractions from the unity of experience. Whitehead attempts to uphold both the autonomy and the interdependence of cultural interests. This is especially true for the interests of religion and science.

Because of Whitehead's strong indictment of the negative effects of modern science upon certain phases of civilized societies, some of his interpreters have failed to stress the actual significance of science to Whitehead's theory of civilization. A. H. Johnson, for example, has stated flatly that, for Whitehead, science is not among the necessary possessions of a civilized society. He makes this claim on two grounds: first, science is not one of the qualities (Art, Adventure, Truth, Beauty, Peace) which define a civilized society, and secondly, there have been civilized societies which have not possessed science as we know it.[3] But this misconceives Whitehead's view of the role of science in culture. For, in the first place, science is not, in Whitehead's terms, a quality of a society, but a particular mode of interest (as are morality, art, religion) which promotes or inhibits the attainment of the five qualities defining a civilization. In the second place, though there may have been civilizations without science in the past, it is doubtful whether there could be one in the present. The context of human experience and expression has been so transformed by scientific theory and practice that science has become an indispensable means of promoting the qualities of civilization. More specifically, science has won a significant, perhaps irreplaceable, position in culture through its maintenance of the qualities of Truth and Adventure, as we shall see.

The most primary and most direct concern of the sciences is Truth. And the kind of truth which science seeks depends upon the "conformal correspondence of clear and distinct Appearance to Reality" (AI 321). Science promotes the attainment of truth through its concern with laws of nature —i.e., with the mutual relations of the final real things, one to another. A discovery of new laws of nature is a discovery of novel relations among actual entities. Each new law of a special science is an addition to the qualitative character of Appearance in a civilized society and enhances the analytic power of individuals in seeking to interpret their concrete experience of the world.

Whitehead claims a three-fold distinction to be important as a basic for philosophic discussion. There are (1) direct, unverbalized intuitions, (2) the literary modes of verbal expressions and the dialectic deductions from these modes, and (3) the deductive sciences so developed that "the network of possible relations with which they deal are familiar in civilized consciousness" (AI 177).

> The sciences under the heading (iii) direct attention for the exploration of the recesses of experience, and also assist in providing the verbal formulae belonging to the heading (ii). The chief danger in philosophy is that the dialectic deductions from inadequate formulae should exclude direct intuitions from explicit attentions. In fact the abstract sciences tend to correct the evil effects of the inadequacy of language, and the consequent dangers of a logic which presupposes linguistic adequacy [AI 177–178].

Two functions of science in promoting the attainment of Truth are noted here. Science "directs attention," and helps to provide explicit verbal formulae from which philosophy makes its dialectical deductions. The function of directing attention is the function of abstraction in general. The abstract patterns of mutual relation which constitute the content of scientific concepts direct attention to the concrete, common characteristics of actual entities.

Science promotes the truth-relation, too, in that the verbal formulae which it develops aid philosophy in its aim at the characterization of a "complete fact" (v. AI 203). Philosophy takes its start from "the generalization of particular factors discerned in particular topics of human interest" (PR 7). And since science, among the other human interests, is the most concerned with rigorous specificity in the formulation of its concepts, philosophy gains critical insight into the inadequacies of unspecialized language in the formulation of certain types of experiences.

Science is important not only because it contributes to the attainment of Truth, but also, and mainly, because it promotes Adventure. As we noted in the discussion of Whitehead's theory of the laws of nature, there are not just a small finite number of sciences which, taken together, exhaust the meaningful patterns of mutual relations between things. There are an indefinite number of abstract sciences. The future of the sciences, therefore, is an open and, from our own present perspective, an almost unlimited one. Adventure, the transcendence of achieved perfections, is one of the primary byproducts of the development of the special sciences.

The story is often told of the attitude of the late-nineteenth-century physicists toward their science. The belief was that the major conceptual and theoretical developments had been made. All that remained was the polishing of its theories and the elaboration of existing techniques. But the discovery of the x-ray and the development of the quantum and relativity theories effected a revolution not only in physics, but in all the sciences as well. The spirit of adventure was substituted for the concern for the maintenance of any single finite set of hypotheses and theories. But the very fact that science entails a constant revision of its concepts and a progressive development beyond theories no longer relevant to its needs can threaten the spirit of the scientific enterprise. The scientist, like the artist and the moral agent, is vulnerable to the sense of dissatisfaction resulting from a realization of the necessarily finite character of his aims and his achievements. This is especially true if the scientist develops a sense of the extreme relativity and limited applicability of scientific theories.

Whitehead thinks that all sciences "depend on an ultimate moral intuition into the nature of intellectual action—that it should embody the adventure of hope. Such an intuition marks the point where . . . every science . . . gains assurance from religion and passes over into religion" (PR 67). For it to be of cultural value, scientists must be able to see more in their work than their own limited aims. How the sciences may "gain assurance" from religion and how they may even "pass over into" religion, without becoming apologies for religious doctrines and thereby giving up their own autonomy, is one of the central problems with which Whitehead's thoughts on science are concerned.

Whitehead is certain that religion and science must find a way of relating one to the other. Writing in 1925, he claimed that "the future course of history depends upon the decision of this generation as to the relations between [religion and science]" (SMW 260). One of the principal relations of the two interests is their shared character of adventurousness.

> Religion is the vision of something which stands beyond, behind, and within, the passing flux of immediate things; . . . something whose possession is the final good, and yet is beyond all reach; something which is the ultimate ideal, and the hopeless quest [SMW 275].

The sense of adventure in both science and religion brings them into close relation. The reason for this shared character is that science, as well as religion, conceives an ideal which is yet a "hopeless quest." It is the infinitude of possible questions, of possible modes of abstractive emphasis, which impresses upon the scientists the realization of the finitude of their attainments. It is the limitless character of the experienced reality "beyond, behind, and within" the passing flux of immediate things which gives to the religious man both the high hope of adventure and the sense of final Peace. Science receives sustenance from religion when it gains the sense of ultimate permanence and completeness in its ideals with which to face the finiteness of its attainments.

But the need of a sense of Peace on the part of scientists is not the result merely of anxiety in the face of the finite and passing character of their achievements. In virtue of their methodologies, the sciences are open to criticism, more often than not, concerning the validity of their entire enterprise. The cardinal sin of the sciences is the acceptance of their own abstractions as characterizations of complete facts. This error Whitehead has labeled the Fallacy of Misplaced Concreteness. But scientific methodology is open not only to this fallacy, but also to the error involved in the construction of irrelevant abstractions—those with little or no basis in concrete, causally efficacious experience. This is a major potential source of uprootedness in a society.

The Fallacy of Misplaced Concreteness consists in accepting abstractions as the concrete data of experience. This fallacy, however, can hide a second error. For the abstractions of the sciences can either be, or not be, germane to the concrete data of experience. In the first case the only error consists in supposing as concrete that which is an abstraction from reality. But in the second case one is not only committing the Fallacy of Misplaced Concreteness, one is taking as concrete that which is not even a valid abstraction. These errors do not plague the artist, the religious man, or the moral agent (as they do the scientist) because their primary emphasis is upon causally efficacious experience, whereas science emphasizes the presentational immediacy of its data.

Most often science maintains the proper germaneness to experience in its data, which means that its principal error, when it is in error, is in the commission of the attribution of concreteness to its abstract data. That this fallacy has had serious ramifications in the development of Western culture is one of the persistent themes in Whitehead's philosophy. By directing attention to things as opposed to values, science has promoted a vision of the world which suffers from extreme abstractness. The objective world of science is uprooted from the subjective world of emotions and purposes which characterize existence in its most fundamental form.

Whitehead has here provided an instance of the vitiating effect of the Fallacy of Misplaced Concreteness. There does not have to be an Appearance–Reality dislocation between scientific concepts and concrete experience in order for the sense of uprootedness to overcome a culture. Even if the scientific concepts are germane, they are germane to only a few selected aspects of the past reality. Without the assistance of the broader and more concrete aesthetic, moral, and religious expressions, there can be no sense of rootedness in the value-aspects of things.

The immediacy of experience is closed to the scientist *qua* scientist. Emotional experiences, as immediate, are not the proper subject matter of the sciences, on Whitehead's view. For when science does deal with emotions, it considers them as "percepta and not immediate passions—other people's emotion and not our own; at least our own in recollection and not in immediacy" (PR 24). The emphasis upon objective data rather than subjective and immediate experience entails the fact that science is primarily concerned with the past. And it is concerned with the future only insofar as it can be an outcome of the data of past experience.

> Science investigates the past, and predicts the future in terms of the forms
> of past achievement. But as the present becomes self-destructive of its in-

herited modes of importance, then the deistic influence implants in the
historic process new aims at other ideals.

Science is concerned with the facts of bygone transition. . . . It is the religious impulse in the world which transforms the dead facts of science into
the living drama of history [MT 103–104].

The orientation of science is toward the past. But religion, with its anticipation of objective immortality and its continual aim at the ideal inherent
in God's lure, is oriented toward the future. Science accepts the past and
constructs its theories and predictions upon it. The religious impulse judges
the past and transforms it in accordance with "new aims at other ideals."
The temporal orientations of religion and science are the reverse of one
another. Science bases itself upon the past; religion, insofar as it is concerned with objective immortality, is grounded upon an anticipated future.
Science predicts the future on the basis of the past; religion judges the past
in terms of its anticipated future. The interdependence of science and religion is necessary in a society which aims to balance the needs of the ordered
control of its environment and the concern for ideals and values.

Whitehead thinks a civilized society can strike a balance between the
two primary pursuits if both recognize the limits implied in their proper
aims. "Science finds religious experiences among its percepta; and religion
finds scientific concepts among the conceptual experiences to be fused with
particular sensitive reactions" (PR 24). One of the chief services of religion to science is expressed in this sentence. Science finds religious experiences among its percepts. The responsibility of science is to resist the
temptation to ignore (or to reduce by extraneous causal explanations) these
data.

Religion, in its turn, cannot ignore the presence of scientific concepts.
They must be "fused with particular sensitive reactions"—i.e., they must
be symbolically referred to the causally efficacious world of primary experience. In rational religion this is done directly. "The final principle of religion is that there is a wisdom in the nature of things, from which flow our
direction of practice, and our possibility of the theoretical analysis of fact"
(RM 137–138).

One of the sources of evidence upon which religion bases this principle
is the successes of the various sciences. For such successes can occur only
if there is a conformation between regions as illumined by sense and the
actual states of those regions—i.e., unless there is a conformation between
Appearance and Reality. Thus religion may utilize the fact of the success
of the sciences to support its belief in the presence in nature of "a tendency
to be in tune, an Eros urging towards perfection" (AI 323).

In the fact of the success of his own methods, the scientist has the basis
for arguments in support of theistic belief. As a scientist, he is unable to
attain the theistic *intuitions* which such arguments could support. Rational
religion, on the other hand, combines the religious intuition of the Eros

with arguments derived from the sciences. One significant responsibility which rational religion has toward the sciences is so to combine intuitions and arguments in the construction of its theories and dogmas as to challenge the limitations of scientific abstractions. In this way, religion may provide the scientists with evidence for the presence in nature of the source of the intuition of Peace which they could not have obtained by their own methods. Such evidence can render acceptable the risks inevitably involved in the adventure of science.

2. THE TECHNOLOGICAL STATE OF MIND

One of the principal characteristics of contemporary culture, outlined in our survey of the cultural problem in Chapter VII, is the dominance of technique and technology. In science, technique has always been supposed subordinate to the theoretical principles which undergird the explanatory theories of the various scientific specialties. One of the most surprising developments of twentieth-century science has been its general capitulation to the technological state of mind which assumes that there is a practical, efficient solution to the problems of men. The impact of the scientific cultural-interest upon society has been, in recent years, increasingly that of the practical instrument of social engineering rather than of the theoretical understanding of the natural phenomena. It is the scientist *qua* social prophet and priest who has come upon the scene as the primary representative of "scientific culture." These contemporary scientists clothe their insights in the jargon of their various specialties but greatly extend the applicability of their theories, applying them to the general conditions of society.

These "scientific" prophets are well represented by such authors as Konrad Lorenz, Robert Ardrey, and Desmond Morris.[4] The reduction of human socialization to motives (aggression, the territorial imperative) having their origin in less complex forms of animal life is found to have astounding implications for the human problems of war and peace, property rights, etc. For example, in Lorenz' *On Aggression*, it is the primary urge toward "intra-specific aggression" which is isolated and found to be the primary motivation from which the social relations of love, brotherhood, compassion, etc., are derived. The analogical leap from the wealth of interesting data concerning the motivations of fish, birds, rats, and geese to those of human beings is as naïve as it is dramatic. It is not a generalization of the data itself which Lorenz seeks; it is the analogical extension of the data to the subject of human beings without adequate attention to the possible sphere of applicability of the principle of aggression. Aggression becomes *the* explanatory principle which is at the root of both the evil and the beneficent aspects of human society.

Accepting the thesis popularized by Robert Ardrey that each living organism is possessed of a territorial instinct which leads it to defend its life-space at all costs, Lorenz characterizes the relations between animals in such a way as to provide what he takes to be a paradigm in terms of which human relations may be discussed. Since the primary explanatory principle is aggression, the tender aspects of human relations, such as love or sympathy, are found to be reducible to a form of intra-specific aggression. "Love," the primary bond between members of the human species is in fact a sublimation of more fundamental aggressive impulses. Love is a technique for the control of aggression—a technique for survival. The implication of such a view is that human society exists in a stable order because of the need to defend property rights (life-space) through aggressive assertion of the territorial imperative. The necessary harmony of intersecting life-spaces which determine conflicts within society is provided by a specialized sublimation of the aggressive instinct manifesting itself as fellow-feeling.

The basis for Lorenz' argument is the concept of *intra-specific* emotions. Not only, therefore, do we find in the aggressive "nature" of man the basis for a theory of property rights and an explanation of the continual resort to violence; we likewise discover that love is naturally directed only to members of the same species. All the ecological disasters consequent upon man's rape of nature find theoretical justification in the work of the biological prophets whose technological minds function in such a fashion as to provide support for the very evils which threaten to destroy civilized order.

In addition to the biological theories of culture, there are those grounded in Freudian principles, which, no less than those of the life-scientists, lay claim to being "scientific." Phillip Rieff's *The Triumph of the Therapeutic*[5] is a brilliant, though necessarily one-sided and reductive, explanation of culture from the Freudian perspective. Rieff's thesis, in part, is that culture functions primarily as a moral-demand system with control and remissive functions. Western culture, the moral-demand system of which has been derived from the Christian theological paradigm, is undergoing a radical change, and religion is no longer the central cultural force. The present period of social chaos signals a transition from a culture dominated by control motifs to one in which remission is primary. If we survive the cultural change, a new therapeutic society will come into being. The "triumph of the therapeutic," according to Rieff, refers to a revolutionary change in society which is "more Freudian than Marxist, more analytic than polemic, more cultural than social." [6] The therapeutic society is one in which releasing and controlling symbolism gives way to symbols which lead a society to eschew commitment to communal purposes and to promote individual commitment to the therapeutic technique. The psychoanalyst inherits the responsibility of social engineering.

Sung in Rieff's brilliant prose, the thesis of such a cultural analysis may not seem at all unpalatable. In fact, the effect of such a therapeutic society would be to subordinate individuals to a non-normative technique of personal self-realization as defined by one class of technicians—the psychologists and psychiatrists—and Freudian psychology, and it alone, would serve as the basis for the new technical psychosocial order. Again this theory of culture is a yea-saying one. The acceptance of the technological order with no sense of nostalgia over the loss of an over-arching set of norms or principles with which to construct a general understanding of society is characteristic of the technological state of mind. The technique sought in this case is the psychotherapeutic analysis whose "how to" orientation expresses the final truth about theory of culture for the mass-man in disguise.

Marxian philosophy has, of course, not been a neglected source for the development of cultural analyses. But clearly contemporary Marxian thought, as a scientific ideology, is inadequate to provide the basis for an assault upon technological society. For as much as any other philosophical theory, as clearly and as fervently as any ideology, contemporary Marxism affirms the ethical neutrality of the structure of technological society. In a capitalist society there is at least the saving grace that at times the profit-motive takes precedence over the free development of technological devices, and the untrammelled progress of technique is impeded by the purchase of patents and by the removal of counterproductive (from the individual capitalist's viewpoint) machines from the economy. Marxist thinking, with its unqualified affirmation of technology, is as little able to serve the needs of a culture overburdened by its technology as any other existing theoretical perspective.

The difficulty is to be found in the centrality of the concept of "alienation" in Marxism. For Marx, in contradistinction to certain existentialists, the term "alienation" has a highly specific meaning relating to economic conditions. Alienation is a function of the labor relations existing in precommunistic systems, in which the worker is alienated from himself, from nature, and from the products of work by virtue of his inability to participate in the ownership of the means of production. For Marx the solution to alienation is not psychological or philosophic; it is an extremely practical, economic solution: when the worker shares in ownership, alienation will begin to decline. Marxist thinkers, such as Erich Fromm, who have attempted to broaden the concept of alienation in the light of existential philosophy's development of the concept, have found themselves with the embarrassing difficulty of relating the Marx of *Das Kapital* with the Marx of the early philosophic manuscripts. Marxian thought provides no better basis for an adequate critique of culture than does the Freudian vision of Rieff which is, in many ways, so closely allied to it.

As if to establish the Hegelian truth that two wrongs, dialectically organized, do in fact make a right, Erich Fromm and Herbert Marcuse rise up to establish a psycho-political point of view (Freudo-Marxian) which compounds the sins of reductionism by casually mining the insights of *two* autonomous semantic contexts. "Alienation" now combines with "repressive de-sublimation" to found diagnostic, prognostic, and therapeutic social theories.

Fromm's insights, developed in a series of widely read books which include *Escape from Freedom*, *The Art of Loving*, and *The Revolution of Hope: Toward a Humanized Technology*, have close relationships to both psychological and sociological categories.[7] In recent years it has been the socialist tradition, particularly the work of the early Marx, which has provided the sources of Fromm's thought. His most popular work, *The Art of Loving*, is evidence enough of his innocence of the effects of technological thinking. Love is an "art," a technique, which can be learned and practiced. The knowledge of the nature of love and its consequences, along with some guidelines concerning the practice of "loving," will provide persons with a frame of orientation from which to organize their interpersonal existence. In *The Revolution of Hope*, Fromm provides a framework for the reorganization of man's relation to technological society. The assumption of the value-neutrality of technology per se makes of the work an extremely naïve analysis of the nature of the technological order which serves, as does *The Art of Loving*, more to intensify than to mitigate our cultural problems.

Marcuse's principal works concerning cultural analysis are *Eros and Civilization* and *One-Dimensional Man*.[8] The former work is as close to Rieff's analysis, from the point of view of man's relation to the technological order, as one could imagine. But between that work and *One-Dimensional Man* there are vast differences. Marcuse made a transition from an optimistic Freudianism to an apocalyptic vision grounded in a disillusionment with the technological order. *One-Dimensional Man* expresses the view that advanced industrial society is closed to transcendence because of the rationality and efficiency of its technological structure. Criticisms, constructive or malign, are automatically absorbed into the system which creates the alternatives for choice as well as placing positive value on a selection of available choices. Life and thought are one-dimensional insofar as no openness to transcendent criticism is possible. The negative implication of this work, which was soon recognized by the New Left, is that destruction of advanced industrial society in its present form is the only solution to the bondage of man within the contemporary social system.

The technological state of mind is in evidence not only in the reductionist writings of our specialized elites, but among the "generalist" approaches as well. Marshall McLuhan, the self-proclaimed generalist, has on many occasions expressed his antipathy toward the specialist. He is opposed to a fragmented intellectual culture. But if most of the other prophetic massmen have illustrated the failure of specialized knowledge over-applied,

McLuhan has certainly shown the limitations of analogical generalization when performed by the amateur. It is this fact which makes the McLuhan impact upon intellectual culture through such works as *Gutenberg Galaxy* and *Understanding Media* so regrettable.[9]

To read one of these theorists is to read them all. The symptoms of the technological state of mind are all too evident in each: (1) the elaboration of a single insight derived from a specialized field of experience, (2) the isolation of the problem implied by that insight as the *fundamental* problem of society, and (3) the naïve and dogmatic employment of the insight to explain or resolve *the* problem.

Obviously, our social problems will not be solved by so-called technicians either of the mechanistic reductionist orientation or of the more streamlined, field-oriented electric generalism of the McLuhan variety. Our problems require for their solution both a knowledge of principles and a healthy respect for the limitations of these principles. The problems we confront are too complex to be solved by the technical mind, since the meaning of the human person in both his private and his public existence is at issue. No special science can grasp the significance of personality via the selective route of scientific, theological, or political concepts. And the "generalist" approach can create only a vague, homeless shadow of man through its abstract analogical conundrums.

The cultural effects of the scientific enterprise are, sad to say, too well illustrated by the "prophetic" voices of popular science. Science, as a theoretical enterprise, has increasingly lost its ideological relevance as it has proliferated specialties. In response to the loss of his role as the "man of wisdom," the scientist has sought from within the provincial boundaries of his own particular interest to comprehend the spectrum of contemporary culture. The condition of uprootedness cannot be overcome by the attempt to extend blunt truth beyond its relevant boundaries. An acceptance of the finitude of one's own special interest, together with the search for hypothetical means of coordinating the insights of the various disciplines is the best path away from the loss of that sense of Eros which seeks to maintain the *fundamentum in re* of cultural experience and expression.

The loss of a significant sense of Peace is evident not only on the popular side of the scientific enterprise but among the elitists as well. Twentieth-century science has moved away from the idea that the theoretical scientist is in search of fundamental "truths" about the nature of things, and toward the pragmatic and operational vision of the scientific enterprise. Thomas Kuhn's *The Structure of Scientific Revolutions*,[10] a timely study of revolutions in the development of scientific paradigms, defends the operational view of scientific theories which has come increasingly to express the scientist's understanding of his activity. The continuity of scientific development is denied. The scientific enterprise is shown to be a successive set of revolutions in theoretical understanding in which the acceptance of a new explanatory paradigm necessarily entails the rejection of an older one. According to Kuhn, science as an activity involves the rejection of any epistemology which understands knowledge to be a construction placed upon raw sense-data and replaces it with the view that a scientific paradigm generates the "facts" which it investigates and provides the tools for the organization and interpretation of those facts. Explanatory paradigms must be mutually exclusive. For example, says Kuhn, "Einstein's theory can be accepted only with the recognition that Newton's was wrong." [11]

At least part of the crisis of science in modern culture, therefore, results from the developing awareness of the relativity of conceptual schemes. The operationalism of contemporary science has led to a methodological awareness which has vitiated the scientist's sense of self-importance by convincing him that a theory or scientific paradigm is merely a way of organizing research techniques and/or of suggesting interesting questions. A theory is seldom considered "true" or "false" by contemporary scientists. It is judged merely in forms of its "fruitfulness." Such sophisticated use of theory often undercuts the scientist's sense of the significance of his task.

The failure of Adventure leads science away from daring and risk toward the cautious implementation of efficiency and order as the fundamental goals defining scientific activity. A science without adventure degenerates into technology as an end in itself. The theoretical explication of morphological schemes and their verification through extended applications is abandoned, and the practical activities of the making of machines and the development of techniques to meet the short-term needs of society is all that remains. Rationality is replaced by ingenuity. Science, dizzy with its success in answering the question "how," forgets to ask the question "why."

The enterprise of science, like that of art, is challenged from the accelerated pace of advanced technological society. Tied as it is to technique and to technical apparatus, and finding its justification all too often in the promise of practical benefits, the structure of the scientific interest is continually being transformed by the effects of technological progress. This accelerated pace produces the phenomenon of the conflict of time-scales between man and his technical apparatus. When machines from automobiles to computers are too rapid in their operations to control safely, then, obviously, "things are in the saddle and ride mankind." Effective control over machines depends upon the exercise of human foresight. But in a computer-oriented society that quality is no longer possible because of the necessity for altogether-too-rapid decisions. According to Norbert Weiner:

> To be effective in warding off disastrous consequences, our understanding of . . . machines should in general develop *pari passu* with the performance of the machine. By the very slowness of our human actions, our effective control of our machines may be nullified.[12]

The challenge of technological society to the scientist is equally great if we consider the problem of differing time-scales in regard to the consequences of scientific discoveries beyond the present. Until recently a scientist responsible for a given discovery could predict with reasonable accuracy the consequences, within his own lifetime, of that discovery. This fact meant that the scientist felt relatively secure in the understanding of the moral consequences of his actions. The tightly interwoven, rapidly changing, relations of the various aspects of contemporary technological society, however, have rendered impossible any effective control of the moral consequences of scientific discoveries. The discoverers of the secrets of the atom lived to see their discoveries used in nuclear warfare. The developers of DDT, and of detergents, lived to see the near-disastrous effects of the use of their scientific discoveries. The demoralizing effect of such unpredicted consequences of scientific and technological developments is sufficient to produce in many scientists a "failure of nerve" in relation to their enterprise.

The sense of finitude threatens the scientist in contemporary society both because of the operational understanding of theory-construction which prevents the scientist from thinking that he will discover universal laws or final truths about the nature of the cosmos and because of the inability to foresee and, therefore, control effectively the moral consequences of scientific discovery or invention. This threat is overcome only by the acceptance of the inevitably finite character of scientific thought and action. Such an acceptance could lead to the realization that science seeks truth beyond the blunt truths of technology; that the scientific enterprise is responsible for Truthful Beauty, as well. Such a realization brings with it the acceptance of the ephemerality of the discoveries of science, since nothing beautiful ever lasts. Adventure in science involves the acceptance of risk. Beauty is that factor expressive of the Eros in existence which makes risk worthwhile.

3. THE BURDEN OF PHILOSOPHY

We have been considering the relations of religion to science, and to the problems of finitude and uprootedness which may be due to science as a cultural interest. As has been the case with our discussions of art and morality, we have found the religious interest to be inextricably bound up in the scientific interest insofar as it aims at civilized ideals. We have now come to our final topic, philosophy.

Philosophy attempts to achieve a system of formal, non-selective abstractions which are adequate to interpret every aspect of experience. There are two ways in which this function of philosophy can promote the qualities of civilization. The first way was investigated in some detail in Chapter V where we constructed a Whiteheadian theory of cultural interests. The value of such a theory, from the Whiteheadian point of view, is that it provides a means whereby the right relative status of any specific set of abstractions from experience may be ascertained. The understanding of the type and degree of abstraction entering into the methods, principles, and subject matters of individual disciplines can provide a way of harmonizing the various interests and activities in the cultural realm. One value of Whiteheadian philosophy, as I have stressed repeatedly, is that it provides the means for constructing a theory of cultural interests which allows the necessary autonomy and interdependence of the various disciplines, avoiding philosophic or scientific reductions of other significant interests, and avoiding, as well, the abandonment of a systematic approach to the understanding of the relationships of the various interests and activities of a society.

In this first function, philosophy promotes the attainment of all the qualities of civilization by providing a means to understand the variety and significance of the aims and interests of a civilized society. There is also a second, more limited, effect which philosophy may have in culture, as it promotes, primarily, the aims of Truth and Adventure.

"Philosophy is the criticism of abstractions which govern special modes of thought" (MT 48–49). The systematic character of philosophy allows it to promote the discovery of new truths as well as to maintain present truth-relations. Philosophy promotes the apprehensions of novel relationships among aspects of experience. In so doing, it may uncover disjunctions and conjunctions, consistencies and inconsistencies. Each mode of thought and action may utilize philosophical principles and methods to clarify, specify, and relate the data with which it is concerned. "By providing . . . generic notions philosophy should make it easier to conceive the infinite variety of specific instances which rest unrealized in the womb of nature" (PR 26). If the special modes of interest utilize philosophic categories in their activities of symbolic reference, the construction of more subtle concepts, which allow a deeper penetration of the reality of concrete experience, may be possible.

The promotion of Adventure is closely tied to the systematic character of philosophy. As long as philosophy recognizes that its function is to provide speculative schemes capable of illumining the insights and expressions of civilized experience, and *not* to elaborate a deductive scheme which seeks to give final answers to ultimate questions, it is able to contribute to the adventure of civilized thought.

> After the initial basis of a rational life, with a civilized language, has been laid, all productive thought has proceeded either by the poetic insight of artists, or by the imaginative elaboration of schemes of thought capable of utilization as logical premises [PR 14].

Speculative philosophy must provide schemes of thought which may be *utilized as logical premises*. Philosophy does not begin with logical premises and arrive at its categories deductively. So there cannot be anything closed or dogmatic about a philosophic system. It must be open to transcendence by more adequate schemes of thought. Through such openness, philosophy contributes to the adventure of thought in culture. The most valuable contribution of philosophy to the adventure of thought comes from the realization within a single philosophic school of the necessity for both an adequate and a consistent expression of its main doctrines.

> Every philosophic school in the course of its history requires two presiding philosophers. One of them under the influence of the main doctrines of the school should survey experience with some adequacy, but inconsistently. The other philosopher should reduce the doctrines of the school to a rigid consistency; he will thereby effect a *reductio ad absurdum*. No school of thought has performed its full service to philosophy until these men have appeared [PR 89].

Locke viewed experience with some adequacy, Hume reduced his insight to consistency. Cartesian thought achieved some adequacy, but at the cost of the inconsistent mind-body dualism which Spinoza and Leibniz variously resolved. Whitehead was, if anything, a philosopher concerned with adequacy. Much of the work of Charles Hartshorne may be construed as an attempt to render consistent the process philosophy exemplified by Whiteheadian thought.[13]

Implied here is that adequacy and consistency are not likely to be attained at the same time by the same system of thought. There is no reason to believe that Whitehead considered his attempt at attaining metaphysical adequacy exempt from some future *reductio*. Whitehead would be inconsistent with the spirit of his own philosophy if he thought that the adventure of the human mind in its search for philosophic adequacy had come to an end with the publication of his own metaphysical works.

The goal of philosophy is attained only if there may be a continual transcendence of inadequate philosophies. The relativity of philosophical systems, and the inevitable obsolescence which is their common fate, pose a significant challenge to the philosopher. Whitehead would have philosophers be both bold and humble in the construction of their speculative schemes—bold in imagination and in argument, humble in the face of logic and of experienced fact. Neither boldness nor humility, however, will preserve a philosophy from eventual irrelevance at some crucial points. "In its turn every philosophy will suffer a deposition" (PR 11).

The failure to recognize the relativity of philosophical systems results, on Whiteheadian principles, not so much from a lack of humility on the part of philosophers, but from an insufficient grasp of the metaphysical implications of *finitude*. Philosophers who construct their speculative systems on the basis of "clear and distinct ideas," or on the inevitability of dialectical transition, or on the concept of self-contained atomic substances, etc., have little trouble in developing theories which, at least to the mind of the philosopher himself, have clarity. Once clarity has been attained, certainty often follows. With Whitehead, however, the principle of process, and the fact of the finitude of all perfections, *systematically* preclude such certainty. The universe is always outrunning the philosopher attempting to enclose it within a speculative system. The philosopher "is always assaulting the boundaries of finitude" (MT 172).

Thus, the philosopher is not exempt from the relativity and finitude which infect all other modes of interest. The assurance of immunity from mutability and decay which belonged to many of the great system-builders in philosophy is not allowed to the Whiteheadian philosopher. The sense of Peace, the assurance of an ultimate permanence beyond and within the relativity of historic process, must serve in the place of the sense of dogmatic finality which was once a chief characteristic of the metaphysician. Thus, the gift of Peace can be one important gift of religion to philosophy.

Philosophy is open to the threat of uprootedness as well. As in science, so in philosophy, uprootedness results from the commission of the Fallacy of Misplaced Concreteness. But, unlike scientists who must settle for selective and incompletely generic concepts and theories, philosophers aim to construct schemes of thought which are adequate to interpret every item of experience. Thus, though the scientist commits the Fallacy of Misplaced Concreteness if he claims that his concepts characterize a complete fact, the philosopher is in danger of committing the fallacy only if he makes such a claim dogmatically.

Dogmatism in philosophy may be expressed either in the claim of systematic completeness in the development of a speculative system, or in the less ambitious claim of completeness in the assemblage of data from which the solutions to philosophical problems are constructed. The former type of dogmatism was considered earlier in relation to the discussion of the effect of finitude upon philosophy. The latter dogmatism involves, according to Whitehead, "The Fallacy of the Perfect Dictionary" (v. MT 173). This fallacy consists in the belief that mankind has invented or entertained all the fundamental notions necessary to interpret its experience. Existing language and philosophical concepts are taken as the fundamental data from which the solutions of philosophical problems are to be constructed. The data of concrete experience are ignored, and there is no longer the recognition of the need for continual symbolic reference to concrete realities. The idolization of Aristotelian philosophy by certain medieval philosophers, and the attitude of many contemporary analytic philosophers in accepting language as the fundamental data of philosophy, illustrate this fallacy. The substitution of philosophical concepts and theories for the concrete realities to which the concepts and theories were meant to be germane threatens all the cultural expressions of a society with uprootedness.

In regard to art, morality, and science, we have noted the importance of the recognition of the Eros in maintaining the relations of Appearance and

Reality proper to each interest. In the case of philosophy, this function is particularly important for the reason that a close relation between the philosophic and religious interests is essential in helping philosophy to achieve its aim, the complete conceptual characterization of experience.

> Religion is the translation of general ideas into particular thoughts, particular emotions, and particular purposes. . . . [It] is an ultimate craving to infuse into the insistent particularity of emotion that non-temporal generality which primarily belongs to conceptual thought alone [PR 23].

The aim of philosophy is to characterize a complete fact. The wedding of generality and particularity at which religion strives makes possible the closest approximation to a complete fact of which human minds are capable. One great service of religion to philosophy is its constant demand that general philosophic concepts find illustration in particular thoughts, purposes, or emotions. In this way, the Eros insures a harmony of Appearance and Reality.

Charles Hartshorne has quoted Whitehead to the effect that, "as physics is the interpretation of our perceptual experiences, so metaphysics is the interpretation of our religious experiences." [14]

Our discussion in Chapter V led to the conclusion that the five principal cultural interests were based upon different kinds of abstractive emphases from the unity of an occasion of experience. The implication of such a unitary basis for all interests is that philosophy, whose task it is to achieve formal concepts adequately interpreting all types of experience, should be able to begin its reflections with any type of abstraction. For, if it is properly rooted in Reality, that abstraction should lead back to the concrete experience from which it derived and should indicate its relationships to other types of abstractive emphases.

But even though, in principle, it is a matter of relative indifference which data are utilized initially to ground philosophic speculation, our theory of cultural interests does imply that there are two types of data which would provide the most immediate and direct information about concrete realities. These are the aesthetic and religious experiences. For only three of the five cultural interests may make any claim to completeness. The completeness of aesthetic experiences comes from their basis in the immediate unity of experience, the completeness of religion, from its reference to the totality of concrete experiencing. Philosophy seeks completeness through developing formal, non-selective conceptual constructions. Philosophy, therefore, seeking to characterize a complete fact, may best begin with aesthetic or religious experiences, since these two provide the most nearly complete repositories of concrete experience.

The priority of religious and aesthetic modes of experience is built into Whitehead's philosophy. This is true not only from the perspective of the phenomenological accounts of the basis of the two types of experience.

The priority of these two modes of interest runs throughout Whitehead's metaphysical discussions. For example, the cosmological problem, discussed in Chapter VII, is seen, primarily, from the religious and the aesthetic perspectives. For the achievement of everlastingness by occasions of the temporal world means that "the sense of worth beyond itself [moral and religious experience] is immediately enjoyed [aesthetic experience] as an overpowering element in the individual self-attainment" (PR 531).

The solution to the cosmological problem is both an aesthetic and a religious solution. As religious, it is an expression of the "dynamic effort of the World passing into everlasting unity, and of the static majesty of God's vision, accomplishing its purpose of completion by absorption of the World's multiplicity of effort" (PR 530). As aesthetic, it is an expression of the universe "as attaining the active self-expression of its own variety of opposites" (PR 531). For human individuals who are concerned about the transience of life and the hope for survival beyond the inevitable passing of temporal immediacy, the cosmological problem shapes itself in its religious character—the desire for everlasting Unity of Adventure. From the perspective of Whitehead's metaphysically elaborated concept of God, the problem is seen from an aesthetic perspective. It is the problem of the adjustment of individual temporal attainments into a perfected unity which provides optimum subjective immediacy.

Religion emphasizes the particularity of emotions. Though abstract generality is lost in religious experience, it maintains a richness of emotion. On the other hand, speculative philosophy gains generality but loses the depth of particular intensity. The task of one seeking to grasp the whole of reality is, thereby, frustrated. He may be *general* but emotionally starved, or *intense* while particular and partial. In the Kantian phraseology: philosophic concepts are blessed with "extensive magnitude," religious experiences and concepts with "intensive magnitude." Both together are necessary for a comprehension of the magnitude of experience. The need to wed intensity with generality is a problem faced by the sensitive man of religion and by the sensitive philosopher as well.

All concepts express some degree of formal abstraction. The full richness of concrete experience cannot be communicated in conceptual form, therefore, because of the formally abstract character of concepts. All experiences share certain general metaphysical characteristics. Only experiences which possess a large number of concrete similarities can allow for comparison in concrete concepts. That is, the greater the commonalities in experienced reality between one entity and another, the greater the evocative meaning which may be grasped. In this way the effective use of evocative concepts may be enhanced. In a human community of common language, customs, etc., there is a relatively great possibility of evocative communication. On the other hand, the less shared the experience, the less the evocative significance which the one experiencing may derive from his experience of another. In this case, the concepts employed must be of a more abstract and general cognitive type.

As a rule, the speculative philosopher seeks to utilize highly abstract concepts which characterize the most generic features of things, but when he deals with intuitions to which his language is inadequate, he must resort to more concrete language of a metaphorical sort. Evocative concepts may be used to evoke the intuition of a generic truth, as Whitehead shows in choosing the line "Abide with me, fast falls eventide" to stimulate the intuitions of the facts of Permanence and Flux (v. PR 318).[15]

No experience can be exhausted by recourse to concepts. The inability of a concept to communicate fully is of the essence of the role of concepts in experience. Only when one deals with notions of the utmost generality can one hope to approximate full communication via concepts. The principal aim of speculative philosophy is to discover cognitive concepts expressive of those most general notions. Religion emphasizes the concrete and evocative character of concepts. Philosophy, on the other hand, strives to achieve a mastery of the most generic cognitive concepts which will allow for a broad-based communication between differing (and partial) sustaining environments. The contrast between religious experience and the entertainment of formal philosophic concepts is the contrast between particularity and generality. Both factors are involved in a complete experience. The tie between the reality of religious emotions and the appearance of philosophical concepts must be made either from the side of philosophy or the side of religion.

A conceptual experience of the whole of things is not an experience of its parts in their particularity, though a particular experience can encompass both itself and the whole in the manner appropriate to both generality and particularity. That is, an individual experiencer can envision a conceptual justification for his religious emotions more naturally than one can evoke religious emotions through entertaining an abstract interpretative construct. Initially, and principally, symbolic reference moves from Reality to Appearance. The more concrete and evocative the symbol or concept, the easier is the reverse move from Appearance to Reality. But at the level of speculative philosophic concepts, the reverse type of symbolic reference is less likely to evoke concrete religious emotions. Thus Whitehead emphasized that it is the task of *religion* to connect rational generality with emotional particularity.

4. THE FALLACY OF THE PERFECT DICTIONARY

In our consideration of the cultural interests of art, morality, and science, we have been concerned to show that the *contemporary* expression of the cultural problem has involved two intricately interwoven phenomena: the failure of absolute standards of rationality and the consequent affirmation of the relativity of thought, action, and passion; and the dominance of technical approaches to theoretical, practical, and productive enterprises. The "death of God" proclaimed by art has been experienced as the loss of Peace and Truthful Beauty throughout contemporary culture. And there is no simple solution to the ensuing cultural problem. Whatever the direction out of our contemporary dilemmas, it is certainly the case that we must proceed in accordance with the rules laid down by our technique-oriented society. Our technical, dynamic, specialized society is here to stay. The attainment of Truthful Beauty in contemporary culture can occur only through the acceptance of the radical sense of finitude imposed upon us by the functional, novelty-seeking, omnicompetent machine of society. In art this means the acceptance of the ephemerality of beauty; in morality, the realization that the goodness achieved through human action and decision may not always be sanctified by a halo of holiness. In science the acceptance of finitude leads to the pragmatic, operational approach to theory-construction suggested by Thomas Kuhn.

Contemporary philosophy is characterized by the general ambivalence toward the finite and relative status of all cultural attainments. In many ways contemporary philosophy may be described in terms of the wholesale commission of the Fallacy of the Perfect Dictionary. The assumption that the assemblage of data in accordance with which philosophic analysis or construction may provide definitive statements amounts to a panic reaction in the face of the continuing threat of relativity flooding in upon human consciousness in our period.

The Fallacy of the Perfect Dictionary is committed in two dramatic ways in contemporary philosophy. The first is that of the analytic philosopher who assumes that the detailed articulation of linguistic structure and usage will be rewarded by some final conclusions concerning language use and abuse. The purpose of the work of such philosophers as the later Wittgenstein, J. L. Austen, and Gilbert Ryle, for example, was both to eliminate conceptual muddles caused by the misuse of language, and to determine rules for correct linguistic usage. The assumption of such philosophers is that language, *as it now exists,* is capable of yielding solutions to the fundamental conceptual problems of human existence. For these philosophers the "perfect dictionary" is, apparently, the *Oxford English Dictionary.* Whiteheadian methodology would not allow for such a rigidly conservative approach to language. Language, like philosophy itself, is always "assaulting the boundaries of finitude," never claiming to have even a simple victory. Linguistic philosophy through its capitulation to the structures of a given language, achieves an abundance of blunt truth, but, as is always the case with narrow scholarship, it brings on a falling away of the past in which all the unclarifiable, unanalyzable aspects of the experienced past are allowed to fade since they cannot be articulated by linguistic methodology. The condition of uprootedness is the obvious result.

But the Fallacy of the Perfect Dictionary is also committed by speculative philosophers. The assumption of dogmatic certainty in the construction of a philosophic system, an assumption we tend to correlate with seventeenth-century rationalism, is still with us. The dogmatic metaphysician, like the dogmatic linguistic analyst, assumes that the assemblage of data necessary for the discovery of truth has been accomplished. But whereas the analyst seeks to articulate the data in order to clarify individual items, the metaphysician wishes to construct a coherent explanatory system from the data which will be true, adequate, and, therefore, final. Thus, the dogmatic metaphysician claims that, in principle, it is possible to construct a metaphysics adequate in every significant regard, and that he has, in fact, accomplished the feat.

Paul Weiss is an example of a contemporary philosopher who makes such claims to metaphysical ultimacy:

> The existence of warring philosophic systems is proof enough that no one of them says all that needs to be said. Rejection of the rest by each is what one might expect from partial systems falsely claiming to be all-inclusive. . . . Only that system can justly claim to be adequate which includes all the rest as partial illustrations of itself, and shows why they, in turn, claim it to be a special case of themselves.[16]

Weiss claims that his is such a system, and he attempts to show how metaphysical counterclaims are reflections and manifestations of his system of thought. This amounts to the claim of having achieved *the* true philosophy. Weiss's philosophy, in effect, envisions a well-defined universe open, in principle, to adequate systematic analysis. Process philosophies, however, are not quite so optimistic. The universe is always outrunning the philosopher attempting to enclose it within a speculative system. For Whitehead the pluralism of philosophies would be seen as an ultimately irreconcilable feature of existence, given the finitude and ignorance of the philosophers in the face of the extreme complexity of the real.

Neither the grand speculative certainty sought by the dogmatic metaphysician, nor the more humble certainties of the linguistic empiricists, can effectively overcome the radical sense of finitude experienced in contemporary society. The quest for certainty is futile: dogmatism can only produce the condition which it seeks to overcome since the result of dogmatic philosophy is, paradoxically, a denial of faith in the efficacy of human reason. For if reason is capable of grasping the most general conceptual categories which interpret existence, then we must assume that such categories have not yet been discovered. The existence of conflict and discord about the adequacy of any given philosophic truth is proof enough that the general agreement among educated men which is presupposed by a faith in reason has not yet been achieved. The dogmatic assumption of truth in any given instance calls into question the reasoning processes of those who do not accept the truth and thereby undercuts any general faith in reason.

232   SOME IMPLICATIONS

Philosophers seeking truth must, as Whitehead has attempted to do, accept the inevitable finitude of every philosophic enterprise. In such acceptance, born of the sense of Peace as the Unity of Adventure, philosophies can be initiated which seek neither to claim that the meaning and value of the universe of things has been encompassed in a single system, nor to collect and classify certain interesting facts upon the way we use words, but to provide a hypothetical interpretative scheme which, at its best, evokes the sense of the importance of those primary modes of experience and expression upon which the achievements of civilized activity depend.

Such a claim about the function of philosophy recalls the discussion of Whiteheadian methodology in Chapter I. Speculative philosophy, for Whitehead, is the speculative development of schemes of thought which interpret civilized experience. This is the philosophy of culture. Perhaps some further explanation of the meaning of the philosophy of culture will secure the exposition of Whitehead's speculative method provided in Chapter I.

It is a truism that wisdom is the knowledge not of facts, but of principles —the beginning points of thought and action. The dominant beginning points are not so often the specific principles of any given discipline as the larger principles which define the broad context upon which cultural activity depends. The pursuit of philosophic understanding is a search for the principles of civilized order.

In the thousand-year history of the Platonic Academy, the character of intellectual culture was indelibly impressed by the Athenian philosophic ideal. The rise of universities in the medieval period illustrated the formative effect of philosophy upon intellectual culture. The *trivium* and *quadrivium* of medieval universities, the foundations of our own contemporary curricular patterns, were based upon the organizations of the disciplines found in Platonic and Aristotelian philosophies. Similarly, the Renaissance ideal of *humanitas* is the foundation of our own belief, only recently beginning to wane, that the study of the humanities, the exposure to the best of what men have thought and done, is the most promising method of becoming creative human beings. By appeal to such a tradition we come to understand the meaning of philosophy within the context of human culture: not that philosophy is one discipline among many necessary to a culture, but that philosophic reflection is the *sine qua non* of the very existence of intellectual culture.

Culture is composed of a complex set of aims and interests defining social activity and its products. A civilized culture is one in which the norms of thought and action are conducive to creative endeavor in the various specialized interests, in which there exists a consciousness of the viable relations among these human interests. Thus, philosophers have the twofold responsibility of mirroring in their work the dominant cultural interests and their proper relationships. The specialized interests express the principles of particular disciplines, but philosophy has as its peculiar subject matter the principles upon which the relationships of these specialized interests are based. Thus the liberally educated man is one who can cite reasons for the fall of Rome while manipulating the binomial theorem, and who can see the relationships between such seemingly disparate facts within the complex of human ideas. A knowledge of such relationships requires an understanding not only of "facts" but of the principles which lead to the discovery and interpretation of these facts. A knowledge of principles comes only from philosophic reflection upon the fundamental relationships of human thought, action, and passion.

A culture without philosophy is a contradiction in terms. It is a "soul-less" entity, lacking any sense of focus and orientation. Philosophy serves the best in human culture by functioning as a critic of the relationships of human interests and activities. Only in philosophy do we find the ideal of a formally adequate, non-selective treatment of man's cultural existence still available. Until philosophy can make good its claim to employment, in conjunction with the sciences of man, as *scientia scientiarum,* the science of the sciences, attempted solutions to social and cultural dilemmas themselves will continue to function merely as additional roadblocks to intellectual progress.

The philosophy of culture is speculative philosophy. It is philosophy which seeks to be a *speculum,* a mirror—or, perhaps better, a map of knowledge—of intellectual culture: of the whole spectacle of human social existence. Philosophy, in its speculative mode, is the disciplined use of analogy. Analogical generalization forms the very core of such philosophy. To see the relationships, dependencies, and mutual adumbrations of things is the goal of synthetic thinking. The aim of speculative philosophy is to guard against each of the types of undisciplined thinking common to a specialized society: the reductive type which employs the ungeneralized principles of a specific discipline as explanatory principles in terms of which to understand human culture, as well as the free-floating analogical method which eschews the necessity of any specialized foundation.

The distaste for speculative thinking characteristic of contemporary philosophy is, from the perspective of the philosopher of culture, one more instance of the technological state of mind. To the extent that this is the case, the philosophical elite must share the blame for the present circumstances of intellectual culture, since it is the responsibility of philosophy as *scientia scientiarum* to promote a vision of the creative interrelationships of the various cultural interests and activities.

At least since Kant's inclusion in the *Critique of Pure Reason* of a brief section on "The History of Pure Reason," philosophers have had some concern with the way in which reason, in its theoretical and practical modes, has been employed in various phases of human culture. Hegel's *Phenomenology* and Dewey's *Quest for Certainty* are two examples of constructive philosophic viewpoints grounded systematically and polemically in an analysis of the history of reason. The philosophic ideal has been a vision which provides for the legitimate claims to autonomy of thought and action, while nonetheless demonstrating the viable relationships of the two modes one to another.

Twentieth-century philosophy has, for the most part, evidenced a reaction against the Hegelian speculative synthesis of cultural interests. Man as willing agent rather than as knowing mind is at question in existentialism and phenomenology, and in pragmatism and language philosophy. Language philosophy seeks no theoretical or speculative synthesis; it seeks rather to accept the ordinary language of mankind, as the frozen products of past intentions, and to analyze these in order to render therapy. Positivism carries on the Humean tradition of sensational atomism in which the disjunct between theory and practice is tentatively maintained as that between hypothetical construct and experimental verification. And, of course, there are those in contemporary philosophy who have continued the Kantian and Hegelian traditions. The Kantian philosophy is strongly entrenched in neo-orthodox Protestant theology which finds the disjunct between theory and practice, between "fact" and "value," convenient in its attempt to construct theologies which affirm Biblical revelation and yet remain respectable in a scientific culture. Hegelian thinkers, where they are still to be found, are fond of citing the "mythical" and symbolic character of religion and art compared to the more final truths of philosophy. The resolution of the conflicts between knowledge and action, fact and value, theory and practice, etc., depend upon the resolution of the conflict existing among philosophers concerning the proper scope of reason. Solutions offered to this date have been such as to solve the conflict at the expense of religion and the arts (Hume and positivists) or of science (Hegel and the existentialists).

The condition of philosophy in the twentieth century has been such as to promote, or at least to fail to alleviate, the breakdown of the fiber of intellectual culture. The failure of philosophy lies, historically, in a failure of nerve occasioned by the aweful achievement of Hegel in the nineteenth century. This last great cultural synthesis functioned as a *reductio ad absurdum* of the aims of philosophy of culture. The effect of Hegel's thinking was to demonstrate that philosophy is the *history* of philosophy;[17] that, indeed, the philosopher is an historian masquerading under an assumed tense. "Culture" is thus rendered a static, completed concept, and philosophy of culture made into a backward-looking discipline.

Philosophers of the twentieth century, sensitive to the dictum, which the Hegelian philosophic system so patently illustrated, that the owl of Athena takes flight only at the close of day, either have sought ways of adjusting with contentment to the assumed *ex post facto* role of philosophy, losing thereby any relevance to a changing culture, or have tried to redefine the task and subject matter of philosophy so as to insure philosophy's rele-

vance to the present, but in so doing have lost the synoptic vision so necessary to a philosophy of culture.

The first reaction has been that of the linguistic empiricists. The analytic
and descriptive methodologies of language philosophers have sent the owl
of Athena on that now too familiar flight from first intentions which ab-
sorbs much of the energies of contemporary philosophy. The language
philosopher, sunk contentedly in second-intensional reveries, reduces philosophic creativity to a trivial set of inter-office memos aimed at the colleague
down the hall, or in the next university.

Equally unfortunate, if not nearly so inconsequential, has been the attempt of twentieth-century philosophy to achieve concreteness and relevance.
The existential rediscovery of the self as concrete subjectivity is, in terms of
the analysis of the cultural problem confronting contemporary men, the
dialectical counterpart of the methods of language theorists; Athena's owl
is brought down to earth and forced to travel the same subterranean route
as the mouse she seeks for food. The compelling immediacy of individual
existence is celebrated by the existentialists, but little attention is given to a
discussion of intellectual culture in all its modes. The *Lebenswelt* is ex-
plored, but the "other culture" is left to the devices of its specialists. It is no
accident that existentialism has found its primary spokesmen and disciplines
outside the academic community. For the purported aim of the university
(as poorly represented as it in fact may be) to serve as a microcosm of intellectual culture is contrary to the anti-intellectualism of the existential bias.

Language philosophers, through their capitulation to a vision of philosophy as a descriptive non-synoptic science, have relegated the idea of human
culture as something more than the arithmetical sum of its component
facets, to their fast-growing collection of category mistakes. Existential
philosophies eschew the abstract objectivity-seeking spirit of speculative
philosophy, and too rarely contain more than vague suggestions concerning
the nature and purpose of intellectual culture. The philosophic sources of
responsible theory of culture are meager indeed.

The failure of philosophy in its role as a critical or evaluational elite is
crucial to the condition of contemporary society. Few philosophers still cling
to the notion that a civilized culture should manifest unity and self-understanding based upon a consciousness of its primary aims and interests and
their mutual relations. And though philosophy is, historically, *scientia scientiarum,* the critic of the principles of the special sciences and that discipline
concerned with an organization of the disciplines, it is hardly so as contemporary activity.

Culturological method must be developed which does not force the philosopher to decide arbitrarily between conflicting self-evidences or to give up
the task of promoting the vision of the unity of intellectual culture. The
method of cultural philosophy must be synoptic and non-reductive in its

characterization of culture. This method should combine an analysis of the development of contemporary notions concerning the proper scope of reason, and a sketch of that vision of the scope of reason which allows for the broadest possible inclusion of the evidences of cultural experience. Such a method requires a radical exercise in speculative thinking.[18]

Contemporary intellectual culture has broken down. And the resulting intellectual chaos of an over-specialized society without normative self-consciousness will go unchallenged until philosophy can again present a vision of the creative organization of cultural interests. The speculative vision of the philosopher should be employed to resolve the fundamental conflicts so much in evidence among our cultural elites. The owl of Athena must sustain a midday flight.

Philosophic reconstruction, the art of rebuilding one's ship while at sea, is the purpose of Whitehead's philosophy of culture. The provision of workable categories with which to understand and evaluate the status and relationships of the various cultural interests is the purpose of philosophy in the role of *scientia scientiarum*. The significance of Whiteheadian philosophy lies in the fact that the close systematic association of the religious vision with the philosophic task means that Whitehead provides both an emotional and a cognitive relationship of philosophy to human culture. For Whitehead, philosophy in the role of *scientia scientiarum* depends upon the concepts of both Eros, insuring the harmony of Appearance and Reality which guarantees Truthful Beauty in the expression of a culture, and the Unity of Adventure which overcomes the threat of the finitude of cultural expression. In constructing these concepts as part of a philosophic system, the philosopher illustrates one part of his function as a civilizing agent in society. In remaining open to the existential experience of that which these concepts interpret, he completes his civilizing function. Philosophy achieves conceptually what religion achieves emotionally. But we must stress again, the task of religion as the sense of Peace is to unite the particularity of emotional experience to the generality of conceptual thought. Whitehead's concepts of religion and of philosophy, as we have detailed them, derive from a philosophic system sensitive to the religious emotions which underlie its categoreal concepts. Thus Whitehead's philosophy is both a faith seeking understanding and an understanding meant to evoke faith. The important experience is "faith," not understanding. That faith from which Whiteheadian philosophy begins, and to which it makes appeal, is the faith in Peace as Eros and the Unity of Adventure which serves as the ground and goal of existence for the perishing occasions in the life of each temporal creature.

NOTES

1. For classic examples of this existential approach to the relations of religion and science, see Karl Heim, *Christian Faith and Natural Science* (New York: Harper & Row, 1957), and John Wild, *Existence and the World of Freedom* (Englewood Cliffs: Prentice-Hall, 1963), especially Chapter V, "The War of the Worlds."

2. See T. R. Miles, *Religion and the Scientific Outlook* (London: Allen & Unwin, 1959). Parts II and III of this work consider the approach of language analysis to the relations of science and religion.

3. A. H. Johnson, *Whitehead's Theory of Reality*, pp. 10–11.

4. See Lorenz, *On Aggression* (New York: Bantam, 1970); Ardrey, *Territorial Imperative* (New York: Dell, 1968) and *Social Contract* (New York: Atheneum, 1970); and Morris, *The Naked Ape* (New York: Dell, 1969) and *Human Zoo* (New York: McGraw-Hill, 1970).

5. Rieff, *The Triumph of the Therapeutic* (New York: Harper & Row, 1968).

6. *Ibid.*, p. 241.

7. See Fromm, *The Revolution of Hope* (New York: Harper & Row, 1970), especially Chapter I.

8. Marcuse, *Eros and Civilization: A Philosophical Inquiry into Freud* (Boston: Beacon, 1955) and *One-Dimensional Man* (Boston: Beacon, 1964).

9. McLuhan, *The Gutenberg Galaxy* (Toronto: University of Toronto Press, 1962) and *Understanding Media* (New York: McGraw-Hill, 1969).

10. Kuhn, *The Structure of Scientific Revolutions* (Chicago: University of Chicago Press, 1962).

11. *Ibid.*, p. 97.

12. Norbert Weiner, "Some Moral and Technical Consequences of Automation," *Science*, 131 (May 6, 1960), 1356.

13. See Hartshorne's *Creative Synthesis and Philosophic Method* (Lasalle, Ill.: Open Court, 1970).

14. Hartshorne, "Whitehead and Contemporary Philosophy" in *The Relevance of Whitehead*, ed. Ivor Leclerc (New York: Macmillan, 1961), p. 25.

15. In this connection, see our discussion in Chapter I of Whitehead's use of metaphor and imagery to provide "existential" analogies discriminating and clarifying vague, but important, experiences.

16. Weiss, *Modes of Being* (Carbondale: Southern Illinois University Press, 1955), p. 381.

17. See Quentin Lauer, s.j., *Hegel's Idea of Philosophy* (New York: Fordham University Press, 1971).

18. I should stress that I have not attempted to produce a philosophy of contemporary culture in this work. What I have done should be seen as a prolegomenon to a future philosophical analysis from a Whiteheadian perspective. I do intend to compose, in the near future, in a more rigorous and complete form, the kind of analysis of contemporary cultural experience adumbrated in the last three chapters.

INDEX